Migration in the Circumpolar North:
Issues and Contexts

Lee Huskey and Chris Southcott
Editors

CCI Press in cooperation with the University of the Arctic

2010

Library and Archives Canada Cataloguing in Publication

Migration in the Circumpolar North: issues and contexts / Lee Huskey and Chris Southcott, editors.

Papers presented at Migration in the Circumpolar North Lessons Learned, Questions Remaining, a workshop held in June 2007 at the University of Roskilde in Denmark. Co-published by the University of the Arctic.
Includes bibliographical references.
ISBN 978-1-896445-48-9

1. Migration, Internal—Arctic regions. 2. Arctic regions—Emigration and immigration. 3. Rural-urban migration--Arctic regions. 4. Indigenous peoples—Arctic regions—Population. 5. Arctic regions—Population.
I. Huskey, Lee II. Southcott, Chris III. Canadian Circumpolar Institute IV. University of the Arctic

HB2155.A3M54 2010   304.80911'3   C2010-904007-4

© 2010 CCI Press in cooperation with the University of the Arctic

All rights reserved
No part of this publication may be reproduced, stored in a retrieval system, or transmitted in any form or by any means—electronic, mechanical, photocopying, recording, or otherwise without the express written permission of the copyright owner/s. CCI Press is a registered publisher with access© the Canadian Copyright Licensing Agency (Publisher Number 3524).

Cover design by art design printing, inc.
Printed in Canada by art design printing, inc.

Occasional Publication No. 64
CCIP ISBN-13 978-1-896445-48-9
CCIP ISSN 0068-0303

Table of Contents

Introduction
Lee Huskey and Chris Southcott ... iii

Chapter 1:
Footprints: Demographic Effects of Out-migration
Lawrence C. Hamilton ... 1

Chapter 2:
The Complex Geography of Native Migration in Arctic Alaska
Lee Huskey and Lance Howe ... 15

Chapter 3:
Migration in the Canadian Arctic: An Introduction
Chris Southcott ... 35

Chapter 4:
Migration and Population Change in the Russian Far North in the 1990s
Timothy Heleniak ... 57

Chapter 5:
Impacts of Regional Labour Market Changes on Migration Trends: Research Examples from Norway
Lasse Sigbjørn Stambøl ... 93

Chapter 6:
Determinants of Migration in Northern Sweden: Exploring Intraregional Differences in Migration Processes
Olle Westerlund ... 117

Chapter 7:
Migration and Population Dynamics in the Regions of Finland: Special Analysis of Lapland
Elli Heikkilä and Maria Pikkarainen ... 133

Chapter 8:
Who Moves and Why: Stylized Facts About Iñupiat Migration in Alaska
Stephanie Martin ... 147

Chapter 9:
Migration and Socio-Economic Well-Being in the Russian North: Interrelations, Regional Differentiation, Recent Trends, and Emerging Issues
Tatiana Vlasova and Andrey N. Petrov ... 163

Chapter 10:
How the North Became Home: Attachment to Place Among Industrial Migrants in Murmansk Region
Alla Bolotova and Florian Stammler ... 193

Introduction

Lee Huskey and Chris Southcott

Migration can have a major impact on the population size, demographic structure, and character of Arctic communities, and is likely to result in long-term changes in towns and villages across the North. Differences in demographic structure, history, and relevant policies have produced different patterns of population movement throughout the North, patterns that have changed over time and will likely change in the future. The papers in this volume reflect an effort to understand both the causes and consequences of this northern migration experience.

The Circumpolar North is an interesting region in which to study migration. This area, which includes the northern regions of Canada, Sweden, Norway, Finland, and Russia as well the state of Alaska and Greenland, shares certain environmental characteristics and an economic base dependent on natural resource production. For the most part, northern regions are relatively poor, but benefit from being located in wealthy democratic countries. Communities in the region are generally small, but the North does contain some cities. Migration patterns relate to rural–urban migration that occurs throughout the world. The importance of place-specific, traditional economic activities among the indigenous population of the North makes the migration stories unique in the developed countries of the world.

The papers in this book were originally presented at *Migration in the Circumpolar North: Lessons Learned, Questions Remaining*, a workshop held in June 2007 at the University of Roskilde in Denmark. As the title suggests, the primary purpose of the workshop was to identify both what we know about migration in the north and what important research questions remain. The motivation for the exchange was a sense that while there is a great deal of research on migration in the North, this research is specific to both discipline and region.

In gathering people from several disciplines and regions of the circumpolar north our intent was to begin to develop a synthesis of this research. Eighteen papers were presented by economists, geographers, sociologists, and anthropologists, describing migration studies from all Arctic nations. One goal of this interdisciplinary, comparative approach was to arrive at a set of stylized facts and hypotheses about northern migration that would be useful in further work. Participants spent a good part of the workshop time discussing the general themes they saw developing throughout.

The workshop was organized by participants in the Boreas project, *Understanding Migration in the Circumpolar North*. Boreas is a program of the European Science Foundation's EUROCORES that has an objective to provide a framework for national research funding agencies to support multinational, multidisciplinary collaborative research. The Boreas program was developed to promote circumpolar research. Two research themes—the relationship between humans and their environment, and population movement associated with community change—were especially relevant to the study of migration.

There were seven projects funded through Boreas. *Understanding Migration in the Circumpolar North* (UMCN) was one of these. The principle objective of UMCN is to improve our understanding of migration flows throughout the circumpolar north. This volume represents one element of the project—the synthesis of migration research from different social science disciplines and from countries throughout the Arctic. UMCN is a collaborative effort of the national science funding agencies of the United States, Canada, and Denmark. The Roskilde workshop was supported by a US National Science Foundation grant (ARC–0639211); the preparation of the book is a joint US–Canada effort.

One obstacle to the study of migration is limited data, both in terms of quantity and quality. Data allowing the description of individual migration decisions is especially limited; therefore, a second objective of UMCN is to develop quantitative information on the determinants and consequences of migration. To this end, individual projects which use similar quantitative approaches were also invited to participate in UMCN. Studies dealing with northern Canada, Greenland, and the Chukhotka region of Russia are the core focus of the UMCN project. Associated projects in Alaska and northern Sweden follow similar study approaches. Several papers illustrate the variety of data availability and quantitative methods used in migration studies.

What did we learn from the three day workshop in Roskilde? Given the variety of disciplines and regions represented, it was possible that no general conclusions would surface. However, a number of lessons did emerge from the presentations and discussions; these can be grouped into seven observations:

The Circumpolar North presents a variety of migration experiences, but the general patterns of migration are similar around the region. The North is currently a sending region; for the most part, more people leave than move to the North. Variation in this pattern over time or in particular places reflects differences in the determinants of migration. This variation provides the basis for examining the role of social, economic, community, and policy factors in migration decisions.

There are a variety of techniques that provide valuable insight into the determinants and consequences of migration. Both quantitative and qualitative approaches were featured that used regression analysis, descriptive analysis of migration data, historical and institutional analysis, and key informant interviews. One benefit of the interdisciplinary approach is that each method informs approaches using other techniques.

A wide variety of population movement types can be considered 'migration.' Short-term movement may be considered migration by some and simply commuting by others. Short-term movement may be for education and training as well as for work. The study of migration also depends on the region examined. Migration within regions might not be counted unless the community is the unit of study. Net migration tells us less about migration than do the population flows into and out of the region.

The geography of migration seems similar in many regions. In the North, larger places seem to gain relative to smaller communities. The draw of larger northern college, science, or administrative centers provides an example of this. Migrants don't always leave the region, and migration between communities reveals an interesting geographic pattern. Finally, there is some evidence that the stepping stone pattern of movement found in many developing countries is also found in the North. Evidence suggests people move in stages to ever larger communities.

Migration throughout the North takes place for a variety of reasons. Bright lights, family, jobs, and education were all isolated as reason for movement. Some temporary movements, such as for education, may result in longer-term 'moves; university centers provide examples of growing communities as magnets for regional residents. The presentations also revealed a number of factors limiting migration from northern communities, such as family ties and the inability of the unemployed to finance moves. For northern communities, the importance of traditional activities such as hunting, gathering, fishing, and herding to the indigenous population both limits out-migration and attracts return migrants.

The North provides ample opportunity to examine the effects of public policy on migration. Migration has not always been voluntary. The northern experience provides examples of forced migration and moves that have been strongly encouraged by the pattern of public service provision. Education, transfer, and development policies all have had intended or unintended consequences on migration.

Migration is not a random event. Across the North, the evidence is that the propensity to move varies across different types of people. Because of this, migration will have long-term consequences for communities. The character of places as well as the number of people will change. A primary example of this effect is the gender gap found in many smaller northern communities; one explanation for this gap is the higher propensity of females to move from the smaller communities. Higher rates of migration among the educated and the young adults will also change the population character of small communities.

This book represents the first step in an ambitious research agenda. Ultimately, the objective is to understand the causes and consequences of migration for various groups in the Circumpolar North. The Roskilde workshop and this book address one of the obstacles to this goal, that is, the fragmented nature of migration research by region and discipline. The dialogue was continued through a series of workshops and meetings supported by Boreas projects. The sharing of ideas across disciplines and regions will contribute to answering research questions, generate new questions, and provide opportunities for future collaboration.

The next steps for the *Understanding Migration in the Circumpolar North* project address two limitations to northern migration research. The first will address the data limits through statistical analysis of individual migration behavior in Alaska, Canada, Greenland, Chukhotka, and Sweden. Modeling and data analysis will be at the individual level. Census data, regional surveys, and data from the recent Survey of Living Conditions (SLiCA) in the Arctic will be incoporated into the study. Using these similar data sources the hypotheses generated through workshop discussions will be tested. For these regions, we hope to develop an understanding of individual, community, and policy factors that influence individual migration decisions.

A second extension of the Roskilde workshop will be the publication of a synthesis volume using a broad range of social sciences to describe the patterns, causes, and consequences of migration in the Circumpolar North. It will describe and compare the migration experiences of various northern

Introduction

regions, whereby similarities and differences will provide an empirical base around which such a synthesis can be organized. This variety of northern experience will allow the exploration of general hypotheses and provide a basis for developing stylized facts about this experience.

Beyond describing the variety of northern migration experiences, this collaborative effort will explore general themes uncovered at Roskilde. This effort will involve an international group of authors and will exlore questions such as: Who migrates? What path does migration follow? What factors influence migration? What role does public policy play in migration decisions? What are the consequences for the migrants and the communities left behind? What do migration patterns tell us about the quality of life of migrants and those left behind? Is northern migration special?

The North provides a laboratory for the study of migration. The lessons learned can be useful both to academics studying the region and to policy makers. Policy approaches to northern regions range from those encouraging the growth of smaller places to efforts to relocate populations to larger communities. The divergent histories and variety of policy and economic experiences in a land of similar environmental circumstances suggest that much can be learned by comparing and contrasting the migration experiences around the region. This volume and the efforts that follow will add to the discussion about migration in both policy and academic circles.

≈

The chapters in this volume are a representative selection of migration research in the North. In the first chapter, Hamilton summarizes research that he and others have conducted in the Circumpolar North since the 1990s. Two main factors are analyzed: the effects of gender and of age on out-migration. Both women and working-age youth are seen to migrate out of northern communities at a higher rate than men and other age groups. This demographic reality leaves a 'footprint' on these communities that impact their day-to-day functioning and development.

Huskey and Howe discuss recent patterns of migration in the northern parts of Alaska, a region with a majority Iñupiat population that has recently been a sending region experiencing net out-migration. While the net out-migration captures the attention of policy makers, Huskey and Howe identify other significant types of migration flows. Return migration and migration between villages are significant in the region. Migration also seems to follow a stepwise pattern, flowing from smaller to ever larger places. An understanding of migration behavior in the north needs to explain these additional types of migration.

Chapter 3 provides an introduction to migration research undertaken in the Canadian North. Southcott points out that, historically, there have been two main types of migration patterns: that of the indigenous population and that of the non-indigenous population. Migration patterns of the indigenous population were largely determined by environmental conditions, traditional activities, and government policies relating to settlement, whereas non-indigenous patterns tended to reflect the needs of natural resource exploitation. An analysis of recent data suggests that indigenousness continues to play a role in determining migration patterns. Gender and age are also playing a role, but in a different manner than that found in other northern regions.

Of all the northern regions that have experienced recent changes in migration patterns, none have been more extreme than Russia in the 1990s. The collapse of the Soviet Union had an enormous impact on the Russian North. The demographic aspects of this collapse are summarized by Heleniak in Chapter 4, where the author describes the impacts of out-migration from the region in the 1990s, and analyzes how it has affected the gender, age, educational, and ethnic composition of the Russian North.

The next chapter discusses migration in Norway with special attention to the northern regions of the country. Stambøl notes the clear trend toward centralization in the national capital region with out-migration from other regions, especially the north. Emphasis is given to the fact that northern migration patterns are also shared by other more rural regions of Norway. The chapter also introduces a new model developed to measure the impact of economic transfers to regions on migration.

The use of population registries, as opposed to census data, yields an extremely rich source of information on migration. This is shown in Westerlund's discussion of migration in northern Sweden. A detailed analysis of the determinants of migration is presented, with special emphasis on the Saami population. Differences are shown between the coastal urban areas and the more rural interior areas of the region. Generally speaking, determinants such as age, education, and presence of children are shown to be of continued importance, although they vary when interior rural areas are compared to coastal urban areas. The Saami population also shows significant differences with the rest of the Swedish population when it comes to migration.

Heikkilä and Pikkarainen describe the migration patterns in Finland and how these patterns are impacting Finnish Lapland. The trends toward centralization noted in other countries are also found in Finland as related to Lapland. A general population decline, despite high levels of natural population growth, masks variations within the North. Certain areas, such as the northern border communities of Tornio–Haparanda, have introduced economic development strategies that can reverse out-migration trends.

Chapter 8 focuses on the migration patterns of a particular population in the Circumpolar North. Martin uses data collected from a recent project to study the migration patterns of the Iñupiat of northern Alaska. Gender differences are highlighted, as women are more affected by the 'pull' of employment and education opportunities outside their traditional communities. Subsistence hunting and fishing make men less likely than women to leave.

Chapter 9 builds on the analysis of migration patterns in Northern Russia described by Heleniak in Chapter 4. Vlasova and Petrov study the particular conditions of post-Soviet migration through an investigation into the impacts of indicators of socio-economic well-being. They show that recent migration patterns in the Russian North are the result of a complex array of socio-economic indicators that go beyond traditional utilitarian models of migration.

Chapter 10 complements the approach of Vlasova and Petrov by showing the importance of an anthropological approach to better understand the complexity of factors influencing migration in the Russian North. Bolotova and Stammler's study of migrants living in the Murmansk area of Russia shows the importance of social, cultural, and other non-material variables that are often excluded from economic analyses of migration. Their work demonstrates the usefulness of combining qualitative methodologies associated with disciplines such as sociology and anthropology with traditional quantitative approaches used by economics.

Migration in the Circumpolar North

1

Footprints: Demographic Effects of Out-Migration[1]

Lawrence C. Hamilton

Introduction

Reports of gold discoveries along the Yukon's Klondike River reached San Francisco in the summer of 1897, setting off a migration stampede that quickly inflated the remote northern area's population from a handful to perhaps 40,000. 'Klondike' has since become a generic term for rapid and sometimes heedless resource-driven growth. The Circumpolar North has seen more than its share of Klondikes, from gold rush days to modern fishing and energy booms. World War II, the Soviet era and the Cold War brought other flows of in-migrants, as have postwar economic and public sector expansions. The arriving newcomers challenge and transform life for longtime northern residents and their traditional settlements.

The highly visible movement of southerners to the North tends to overshadow an opposite flow that also shapes these places: northern-born people moving south. Unlike southerners moving north, the northerners moving south have not written a broad literature about their experiences, or so visibly changed their destination communities. Often, these reverse flows are not easily counted or tracked. Departures do, however, leave footprints in the altered profiles of the places left behind. This chapter brings together some results from a series of studies that, incidentally at first, followed the demographic footprints of out-migration from the North. We use the terms 'North' and 'South' somewhat loosely; social gravity pulls toward larger, more diverse communities, which are often but not necessarily in lower latitudes.

---

[1] The research described here was supported by grants from the Arctic Social Sciences and Arctic System Science programs at the U.S. National Science Foundation (OPP-0638413, OPP-0531354, OPP-9912004, OPP-9515380, OPP-9319921 and DPP-9111675). Many colleagues contributed, including Carole Seyfrit, Rasmus Ole Rasmussen, Oddmund Otterstad, Richard Haedrich, Helga Ögmundardóttir, Cliff Brown, Cynthia M. Duncan, Igor Belkin, Chris Colocousis and Melissa Butler.

As with any migration flow, out-migration from northern communities is not random. Migration decisions vary both with individual characteristics (e.g., Seyfrit and Hamilton 1992; Hamilton and Seyfrit 1994a; Seyfrit *et al.* 1998) and with socioeconomic conditions (e.g., Hamilton 2007; Hamilton *et al.* 1999, 2000, 2003, 2004a–c). More energetic and mobile individuals, including those with portable skills, are more likely than others to move, and especially to do so when their opportunities seem better elsewhere. To whatever extent movers differ from those who stay behind, out-migration reshapes the source community. Effects of out-migration can be particularly strong in northern communities, where populations are not large relative to migration flows (e.g., Hamilton and Mitiguy 2009).

Although everyone in a small place knows people who have left, or talk of leaving, broader patterns sometimes go unrecognized until we take a step-back, statistical view. Patterns of out-migration from small places change the population structure of source communities. For example, many small northern communities have experienced a gradual, disproportionate out-migration by women in recent decades. In times of economic difficulty in particular, young adults of both sexes often leave. These two patterns of out-migration leave demographic footprints in their source communities that might not be apparent on the street, but stand out in statistical analysis and have broad consequences for community life.

Outmigration Effects on Sex Ratios

During the course of survey research on the aspirations of high school students in two predominantly Native regions of rural Alaska, Carole Seyfrit and I noticed a pattern. Girls, more often than boys, told us that they expected to live most of the rest of their lives elsewhere. High proportions among students of both genders expected to leave, but the gender gap proved robust across 15 communities and follow-up interviews with high school graduates (Hamilton and Seyfrit 1993, 1994b). A replication survey several years later confirmed this pattern, adding several new communities and showing also that the gender gap was widest among Alaska Native students (Seyfrit *et al.* 1998).

The students themselves suggested a number of push and pull factors, even before learning about the gender gap in our survey. We heard repeatedly that "school is a girl kind of thing," an attitude they extended toward post-secondary education, and hence to jobs requiring some higher education as well. High school girls voiced an interest in 'careers,' not just 'jobs' or 'work.' Their choices for careers looked better in cities than in their present small villages or towns. Women's roles in a village seemed more narrowly constrained, and careers almost non-existent. In describing positive aspects of village life, students spoke enthusiastically about

Chapter 1: *Footprints: Demographic Effects of Out-Migration*

hunting, fishing, snowmobiling and basketball—activities that appealed more strongly to boys than to girls. Among the negative aspects were social problems (often related to alcohol) that created pressures on women and girls. Marriage between local women and outsider men opens another common path for outmigration (Hamilton and Seyfrit 1994c).

Were women really voting with their feet, then, and disproportionately moving away? We reasoned that gender-biased migration from such small communities should leave clear footprints in the Census. Specifically, the high-school survey findings led us to hypothesize that there should be fewer young-adult women than men among the villages' Native populations (Iñupiat or Yupik, and mostly local-born). A look at 1990 Census data generally supported this hypothesis, revealing a characteristics scatterplot pattern. Among young-adult age groups, small communities (migration sources) generally had more men than women. In larger communities (migration destinations), there were often more women. We confined our analysis, initially, to Alaska Native populations to reduce the impact of newcomers (typically more men than women) moving *in* to these small northern places.

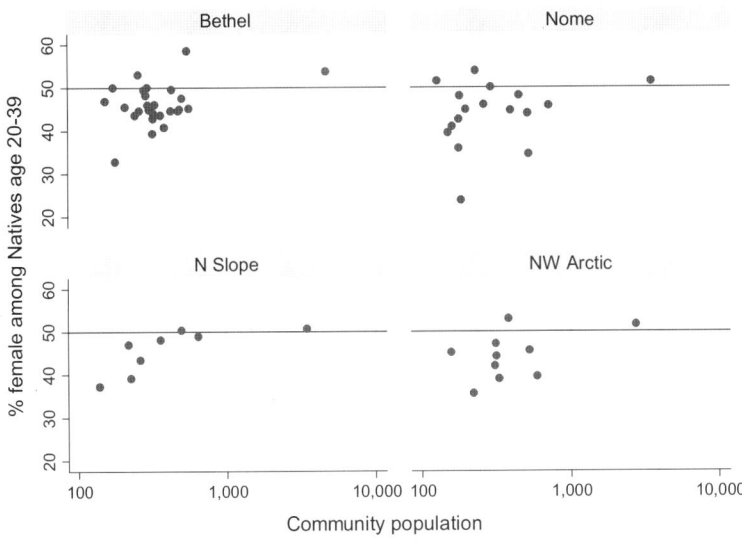

Figure 1: *Percent female among Alaska Natives age 20–39 vs. community size in four rural regions of Alaska (1990 Census).* See Hamilton and Seyfrit (1994c).

Figure 1 depicts such 'footprint' scatterplots for four regions of rural Alaska. Each point in the plots represents one village or town, graphed according to the percentage of females among their Native population aged

20–39, and the total community size (note logarithmic scaling). Within each of the four regions, we see a scattering of small villages at lower left, which have total populations below 1,000 and fewer than 50% women. Also within each region its hub town (Bethel, Nome, Barrow or Kotzebue) appears toward the upper right, with more than 1,000 people and slightly more than 50% women. Offering a wider range of job and educational choices, hub towns provide an attractive destination for many Natives leaving small villages.

The footprint pattern generalizes to the Alaskan Native population statewide, as shown in Figure 2. Points in this graph represent all Census places in Alaska with at least 100 Native residents. There is a positive correlation ($r=.37$, $p<.001$) between the percent female among Natives 20–39, and the logarithm of total place size. Anchorage, the largest city, shows at far right with about 56% female among young-adult Natives. The bulk of smaller places (fewer than 1,000 people), have fewer than 50% women. Towns with a few thousand people are in-between. This gradient reflects a pattern of migration by proximate steps: village residents moving to towns, town residents moving to cities, and city residents moving out of the state.

Of course, with respect both to places and people, such generalizations describe statistical patterns and not laws. Figure 2 shows many communities that do not follow the up-to-right trend.

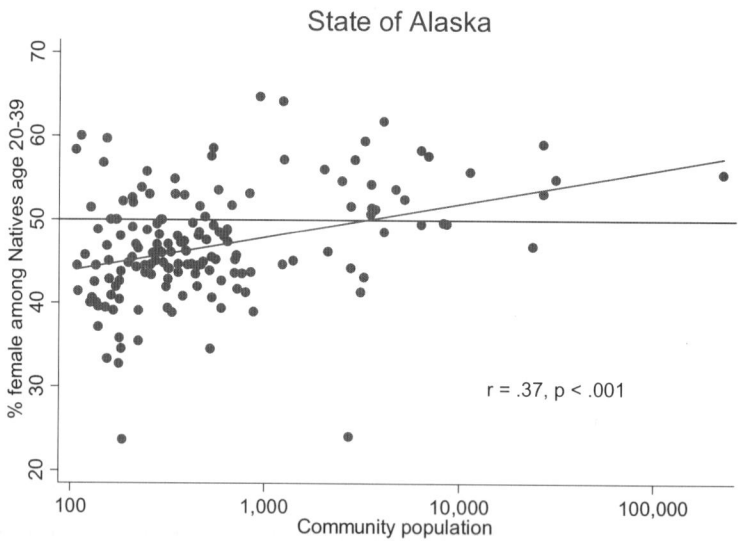

Figure 2: *Percent female among Alaska Natives aged 20–39 vs. community size in Alaska communities with at least 100 Native residents (1990 Census). See* Hamilton and Seyfrit (1994c).

Chapter 1: *Footprints: Demographic Effects of Out-Migration*

The deficit of Native females in many places becomes more striking if we take differential mortality into account. Males suffer higher death rates, and this factor alone should lead to a growing excess of females after about age 25. Migration more than offsets the substantial mortality differences, resulting in an excess of males (Hamilton and Seyfrit 1994c).

After seeing these sex-ratio patterns for Alaska in the 1990s, we began to wonder when the imbalance began historically, and where else it might occur. An exploration of limited historical data found no evidence of an earlier 'stable state' with approximately equal males and females. Sex ratios among Natives have fluctuated substantially in the past, responding to various environmental, health and social forces—of which differential migration is only the most recent (Hamilton *et al.* 1997). Earlier gender-roles-linked differences in mortality (such as the dangers to males hunting on ice, or to females exposed to tuberculosis and other illness) had contributed to widely off-center sex ratios in various historical periods.

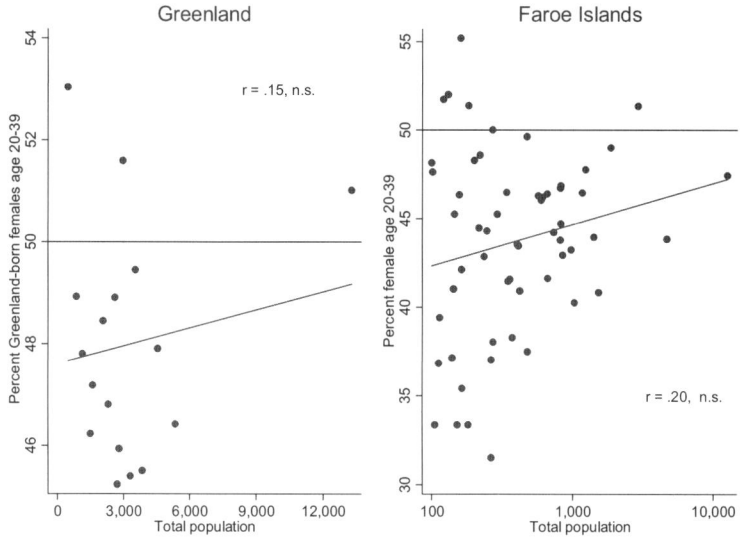

Figure 3: *Percent female among Greenland-born population (left) or Faroe Islands population (right) vs.community population in Greenland and the Faroe Islands (ca. 2005).*

Inuit communities of Canada and Greenland have some parallels to their counterparts in rural Alaska, providing avenues for replication. We found a generally similar patterns reflecting female out-migration from

Greenland (left scatterplot in Fig. 3). Population registry statistics confirmed this flow directly, and also showed a gender bias in out-migration by Greenlanders to more urban destinations in Denmark (Hamilton *et al.* 1996; Hamilton and Rasmussen 2010). Another former Danish colony, the Faroe Islands, exhibits a similar pattern of excess males in the smallest municipalities (right plot in Fig. 3). Unlike the Inuit Greenlanders, however, the Faroese are culturally Nordic. Their movements to and from Denmark tend therefore to be simpler, and an excess of men in small Faroese places could reflect in- as well as out-migration.

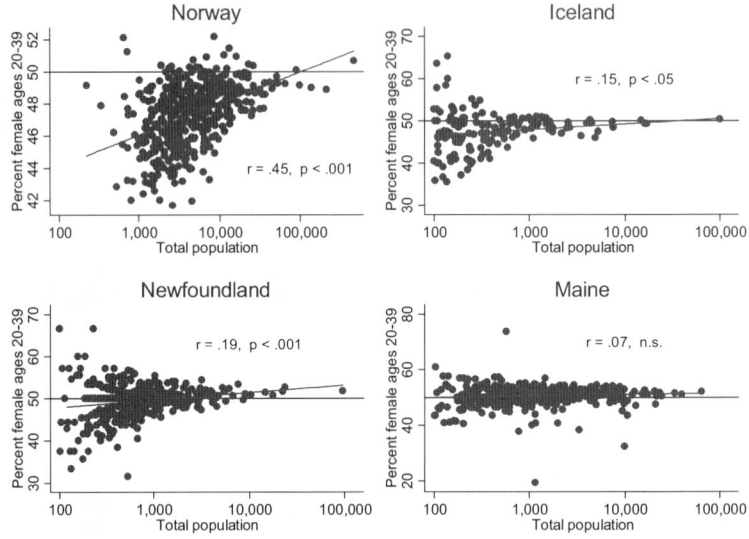

Figure 4: *Percent female age 20–39 vs. total population in municipalities or communities of Norway, Iceland, Newfoundland and Maine (ca. 1990).* See Hamilton and Otterstad (1998a).

Several other northern societies without strong cultural divisions exhibit this pattern of too few women in small places. Out-migration plays a substantial although not exclusive role in shaping these sex ratios. Figure 4 gives four examples. Among Norwegian municipalities, the up-to-right pattern is striking. Icelandic municipalities also show this pattern, but with more random variation among the smallest places. Canadian evidence is problematic—data on the populations of small places were available to us only in a rounded-off form that defeated Alaska or Greenland-style analysis of the Inuit regions in northeastern Canada. The larger province of Newfoundland shows some signs of female out-migration, obscured by a rounding effect that sweeps data points to erroneous locations on the left third of the graph. The U.S. state of Maine, in contrast, exhibits no significant correlation between percent female and community population.

What are the consequences, if more women than men leave? One obvious result for source communities is that men have reduced prospects to find long-term partners and form families—the key transition to adulthood for many. Some Alaska informants described increased pressures on teenage girls, creating problems for them and further incentives to leave. In migration–destination communities there could be gender mismatches within culture/age-cohort groups too, although the total population tends to be larger and more diverse.

In summary, the motivations for female out-migration apply to many small northern communities. Aggregate data appear widely, although not universally, consistent with the hypothesis that disproportionate net outmigration does occur, and has shaped the populations left behind—perhaps with complex social consequences. Disproportionate in-migration by outsider males certainly can shift sex ratios too, but in many places this is not the main force. Case studies and individual-level research on who comes and goes, and what happens to those who leave, invite further study.

Out-migration Effects on Age Structure

Disproportionate female out-migration from small northern places reflects broad social conditions such as gender roles, attitudes toward education and careers, marriage patterns, and the availability of amenities and jobs. In some of these same places we also saw another out-migration pattern, not so gender biased, that responded more immediately to economic development. Sharp declines in jobs tend to drive out-migration by the most mobile age groups—young adults and families. Age-biased migration causes a rapid 'aging' of the population left behind.

Fisheries-dependent communities of the North Atlantic, beset by resource crises during the 1980s and 90s, experienced out-migration of this type. Looking at demographic changes in Norway, Hamilton and Otterstad (1998b) noted a median population loss of 10% among fisheries-dependent municipalities from 1980 to 1990. During the same period, other municipalities experienced a median gain of 1.2%. Median age went up by more than 3 years in the fisheries-dependent municipalities, but less than 2 years elsewhere. Population loss and aging resulted not simply from net out-migration, but also from social changes that brought rural birth rates down from their formerly high levels (which historically somewhat offset out-migration) to low levels closer to the rest of the nation—hence, no longer able to offset out-migration. Similar demographic changes occurred in the most fisheries-dependent regions of Newfoundland, in connection with 1980–90s fisheries troubles (Hamilton and Butler 2001; Hamilton *et al.* 2004b).

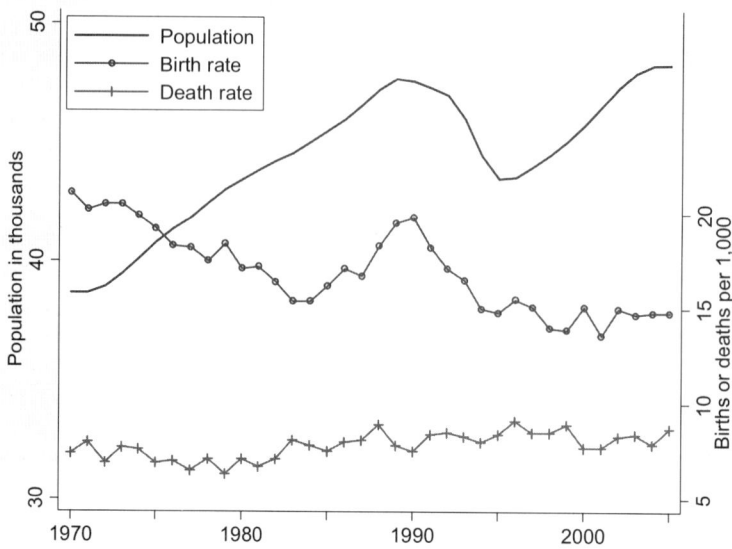

Figure 5: *Faroe Islands total population, birth and death rates 1970–2005.*

The Faroe Islands, among the most fisheries-dependent societies in the world, provide a striking example of resource-driven out-migration. Catches of cod and other groundfish species declined steeply during the late 1980s and early 1990s, setting off an economic crisis that caused many Faroese to leave the islands. Net migration shadowed the falling and rising fortunes of the cod fishery, with a lag of 0–2 years. The Faroe Islands population had grown by 23% between 1970 and 1988, mainly due to natural increase while net migration hovered around zero. Lower in-migration, combined with rising out-migration (strongest in 1993–95), eroded half of the 19-year gain in just 6 years, from 1989 to 1995. After 1995 the flow reverses—in-migration, mostly returning Faroese, increased while out-migration declined. Rising catches of other species in the late 1990s partially offset the decline in cod landings. Moreover, the Faroese economy as a whole, having gone through bankruptcies and a painful restructuring, emerged more efficient and less fragile after the crisis (Hamilton *et al.* 2004a). Figure 5 graphs the down-and-up path of total population, together with shifting birth and death rates.

Faroese outmigration both shrank and 'aged' the population left behind as it had in fishing communities of Norway and Newfoundland. The late-1980s crisis marked a clear discontinuity, where the proportion of young adults began falling steeply, and the proportion of children (leaving with their parents, or simply not born in the Faroes because adults of family-starting age had moved elsewhere) also declined. The proportion of individuals 40 years and older increased from 36% in 1988 to 43% in 2000. Birth rates fell with the departure of young adults, while death rates rose as the proportion of elders increased.

Population pyramids depicting Faroese society just before, during and after the crisis show the demographic reshaping that occurred. In Figure 6 (1988), just before the crisis, the pyramid is relatively fat-bottomed, characteristic of a society growing rapidly through natural increase (excess of births over deaths). Birth rates had been declining gradually in the preceding decades (*see* Fig. 5), making the births registered in the late-60s the largest cohort—albeit only marginally.

At the demographic low point after seven years of net out-migration, the Faroe Islands population pyramid (Fig. 7, 1995) had slimmed overall and developed a pronounced waist due to the missing 20-something adults. After the crisis, some but not all returned, leaving a noticeable gap in the pyramid between children under 18, and adults approximately 38 years of age and younger (Fig. 8, 2006). A continuous animation of pyramids through theses years shows the 'bite' of the crisis even more clearly.

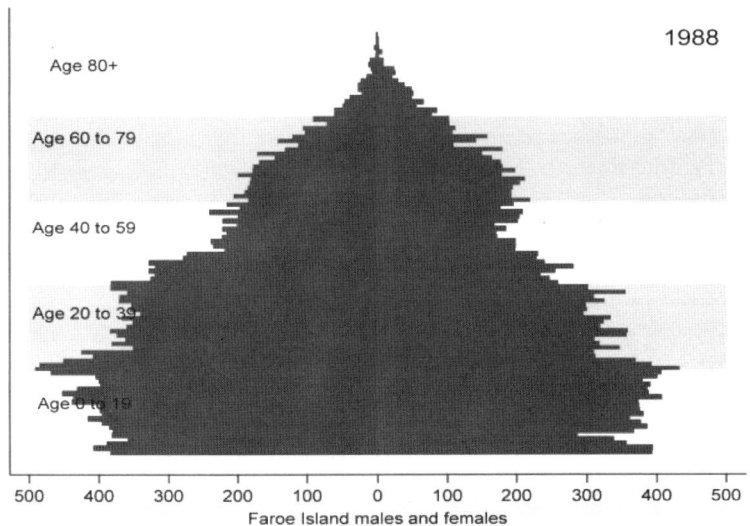

Figure 6: *Age-sex distribution of the Faroe Islands population in 1988, before the crisis. [Legend: males (left of 0); females (right of 0)].*

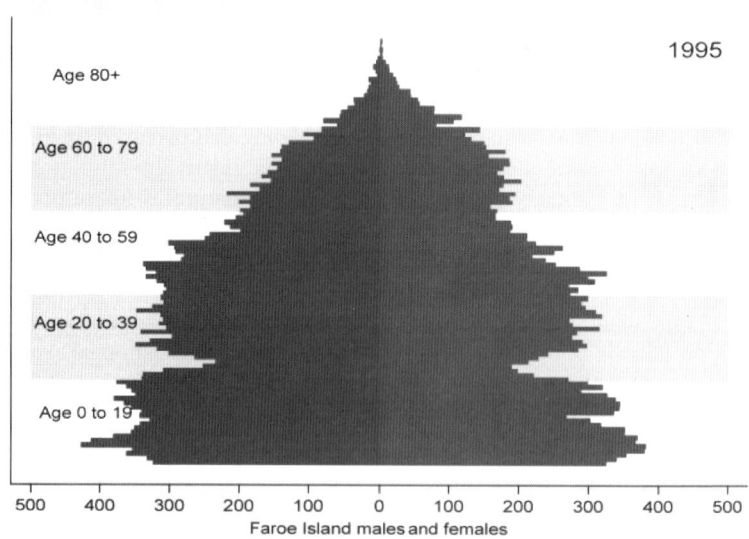

Figure 7: *Age-sex distribution of Faroe Islands population in 1995, after net out-migration. [Legend: males (left of 0); females (right of 0)].*

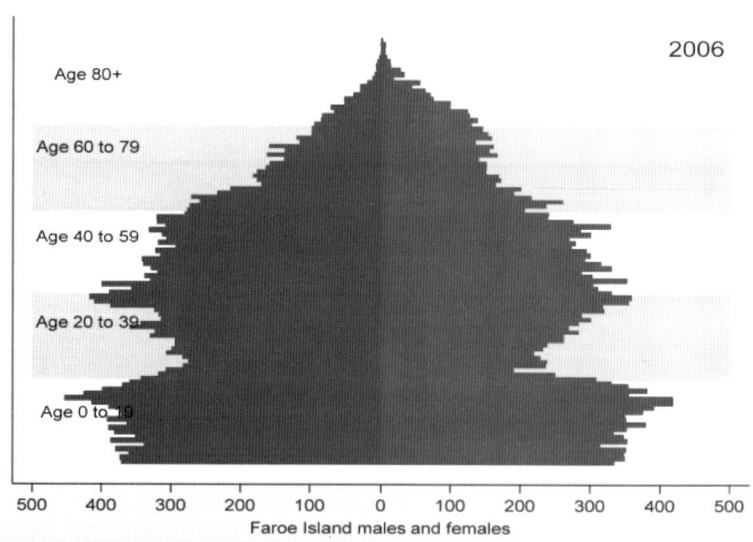

Figure 8: *Age-sex distribution of Faroe Islands population in 2006, after recovery from the crisis. [Legend: males (left of 0); females (right of 0)].*

Chapter 1: *Footprints: Demographic Effects of Out-Migration*

Sex ratios are less obvious in the pyramids of Figures 6–8, but such ratios nevertheless reflect the more persistent, non-crisis patterns mentioned earlier. At almost all ages below about 60 (in 1988) or 70 (by 2006), the Faroese population has a relative excess of males (Figs. 9–11). In many age cohorts there are more than 120 men per 100 women.

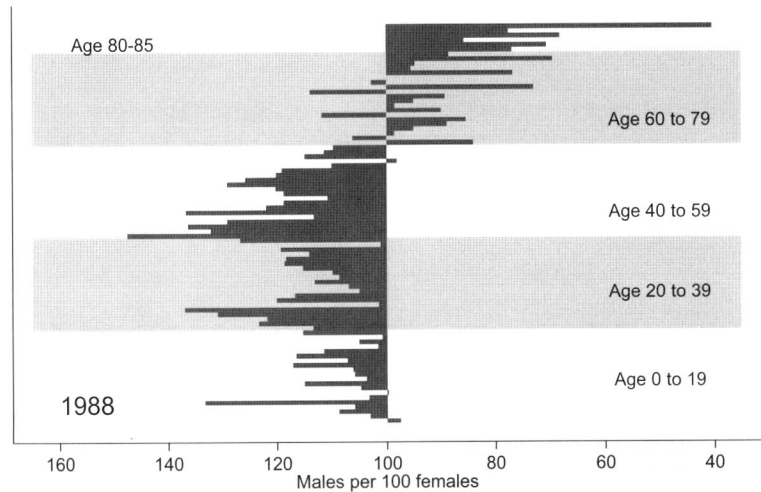

Figure 9: *Sex ratio by age in the Faroe Islands population in 1988.*

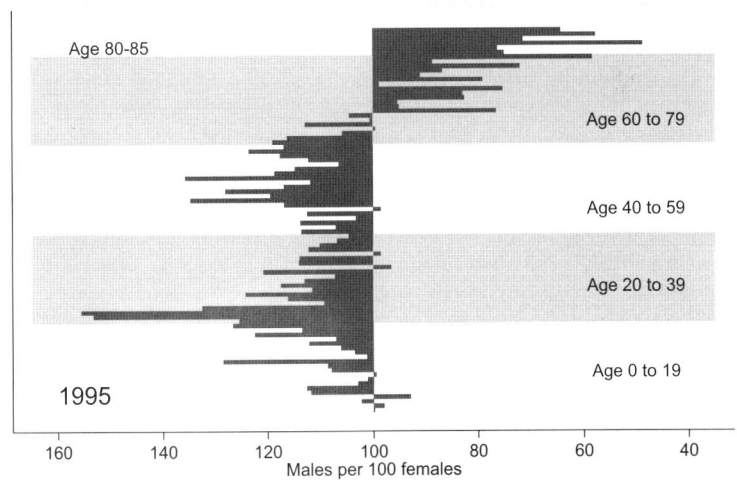

Figure 10: *Sex ratio by age in the Faroe Islands population in 1995.*

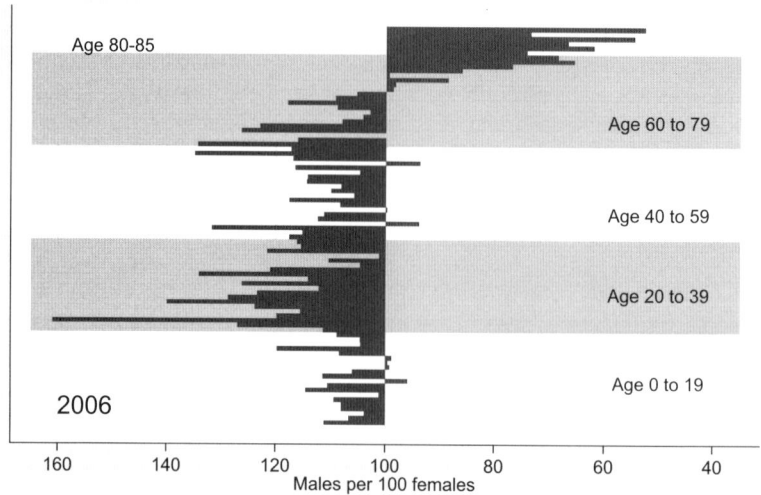

Figure 11: *Sex ratio by age in the Faroe Islands population in 2006.*

Conclusion

Individual migration decisions are non-random along dimensions more personal than the simple demographic patterns displayed here. Such decisions select for energy and ambition, or people who believe they could do better somewhere else. Departures related to these less tangible qualities might not leave such clear footprints in demographic statistics, but their consequences will be no less real.

Understanding this, northern residents often look for ways to make their communities more attractive, specifically to retain local youth. Government investments to create jobs or expand educational choices have been effective in some places, particularly those functioning as regional government, transportation, and educational centers. At the high end, universities seem to be a new growth engine. Stimulating private enterprise, even with subsidies, has had mixed success in remote area where labor and other market conditions were not competitive to begin with. More persuasively, the need for jobs to retain youth has provided arguments for encouraging industrial development of natural resources. Future studies could more systematically examine how migration and demographic indicators respond to policy initiatives.

The challenges of reducing out-migration from small places are by no means unique to the Circumpolar North. A recent survey of 7,800 residents in selected rural counties of 9 U.S. states (not including Alaska; *see* Hamilton *et al.* 2008) asked the following question:

If your own teenage child, or the child of a close friend, asked you for advice, would you recommend that they should plan to stay in this town as an adult, or move away for opportunities somewhere else?
Recommend they stay here?
Recommend they move away?

More than two-thirds of the survey's respondents said that they would advise their teenager to move away. Looking at the other side of this conversation, the high school student surveys described earlier (Seyfrit and Hamilton 1992; Hamilton and Seyfrit 1993, 1994a,b; Seyfrit *et al.* 1998) found that many northern teenagers, often the majority, shared (realistically or not) a similar hope of moving away. Out-migration is an area where individual and community self-interest can pull in opposite directions. Policies might influence their choices, with outcomes revealed by how people vote with their feet.

References

Hamilton, L.C. and C.L. Seyfrit (1993). Town–village contrasts in Alaskan youth aspirations. *Arctic* 46(3): 255–263.
Hamilton, L.C. and C.L. Seyfrit (1994a). Resources and hopes in Newfoundland. *Society and Natural Resources* 7(6): 561–578.
Hamilton, L.C. and C.L. Seyfrit (1994b). Female flight? Gender balance and outmigration by Native Alaskan villagers. *Arctic Medical Research* 53(Supplement 2): 189–193.
Hamilton, L.C. and C.L. Seyfrit (1994c). Coming out of the country: Community size and gender balance among Alaskan Natives. *Arctic Anthropology* 31(1): 16–25.
Hamilton, L.C., RO. Rasmussen, N.E. Flanders, and C.L. Seyfrit (1996). Outmigration and gender balance in Greenland. *Arctic Anthropology* 33(1): 89–97.
Hamilton, L.C., C.L. Seyfrit, and C. Bellinger (1997). Environment and sex ratios among Alaska Natives: An historical perspective. *Population and Environment* 18(3): 283–299.
Hamilton, L.C. and O. Otterstad (1998a). Sex ratio and community size: Notes from the northern Atlantic. *Population and Environment* 20(1): 11–22.
Hamilton, L.C. and O. Otterstad (1998b). Demographic change and fisheries dependence in the northern Atlantic. *Human Ecology Review* 5(1): 16–22.
Hamilton, L.C. and R.L. Haedrich (1999). Ecological and population changes in fishing communities of the North Atlantic Arc. *Polar Research* 18(2): 383–388.
Hamilton, L.C. and C.M. Duncan (2000). Fisheries dependence and social change in the northern Atlantic, pp. 95–105 in Symes, D. (ed.), *Fisheries Dependent Regions*. Oxford: Fishing News Books.

Hamilton, L.C. and M.J. Butler (2001). Outport adaptations: Social indicators through Newfoundland's cod crisis. *Human Ecology Review* 8(2): 1–11.

Hamilton, L.C., B.C. Brown, and R.O. Rasmussen (2003). West Greenland's cod-to-shrimp transition: Local dimensions of climatic change. *Arctic* 56(3): 271–282.

Hamilton, L.C., C.R. Colocousis, and S.T.F. Johansen (2004a). Migration from resource depletion: The case of the Faroe Islands. *Society and Natural Resources* 17(5): 443–453.

Hamilton, L.C., R.L. Haedrich, and C.M. Duncan (2004b). Above and below the water: Social/ecological transformation in northwest Newfoundland. *Population and Environment* 25(3): 195–215.

Hamilton, L.C., S. Jónsson, H. Ögmundardóttir, and I.M. Belkin (2004c). Sea changes ashore: The ocean and Iceland's herring capital. *Arctic* 57(4): 325–335.

Hamilton, L.C. (2007). Climate, fishery and society interactions: Observations from the North Atlantic. *Deep Sea Research II* 54: 2958–2969.

Hamilton, L.C., L.R. Hamilton, C.M. Duncan, and C.R. Colocousis (2008). *Place Matters: Challenges and Opportunities in Four Rural Americas.* Durham, NH: Carsey Institute, University of New Hampshire.

Hamilton, L.C. and A.M. Mitiguy (2009). Visualizing population dynamics of Alaska's Arctic communities. *Arctic* 62(4): 393–398.

Hamilton, L.C. and R.O. Rasmussen (2010). Population, sex ratios and development in Greenland. *Arctic* 63(1): 43–52.

Seyfrit, C.L. and L.C. Hamilton (1992). Who will leave? Oil, migration, and Scottish island youth. *Society and Natural Resources* 5(3): 263–276.

Seyfrit, C.L. and L.C. Hamilton (1997). Alaska Native youth and their attitudes towards education. *Arctic Anthropology* 34(1): 135–148.

Seyfrit, C.L., L.C. Hamilton, C.M. Duncan, and J. Grimes (1998). Ethnic identity and aspirations among rural Alaska youth. *Sociological Perspectives* 41(2): 343–365.

2

The Complex Geography of Native Migration in Arctic Alaska[1]

Lee Huskey and Lance Howe[2]

In recent times, Alaska's north has been a sending region; more people move from the region than move to it. This pattern of movement is especially important for the majority Iñupiat population. As a number of papers in this volume suggest, this has been the common experience of the northernmost parts of most Arctic nations. This paper examines the recent pattern of migration of Alaska Native residents of the Arctic region.

The regional pattern of net out-migration is consistent with the theory that migration is a means of adjusting to economic conditions. The people of Alaska's rural regions engage in a significant subsistence economy, which provides the traditional economic base for many small communities. However, the monetary economy of Alaska's northern communities offers relatively few jobs or other income-earning opportunities. If people move to improve their economic well-being, then net out-migration seems an appropriate response to the region's economic condition.

The actual pattern of northern migration is more complicated than the story told by net migration. People move into as well as out of the region. Return migration is an important flow in the north; therefore, population movement within the region must also be considered. People move between communities within the region, even when these communities offer no real

---

[1] The research that forms the basis of this paper was conducted while the authors were Special Sworn Status researchers of the US Census Bureau at the Center for Economic Studies. Research results and conclusions expressed are those of the authors and do not necessarily reflect the views of the Census Bureau. The data used in this paper has been carefully screened by the US Census to insure that no confidential data are revealed.

[2] The work on this paper was supported by an award from the National Science Foundation (ARC-0457662), *Migration in the Arctic: Subsistence, Jobs, and Well-Being in Urban and Rural Communities.* Any opinions, findings, and conclusions expressed are those of the author and do not necessarily reflect the views of NSF.

improvement in income or employment opportunities. In addition, population movement between communities seems to follow a pattern. The stepping-stone pattern characterized by movement to ever bigger places, which is common in other parts of the world, also occurs in the North. This contribution describes the more complex pattern of migration in Alaska's north.

Understanding the patterns, determinants, and consequences of migration will be helpful in a number of policy debates, as migration may change the character and demographic structure of small northern places (Hamilton and Seyfrit 1994). Migration patterns will both affect and be affected by public decisions about the availability and distribution of local resources. For example, the welfare-improving effects of transfers, public investment and other public spending in rural communities may be limited by their effects on mobility (Knapp and Huskey 1988). The migration response may be a central consideration in decisions about the costly relocation of villages in response to changing sea and ice conditions along the Arctic coast.

This paper is organized in four sections. The first provides an overview of the region and its special demographic and economic character. This is followed by a discussion of the dominant economic explanations of migration found in the literature on migration in the northern regions of North America. The next section describes the recent history of Arctic Alaska as a sending region. The complicated pattern of migration in Alaksa's North is discussed in the fourth section. Finally, the findings and research questions raised by this are summarized.

Alaska's Arctic Region

The Arctic region examined for this study is a vast area that contains three of Alaska's most northern census areas (*see* Fig. 1). Two of these areas (the North Slope and the Northwest Arctic Boroughs) are organized as local governments or boroughs, while the third (the Nome census area) has no regional government. The region is sparsely settled. In 2004, approximately 24,000 people lived in an area measuring 146,000 square miles. The communities are connected only by air and seasonal river travel, since the region lacks any significant road connections. (Much of the following is based on Fried and Windisch-Cole 2005).

Fried and Windisch-Cole examined the region in the first years of the decade. Alaska's Arctic is younger, more male, and more Alaska Native than the state as a whole. The median age in the three census areas was six to ten years younger than that for the state. In the Arctic, the ratio of men to women was higher than the State's ratio of 107 men for every 100 women. For example, the Nome census area had the highest, at 117 men to 100 women. At least 70 percent of the population in each of the three census

Chapter 2: *The Complex Geography of Alaska Native Migration in the Arctic*

areas was Alaska Native, while only 16 percent of the state's population in 2000 was Alaska Native. The state's northern areas are demographically different from the state as a whole, a difference that reflects the consequences of migration but that also influences the pattern of northern migration.

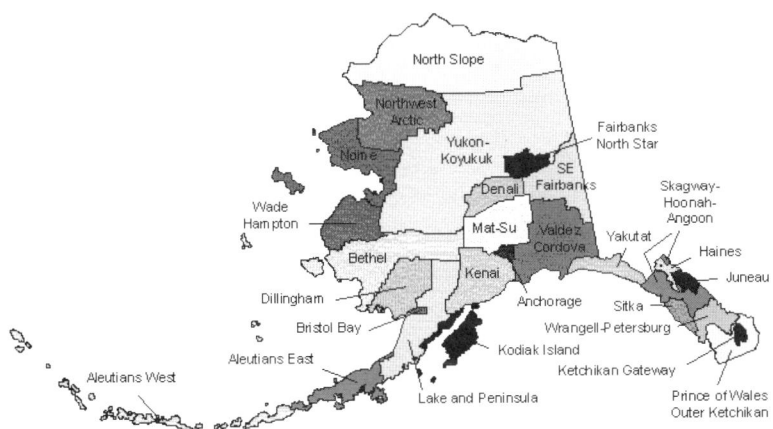

Figure 1: *Map of Alaska Census Regions.* Source: Alaska Department of Labor (http://146.63.75.50/research/cgin/cenmaps/statemap.htm)

The region's rural character is reflected in its economic geography. In 2000, approximately one half of the region's population lived in one of three regional centers, each having a population of at least 3,000; the population of the largest (Barrow) was about 4,600. Of the three regions, the North Slope was the most 'urbanized' with about 62 percent of its population centered in Barrow. The population outside the regional centers lived in 34 smaller communities; the majority of these had less than 500 people. The scale of these communities determined the type of services available and the character of the community; both of these are likely to influence migration.

Like most rural areas in Alaska, the community economies of the Arctic region are based on three factors: the market economy, the public sector economy, and the traditional or subsistence economy. The public sector economy is a major component of the local monetary economy: it provides employment, social services, and real income subsidies. In 2003, direct public sector hiring accounted for at least 42 percent of employment in all regions of Arctic Alaska. The impact of the public sector is even greater once spending through non-profits and the provision of social services is included.

In all three regions, local economies are tied to the international market economy through major resource development. The North Slope Borough contains a major area of petroleum activity, including the large Prudhoe Bay oil fields. In the Northwest Arctic Borough, Red Dog Mine is a world-scale zinc operation. Nome region communities are tied to the world economy through local Community Development Quota Corporations that participate in the Bering Sea fishery. Resource production contributes employment opportunities and local resource ownership to local economies. Most importantly, resource production provides tax revenue to local governments resource projects provide a major source of revenue for both the North Slope and Northwest Arctic Boroughs.

Despite the location of these major resource operations, convential economic indicators tell a similar story of relatively poor economic performance throughout the region. In 2003, while the state's unemployment rate was about eight percent, the unemployment rate in the Northwest Arctic Borough was close to 20 percent. While unemployment was not as high in the other two areas, it was significantly higher than the state average. Real rates of unemployment were likely much higher in these small labour markets since the number of discouraged workers was likely to be high.

While there was some variation throughout the North, wage incomes were much lower in the Arctic. All three census areas in 2000 had much higher poverty rates than the 6.4% found in Anchorage, Alaska's major city. The per-capita income picture was mixed: in 2002, it was $32,799 in Alaska, while in both Nome and the Northwest Arctic Borough it was close to $25,000. Per capita income in the North Slope Borough was almost $3,000 higher than the state average; however, income differences underestimate comparisons of Arctic economic welfare with that of urban areas of the state, since they ignore the significant cost-of-living differences. The Arctic is a high-cost region; for example, food costs in Barrow were estimated to be 150% of the cost in Anchorage (Robinson and Fried 2005).

The relatively poor monetary economy in the region is moderated by the region's active subsistence economy. The harvesting of wild fish and game provides a significant source of real income to residents of the Arctic region. According to the Alaska Division of Subsistence (Wolfe 2000) most rural families in Alaska depend on subsistence hunting and fishing. For surveyed communities in the Arctic, nearly 78% of households participated in the harvest of fish and 63% harvested game. Since subsistence foods are widely shared, more residents used resources than harvested them— approximately 96% of the region's population used fish and 92% used game resources.

Wild food harvest in the region during the 1990s averaged 516 pounds per person per year. This is significantly greater than the estimated 375 pounds harvested in the rural areas of the state. These harvests provided an important portion of dietary needs; residents received over 300% of the Recommended Dietary Allowance of protein and about half of their required calories from subsistence fish and game harvests (Wolfe 2000). Therefore, subsistence activities add significantly to the real income of residents of the Arctic.

The Arctic region of Alaska presents a puzzling economic picture. The region is a central location for the state's major resource industries. Prudhoe Bay, Red Dog mine, and the Bering Sea fisheries are significant contributors to the state's economy. Yet by most monetary indicators the region is one of limited economic opportunity.

The relatively poor regional wage economy provides the circumstances that create a sending region. However, the significant subsistence economy, providing another impotant source of real income, may limit the tendency to move from the region, since it provides a significant source of real income and is likely to require skills that do not transfer well to other regions of the state. The importance of the region's transfer or public assistance may also dampen the migration pressures created by the wage economy by providing social services, such as education and housing, at relatively low costs.

Migration in the North

Population movement has always been a factor in rural Alaska. Traditionally, Alaska Natives moved to follow subsistence opportunities (Nelson 1973). The modern era brought increased connections with other regions and social and economic changes which were accompanied by migration into and out of rural Alaska (Alonso and Rust 1976). In this section we consider the historic pattern of Alaska Native population. Since the literature on Alaska Native migration is limited, literature on indigenous population movement in the Canadian north is also examined.

Alonso and Rust (1976) described the increased flow of Alaska's Native population to the state's urban areas between 1950 and 1970. The share of Alaska Natives in the state's cities grew from 5.3 percent in 1950 to almost 24 percent by 1970. Alonso and Rust predicted that this urbanizing trend would continue, especially as the large cohort of children reached the age of mobility. However, the rural–to–urban migration flows were not one-way. Alonso and Rust found considerable migration from the state's urban to rural regions and predicted that as the connection between urban and rural Alaska increased, the gross population flows between the regions would also increase.

Alonso and Rust also predicted a decline of Alaska's smallest villages and a concentration of the rural population in regional centers. In 1950 almost half of the places in north and west Alaska had 100 or fewer people, while there were only two places with populations over 1,500.

Between 1950 and 1970 the number of villages in this region also fell by seven percent, and by 1970, fewer than one-third had populations of less than 100 people, and 6 places had populations greater than 1,500. The growth of the large places reflected the concentration of administrative activities in regional centers and larger villages.

Kruse and Foster (1986) generally supported the trends found by Alonso and Rust through 1970. However, they found a reversal of one of these trends in the 1970s and first part of the 1980s. Based on an examination of Census and Vital Statistics data, they found increased in-migration by Alaska Natives to the state's smallest places. During this period there was a continued out-migration of rural Alaska Natives that was matched by an accelerated in-migration of non-Natives to rural regions. Their analysis suggested that Native migration to both the smallest places and to the state's urban areas came from the larger rural communities.

In contrast to the Alaska experience, migration does not seem to have been as important for the Native population of the Canadian North. When he reviewed population change in the 1980s, Stabler (1989) found little movement by the Native population in the Northwest Territories. Migration of the non-Native population was influenced by changes in economic conditions, but economic conditions had little influence on the Native population. The difference between the experience of Alaska and northern Canada likely reflects differences in the costs and benefits of moving and not differences in preferences. Alaska's cities are closer to the villages and have relatively larger Native populations than Canadian cities. These make both the economic and social costs of rural–to–urban migration lower in Alaska than in Canada.

Though limited, the existing literature on Alaska Native migration can provide some indication of the reasons for migration among the northern indigenous population. Marshall (1993) found that improving job opportunities and the chance of finding work were the reasons most frequently cited for moving among inter-community migrants on Alaska's North Slope. Kuo and Lu (1975) and Wonders and Brown (1984) found that looking for work was also an important reason for Native migration within the Canadian North. When examining Alaska Native migration in the 1990 Census, Huskey et al. (2004) found the potential for high earnings (wage time hours worked) influenced the movement of Native men and women from rural to urban areas.

Age and gender also affect the propensity to migrate among the northern indigenous population. Young adult Natives had relatively higher migration rates and made up a larger proportion of migrants in Northern Canada and Alaska (Kruse and Foster 1986; Kuo and Lu 1975; Wonders and Brown 1960). According to Huskey et al. (2004), young, single Alaska Natives are more likely to move from rural to urban regions in Alaska. Hamilton and Seyfrit (1994) suggest that the greater propensity of women to move from village to regional centers and urban areas was responsible for a gender gap in Alaska villages.

The continued attraction of small communities and rural regions for the Native population of Alaska and the Canadian North reflects the importance of subsistence opportunities and social connections. Subsistence hunting and fishing provide real income for rural residents and likely involve place-specific human capital. A number of Canadian studies found opportunities to improve subsistence activities affected migration decisions (Kuo and Lu 1975; Wonders and Brown 1984; Gardner 1994). Marshall (1993) found social reasons, such as marriage, housing, being with family and friends, were as important as jobs in determining migration within Northern Alaska.

Public policy also influences migration patterns. Public spending can make a community a better place to live by the provision of infrastructure and services (Kruse and Foster 1986; Wonders and Brown, 1984). Public spending can also influence income opportunities in a place through the creation of employment and direct transfer payments (Stabler 1990). Knapp and Huskey (1988) estimated that the transfer economy of Coastal Western Alaska discouraged population movement and increased the population by thirty percent above what it would have been without such social transfers.

Public policy also affects migration from rural regions through spending on education. Increased spending on local schools improves the amenities that communities offer. Kruse and Foster (1986) suggested that spending on village schools influenced migration to smaller Alaska communities in the 1980s. In Canada, Stabler (1989) suggested that migration rates from rural regions would vary with levels of education; limited education decreased the probability of getting permanent employment and therefore the benefits of migration. Other Canadian research supported a positive effect of education on permanent migration from rural communities (Kuo and Lu 1975; Wonders and Brown 1984). Huskey *et al.* (2004) found a pattern of migration that suggested young people may actually move from rural to urban regions to acquire training and education.

In many ways, the history of migration in the North American north seems a standard story. People move for employment opportunities; the young and educated are more likely to move; and place matters. The role of subsistence in migration decisions enriches the northern migration story. Subsistence harvests increase real incomes in the region, reducing the benefits of moving, and place-specific subsistence skills increase the cost of moving. Examining the patterns and determinants of past migration is useful for anticipating the future of the region's population.

The Alaska Arctic: A Sending Region

The pattern of net out-migration experienced throughout Alaska's Arctic region is not surprising to an economist. The notion that migrants move to improve their economic welfare has a long history in economics (Lucas 1997). Sjaastad (1962) formalized the idea that people moved for higher income opportunities when he described the migration decision as a human capital investment. Todaro (1969) restated Sjaastad's model and described migration decisions based on the expectation of improved economic well-being. Todaro's story of migration has been widely accepted as the description of rural–to–urban migration in developing countries by both economists and policy-makers.

According to these models, the pattern of regional migration can be explained by a pattern of relative economic opportunity. People move from regions of limited opportunity to regions of greater opportunity. This is consistent with the economic principle that people will act in such a way as to improve their situation. The pattern is also consistent with the great modern population movements from the southern to the northern hemisphere and from eastern to western Europe. From this perspective, the net out-migration from the Alaskan Arctic can be simply explained as a movement from a region of limited economic opportunity.

Table 1. Net Migration Arctic Region.

Decade	Starting Population	Natural Increase	Net Migration
1970-1980	13,248	3,547	-228
1980-1990	15,567	4,654	+159
1990-2000	20,380	4,328	-919
2000-2007	23,759	2,940	-3046

Source: Alaska Department of Labor and Workforce Development, Table 2.3, 2008

The Arctic region of Alaska has a mixed history of being a sending region (*see* Table 1). Between 1970 and 2000, the region experienced two decanal periods of net out-migration (1970-1980 and 1990-2000) and one decade of net in-migration (1980-1990)[3]. The region experienced negative net out-migration over this entire period. But in fact, migration had a limited effect on population growth in many of these decades. High rates of natural increase were the dominant demographic change throughout these three decades—more than ten times as great as total net out-migration. The

---

[3] This section examines the change in total regional population. Population estimates were made by the Alaska Dept. of Labor and Workforce Development. Both Alaska Native and non-Native populations are included in these estimates of population change.

higher rates of natural increase meant that between 1970 and 2000, the regional population increased even though the Arctic was a sending region.

This demographic pattern changed after 2000. For the whole of the Arctic region, the population declined between 2000 and 2007. For this period, net out-migration was greater than natural increase. The estimated decline in population was relatively small—less than half of one percent of the 2000—population but it did suggest a change in demographic relationships. The change resulted from a decrease in the rate of natural increase and a concomitant an increase in the rate of net out-migration. The rate of natural increase fell from 17.5% of the starting population in the 1990s to 12.4% for the period between 2000 and 2007. Comparing the same time periods, the rate of net out-migration rose from 4.5% to 12.8%.

The migration experience differed throughout the region during these four time periods (*see* Table 2). The Northwest Arctic Borough experienced net out-migration throughout the entire time period. In each decade, net migration rates were significant, and never lower than about four percent of the population. The migration experience of the Nome Census region was similar to the region as a whole. The region experienced net in-migration during the 1980s, followed by relatively higher rates of net out-migration through to the end of the period.

Table 2. Net Migration Across the Arctic Region.

Decade	Nome Census Area	North Slope Borough	Northwest Arctic Borough	Arctic Region
1970-1980	-247	+167	-148	-228
1980-1990	+48	+420	-309	+159
1990-2000	-755	+166	-330	-919
2000-2007	-741	-1,557	-748	-3,046

Source: Alaska Department of labor and Workforce Development, Table 2.3, 2008

For the first three decades, the North Slope Borough experienced positive net migration; the rate ranged from almost three percent during the 1990s to ten percent during the 1980s. After 2000, this pattern changed and the North Slope Borough experienced significant net out-migration (estimated at approximately 20 percent of the 2000 population). The North Slope was the only part of the Arctic region that experienced a decline in population because net out-migration was greater than natural increase.

For the region as a whole, population fell after 2000 because net out-migration exceeded natural increase. Net out-migration was the pattern in all parts of the Arctic region, but the significance of the out-migration from the North Slope Borough caused the population of the entire region to decline. There are two possible explanations of the pattern of net migration found in Alaska's Arctic region which illustrate the consequences of past migration. First, net out-migration may reflect an aging of the population. As the young migrate from a region, the regional birth rate will drop, death rates will increase, and natural increase will decline. A second explanation reflects the relationship between economic health and migration. The net in-migration experienced in the North Slope Borough prior to 2000 likely reflected a relatively strong economy. The economy of the Borough has struggled since 2000 (Fried and Windisch-Cole 2005). Employment-driven migrants into a region are most likely to move at times of economic decline.

Arctic Alaska Migration: A Complex Process

A number of interesting research questions arise from the pattern of net migration in Arctic Alaska. A better understanding of the economic determinants of migration may be derived by comparing the varying pattern of net migration over time and across regions with changes in regional economic welfare. While these may be important questions, focusing on net migration provides too simple a story of migration in the north. This section examines a more complicated set of migration patterns that are hidden by a focus on regional net migration.

Net migration stories are useful to our understanding of migration. According to Greenwood *et al.* (1991) net-migration models emphasize the equilibrium-seeking tendency of population movement. Net migration models assume that population will move toward more desirable locations. In equilibrium, theory suggests, all places will provide equal well-being. Continual net movement from one place has been explained by changes in age, income, and tastes of a region's residents which change their evaluation of the region's economic opportunities and quality of life. Net migration studies have contributed to our understanding of the value of regional differences (Evans 1990). Greenwood and his co-authors suggest that net migration models are more appropriate when the concern focuses on the stable population structure. However, net migration models may not be best suited to the study of Arctic Alaska where significant migration and demographic change has been occurring.

Net migration patterns in Alaska's Arctic provide only part of the story. When these patterns are examined at the scale of the community or small region we see that migration is a complicated process. Consequently, explaining the northern Alaska pattern only in terms of net migration leaves many important patterns unexplained and important questions unanswered. This section examines the complex pattern of migration in Arctic Alaska, and specifically the importance of return migration, village-to-village migration, and stepwise migration. These patterns broaden the need for explanations beyond relative economic opportunity in order to explain the choices made by Alaska Natives moving into, out of, and within Arctic Alaska.

Chapter 2: *The Complex Geography of Alaska Native Migration in the Arctic*

The decision to study net migration often reflects the availability of data. Economic studies of migration are frequently empirical studies, and net migration is the most widely available data. The more complex patterns of Native migration in the Alaska Arctic were studied using a special data source based on work undertaken at the California Research Census Data Center.These data are based on the migration question in the 1990 and 2000 decennial US Census where respondents were asked "where did you live five years ago?" Using decennial census micro-data, origin and destination tables can be generated for arctic villages, regional centers, and urban areas. Migrants are people over five years old who lived in a different community sometime in the previous five years. Migration rates reported below are for Alaska Natives older than five years old.

The numbers reported are estimates. Census disclosure rules censor data from small places. In addition, the migration question only appears on the Census long-form and so reported migration numbers are estimates based on this sample. In our study region, roughly 50% of households were targeted for long-form surveys. Thus, while sampling and non-sampling error are problems to be considered, they are less of an issue because of the relatively large sample.

Return Migration
Net migration highlights the dominant flow of population in one direction. For sending regions, it emphasizes that people are leaving the region. But people move into as well as out of regions, so there will be migration into Arctic communities even when the net flows are away from these communities. For Alaska Natives moving into the Arctic region this is likely to be return migration, which is significant in Alaska's north.

Table 3. Population Churning in Arctic Regions, 1995-2000.

	In-migrants	Out-migrants	In/Out Migrants
North Slope Borough	1156	1465	0.79
Northwest Arctic Borough	877	1231	0.71
Nome Census Area	1073	1866	0.58

Source: Regional flows from County to County Migration Flow Files, US Census 2000. Population flows include Native and non-Native movers.

To understand migration behavior we need to understand the patterns and determinants of both these counter-balancing population flows. The factors that influence in-migration are likely to differ from those influencing out-migration decisions. For example, in other parts of the U.S. a region's economic welfare has been shown to have a greater influence on in-migration decisions to the region than on the decision to migrate from the region (Greenwood 1997). The explanations of return migration will not simply be the inverse of the reasons given for out-migration decisions.

Table 4. Population Churning in the Arctic, 1995-2000.

	In-migrants	Out-migrants	In/Out Migrants
North Slope Borough			
Barrow	400	380	1.05
Villages	215	335	0.64
Northwest Arctic Borough			
Kotzebue	395	570	0.69
Villages	400	520	0.77
Nome Census Area			
Nome City	335	455	0.74
Villages	385	500	0.77

Source: US Census, Center for Economic Studies, Decennial Census Data.

Alaska Native in-migration to the Arctic is significant when compared to out-migration flows. Tables 3 and 4 compare the flows of migrants between 1995 and 2000 for the regions, regional centers, and villages of Arctic Alaska. For each region, return migration replaces at least half of the population that left during the period. The regional population flows in Table 3 include both Native and non-Native populations. The same patterns exist for regional centers and villages in the Arctic region. During this period, Barrow actually experienced net in-migration of Alaska Natives. For regional centers and villages, both in- and out-migrants may have moved from within the region as well as from outside.

We need to explain return migration, and explore why people move back to a sending region. There are three possible hypotheses. First, this movement may reflect the structure of the regional job market. People have different skill sets and different preferences for types of jobs; migration might occur as a means to match people with types of employment available in the region. People may leave a region when jobs are available because they do not have the skills or tastes for those particular jobs. A second hypothesis relates to the role of life cycle in migration decisions. People may move away when they are young to acquire human capital, to seek the bright lights, or for income. They move back once they have the required skills or income. Lucas (1997) points out that temporary and circular migration are important flows in developing regionswhere these short-term moves may be part of a household's informal insurance mechanism (Rosenzweig and Stark 1989; Stark and Lucas 1988). Finally, migration is often based on the expectation of improved welfare. Return migrants may have found that the new place did not meet their expectations. This is one reason research evidence suggests that people who leave a region are likely to have a greater propensity to move back (Greenwood 1997).

Village-to-Village Migration
The research focus in developing regions of the world has been on rural-to-urban migration. However, according to Lucas (1997), in regions where it has been documented, rural-to-rural moves take place at a greater rate than rural-to-urban moves. The primary research problem in other regions is that these moves are not well-documented. Census micro data provide a means by which to describe this type of migration.

Villages are the smallest types of communities in rural Arctic Alaska. In 2000, there were 23 villages of less than 500 people and nine villages with a population of between 500 and 1,000. The Arctic region had three places with over 3,000 people that would qualify as regional centers (Williams 2006). Village-to-village movement is similar to the intra-rural migration referred to by Lucas. Table 5 illustrates the importance of this movement in the Arctic region where migration is not always up the place hierarchy or out of the region. Migration between villages was significant in both 1990 and 2000.

The relative importance of village-to-village migration varied across Arctic regions, but it was a significant share of migration flows in all regions. In-migrants from other villages accounted for almost half of the in-migrants to villages in the Northwest Arctic Borough in 2000. The smallest share of in-migrants moving from other villages was 20 percent in the North Slope Borough in 2000. In all cases, the share of village out-migrants moving to other villages (vs. moving to larger communities) was lower than the share of in-migrants moving from other villages; this share ranged from 10 percent in the North Slope Borough village in 2000 to 32 percent in the Northwest Arctic Borough in the same year. Village-to-village migrants are also more likely to move to villages within the same region of the Arctic (Howe and Huskey 2007).

Table 5. Migration to and from Arctic Villages, 1995-2000 and 1985-1990.

	North Slope Villages	Nome Villages	NW Arctic Villages
1990			
Village-to-Village migration	50	120	110
Share of total in-migrants to Arctic villages	23.8%	37.5%	32.8%
Share of total out-migrants from Arctic villages	13.3%	19.2%	29.7%
2000			
Village-to-Village migration	35	130	165
Share of total in-migrants to Arctic villages	19.4%	34.7%	47.1%
Share of total out-migrants from Arctic villages	10.4%	26.0%	31.7%

Source: US Census, Center for Economic Studies, Decennial Census Data.

How do we explain these important moves? Village-to-village movement means that people are choosing not only to stay in a sending region but also to stay in the same type of settlement. This could be because some villages offer better economic opportunities, or because villages differ in public amenities, or because of other factors that influence quality of life. Marriage and other family matters are more likely to be reasons for these types of moves. Understanding the role of geography is also important in these large, poorly connected regions. Village-to-village moves are significant and a full understanding of migration behavior in the region needs to explain these moves.

Stepwise Migration
In much of the developing world, households rarely move directly from remote rural settings to urban centers; rather, it usually happens in a stepwise pattern. An idealized pattern has population moving up a place size hierarchy from the smallest to ever larger communities. This pattern has been called by a variety of names: stepwise migration, stage migration, and chain migration (Conway 1980).

The idea that migration proceeds in a stepwise manner was introduced over 120 years ago in Ravenstien's *Laws of Migration* (Ravenstien 1885; Lee 1966). Ravenstein stated that most moves occur over short distances and that migration from smaller communities fills gaps created as residents of larger communities move to take advantage of opportunities in ever larger places. People moving up the place hierarchy characterized the pattern of migration in the U.S. through the 1950s, a pattern that continues to describe migration in many developing countries (Plane *et al.* 2005).

Table 6. Migration to and from Arctic Villages and Arctic Regional Centers.

		North Slope Villages		Nome Villages		Northwest Arctic Villages	
		No.	Share of Total In or Out Migrants	No.	Share of Total In or Out Migrants	No.	Share of Total In or Out Migrants
1985-1990	Moved to the village from the regional center	45	21.4%	70	21.9%	80	23.9%
1985-1990	Migration out of the village to the regional center	150	40.0%	180	28.8%	130	35.1%
1995-2000	Moved to the village from the regional center	35	16.3%	60	15.6%	90	22.5%
1995-2000	Migration out of the village to the regional center	160	47.8%	100	20.0%	145	27.9%

Source: US Census, Center for Economic Studies, Decennial Census Data.

The geography of Alaska as described in the last section includes small villages, larger regional centers, and urban areas. Migrants from villages and regional centers have the option to move to any of these types of places. They may also move out of state. A stepwise migration pattern would result in the dominant flows up the hierarchy of places and the majority of flows to places closest in size.

The stepwise pattern of movement seems consistent with migration in Arctic Alaska. Table 6 describes migration between villages and regional centers in three regions of Arctic Alaska. In each region and time period, there is net migration from the village to the regional center. The relative importance of regional center migrants to the villages is similar in Nome, the Northwest Arctic Borough, and The North Slope Borough, where between 15 and 24 percent of village in-migrants are from the regional center. The importance of the regional center as a destination for people leaving the villages varies more greatly. Almost half of the out-migrants from villages move to the regional center in the North Slope, while in Nome only one in five village movers migrate to the regional center. This variety of experience is consistent with the fact that the North Slope is the most 'urbanized' of the Arctic regions, and the relative greater importance of village-to-village migration in Nome (*see* Table 5).

Table 7. Regional Center Out-Migration, 1995-2000 and 1985-1990.

		Out-Migration From (1995-2000)			Out-Migration From (1985-1990)		
		Barrow	Nome	Kotzebue	Barrow	Nome	Kotzebue
Out-Migration To:	North Slope Places	35	0	30	45	4	20
	Barrow	---	0	5	---	4	15
	Nome Places	0	60	15	4	70	10
	Nome	15	---	20	15	---	105
	NW Arctic Places	5	0	90	4	4	80
	Kotzebue	30	5	---	0	4	---
	Anchorage	145	145	250	95	35	135
	Fairbanks	20	0	20	0	35	0
	Other Alaska	90	170	95	105	50	25
	Subtotal Alaska	*340*	*380*	*530*	*270*	*210*	*390*
	Other State	40	75	35	40	50	30
	TOTAL	**380**	**455**	**570**	**310**	**260**	**425**

Source: US Census, Center for Economic Studies, Decennial Census Data.

Table 7 shows that out-migration from the regional centers also fits the stepwise pattern. Between 1995 and 2000, only Kotzebue showed significant out-migration from the regional center to the villages; village movement from Kotzebue was about 25 percent of the total. In both the

North Slope and Nome, out-migration to the villages was less than 15 percent. During this period, most migrants from Arctic regional centers moved to Anchorage, Fairbanks, or a collection of smaller urban areas in Alaska (other Alaska in Table 7); this type of move accounted for 67 percent of out-migration from the regional center. A similar pattern held in the earlier period, although there was more significant movement between regional centers.

The basis for the stepwise pattern of migration likely depends on the region examined, but some similarities exist across places. In developing countries, opportunities for both earnings and education are often greater in larger centres, resulting in movement up the hierarchy of places (Zhang 2002). Lucas (2001) describes the potential influence of distance as a determinant of this pattern. Distance affects the cost of a move—monetary, social, and psychic—which increases the potential for short moves. Psychic costs might be lesser because slightly larger centres would not be radically different from the place of emigration. Places not too distant or too different from the place of emigration may have relatively similar economies, which would allow work skills to be more easily transferred Finally, Lucas suggests that close moves make it easier to return to the place of origin if the move does not work out or in the face of a crisis. Moves close on the hierarchy may also follow friends and relatives reducing the social costs. Geib (2001) argued that for movement within or between reservation areas in the U.S., informal social safety nets and cultural ties are extremely important in the migration decision, even dampening the effects of transfer payments and other economic incentives.

All of these factors are likely at play in the migration decisions of Alaska Natives in the Arctic region as they move along the hierarchy. In addition, transportation connections may play a role in the choice of migration decisions; transport is expensive and operates on a hub-like system with connections to Alaska's cities primarily through the regional center. The importance of subsistence in rural Alaska also argues for moves to close, similar places. Just as Lucas suggested for employment, the value of subsistence skills will be maintained in similar environments.

Conclusions

Arctic Alaska is a sending region. Throughout most of the period after 1970 the region experienced net out-migration. Since the region is generally poorer and younger than the urban areas of the state, this pattern is consistent with the idea that migration is a way to pursue improved economic opportunity. This simple observation identifies the patterns, determinants, and consequences of Arctic migration. The story of the sending region can be used for future public and private decision-making.

There are, however, two facts which limit an easy interpretation of the region's net migration patterns. First, while the region may have a relatively poor monetary economy, there is an active and rich subsistence economy. Subsistence activities provide a local source of real income, and subsistence human capital may not be easily transferable to urban areas or even other areas of the region. The long-term pattern of Arctic migration may differ from past patterns because of the evolution of subsistence and the monetary economy.

The second limiting factor is that migration is a complex behavior. This paper has shown that the actual pattern of northern migration is more complicated than the story told by net migration. People move into, as well as out of, the region. Return migration is an important population flow which needs to be included in the story. Village-to-village migration is important; people move between communities in the region, even when these communities offer no real improvement in income or employment opportunities. Finally, population moves between communities follow a pattern. The stepwise pattern of migration to ever larger places, which is common in other parts of the world, also occurs in the north.

To arrive at an understanding of migration that will be helpful to both private and public decision-makers, migration behavior must be considered in the richness of all possible choices. The purpose of this chapter was to identify the dimensions of migration behavior in the Arctic. The variety of this experience may not fit any single story of migration decision-making perfectly, but this variety does provide the data from which to develop an understanding of the factors that influence migration behavior in the Arctic.

References

Alaska Dept. of Labor and Workforce Development (2008). Population estimates, characteristics of boroughs and census areas, components of change by region, 1970-2007. (retrieved May 29, 2008) http://almis.labor.state.ak.us.

Alonso, W. and E. Rust (1976). *The Evolving Pattern of Village Alaska. The Federal-State Land Use Planning Commission for Alaska*. Study No. 17. Anchorage.

Conway, D. (1980). Step-wise migration: toward a classification of the mechanism. *International Migration Review* Spring: 3-14.

Evans, A. (1990). The assumption of equilibrium in the analysis of migration and interregional differences: a review of some recent research. *Journal of Regional Science* 30: 515-531.

Fried, N. and B. Windisch-Cole (2005). The Northern Region. *Alaska Economic Trends,* March.

Gardner, P. (1994). Aboriginal community incomes and migration in the NWT: policy issues and alternatives. *Canadian Public Policy* 20: 297-317.

Geib, R. (2001). Do reservation Native Americans vote with their feet? A Re-Examination of Native American Migration, 1985-90. *American Journal of Economics and Sociology* 60: 4.

Chapter 2: *The Complex Geography of Alaska Native Migration in the Arctic*

Greenwood, M., P. Mueser, D. Plane, and A. Schlottmann (1991). New directions in migration research: perspectives from some North American regional science disciplines. *The Annals of Regional Science* 25: 237-270.

Greenwood, M. (1997). 'Internal migration in developed countries,' pp. 647-720 in M. Rosenzweig and O. Stark (eds.), *Handbook of Population and Family Economics*. Amsterdam: Elsevier Science.

Hamilton, L. and C. Seyfrit (1994). Coming out of the country: community size and gender balance among Alaska natives. *Arctic Anthropology* 31: 16-25.

Howe, L. and L. Huskey (2007). Migration decisions in the Arctic: empirical evidence of the stepping stones hypothesis. Western Regional Science Association Annual Meetings, Los Angeles.

Huskey, L, M. Berman, and A. Hill (2004). Leaving home, returning home: migration as a labor market choice for Alaska Natives. *The Annals of Regional Science* 38: 75-91.

Knapp, G. and L. Huskey (1988). The effects of transfers on remote regional economies: the transfer economy in rural Alaska. *Growth and Change* 19: 25-39.

Kuo, C. and C. Lu (1975). 'A study of migration behavior in the Mackenzie District of northern Canada.' Policy and Planning ACND Division, Northern Policy and Planning Branch. Ottawa: Indian Affairs and Northern Development.

Kruse, J. and K. Foster (1986). Changing Rural Settlement Patterns. *Alaska Review of Social and Economic Conditions* 23: 1-16.

Lee, E. (1966). A theory of migration. *Demography* 3: 47-57.

Lucas, R. (1997). 'Internal migration in developing countries' pp. 721-798 in M. Rosenzweig and O. Stark (eds.), *Handbook of Population and Family Economics*. Amsterdam: Elsevier Science.

Lucas, R. (2001). The effects of proximity and transportation on developing country population migrations. *Journal of Economic Geography* 1: 323.

Marshall, D. (1993). Migration and oil industry employment of North Slope Natives. US Dept. of the Interior, Minerals Management Service, Study MMS 92-0061.

Nelson, R. (1973). *Hunters of the Northern Forest*. Chicago: The University of Chicago Press.

Plane, D., C. Henrie, and M. Perry (2005). Migration up and down the urban hierarchy and across the life course. PNAS 102: online.

Ravenstein, E. 1885. The laws of migration. *Journal of the Royal Statistical Society* 68: 167-227.

Robinson, D. and N. Fried (2005). The Cost of Living in Alaska. *Alaska Economic Trends*, June.

Rosenzweig, M. and O. Stark (1989). Consumption smoothing, migration and marriage: evidence from rural India. *Journal of Political Economy* 97: 905-926.

Sjaastad, L. (1962). The costs and returns of human migration. *Journal of Political Economy* 70: 80-93.

Stabler, J. (1989). Dualism and development in the Northwest Territories. *Economic Development and Cultural Change* 37: 805-839.

Stabler, J. (1990). Native participation in Northern development: the impending crisis in the NWT. *Canadian Public Policy* 16: 262-283.

Stark, O. and R. Lucas (1988). Migration remittances and the family. *Journal of Economic Development and Cultural Change* 36: 465-481.

Todaro, M. (1969). A model of labor migration and urban unemployment in less developed countries. *American Economic Review* 59:138-48.

U.S. Census (2000). County to county migration flow files. (retrieved June 1, 2008) www.census.gov/population/www/cen2000/ctytoctyflow.html.

Williams, G. (2006). 'Alaska Population Overview, 2003-2004 Estimates.' Juneau: Alaska Dept. of Labor.

Wolfe, R. (2000). Subsistence in Alaska: A year 2000 update. Juneau: Division of Subsistence, Alaska Department of Fish and Game.

Wonders, W. and H. Brown (1984). Aklavik, Northwest Territories: The town that did not die, pp. 405-424 in: Olson R., R. Hastings, and F. Geddes (eds.), *Northern Ecology and Resource Management*. Edmonton: University of Alberta.

Zhang, J. (2002). Urbanization, population transition, and growth. *Oxford Economic Papers* 54: 91-117.

3

Migration in the Canadian Arctic: An Introduction

Chris Southcott[1]

One of the fundamental assumptions underlying discussions of human society in the Canadian Arctic is that it has been an extremely mobile population. Environmental conditions in the region meant that the indigenous population moved often to ensure their survival. The non-indigenous population's presence was determined by the boom and bust cycles of natural resource exploitation. Their migration into, within, and out of the region was dependent upon the rapidly changing conditions of resource discovery, depletion, and fluctuating market prices. Despite the recognized importance of migration in the Canadian Arctic, very little has been written that addresses it directly. Several explanations can be suggested for this absence of analysis. The first is that discussion of indigenous migration, while rarely treated independently, has nonetheless been discussed and analyzed in the relatively plentiful archeological, anthropological, and ethnographic research undertaken in the region. This research has tended to focus on migration patterns in the pre-contact and early contact eras, and a good deal explained mobility based on environmental conditions or social conflicts. Recently, attention has been devoted to migrations imposed on the indigenous population by the federal state, or forced migration.

Migration of the non-indigenous population by and large has been left to regional historians and has been explained by the discovery of whales, gold and other minerals, and the military needs of southern societies. Little attention has been given to trying to understand the reasons people move into, around, and out of the region. It may be that such research was deemed unnecessary; the standard utilitarian models of migration adequately account for any and all movement of the non-indigenous population of the region—non-indigenous people move into the region to find employment and higher incomes, they move within the region

---

[1] Research for this chapter was made possible with funding from the Social Sciences and Humanities Research Council of Canada (Grant # 863-2006-0002).

to maximize their income, and they leave the region to maximize their income.

While relatively few works tended to isolate migration as a distinct phenomenon, the available analyses seem to provide a sufficient understanding of migration for the historical period prior the 1970s. The trends of globalization, post-industrialism, new communications technology, the knowledge society, and political empowerment indicate that new migration patterns may be developing which need to be analyzed (*Arctic Human Development Report* 2004). This chapter hopes to lay the groundwork for this analysis by summarizing previous research undertaken on migration in the Canadian Arctic and providing an initial investigation into the recent conditions of migration in the region.

It begins with a discussion of the migration patterns of the indigenous population in both pre-contact and early contact periods, followed by a comparison with migration patterns of the non-indigenous population. The literature dealing with more recent migration patterns is then examined. The empirical investigation into contemporary migration patterns in the region starts with an investigation into general population changes in the Yukon, Northwest Territories, and Nunavut over the past 90 years using short-form census data. Taxfiler data and long-form census data is then examined in order to determine how migration conditions in the north vary from the national norm and to isolate characteristics of northern migrants.

Traditional Migration Patterns

As stated above, while there are few works dealing independently with questions of pre-contact and early contact migration patterns in the Canadian Arctic, there is a wealth of archeological, anthropological, and ethnographic research that deals with the question. The classical work of Boas, Stefansson, Jenness, and Rasmussen all deal with the migration patterns of the Inuit and other indigenous peoples. As concerns the Inuit in particular, much of the archeological work is dealt with by McGhee (2005) and the anthropological work is summarized by Rowley (1985).

The initial migration of the ancestors of the Inuit into the Canadian Arctic was previously explained by the 'Thule migration' theory (McGhee 2005:121), which postulated that a warming trend occurred about 1,000 years ago that allowed the whale-hunting Thule Inuit people to spread across the Canadian Arctic. According to McGhee, evidence now challenges this theory. He suggests that while the search to exploit new whale-hunting areas may be a partial explanation of the movement of these people from Northwestern Alaska across the Canadian Arctic, a more logical explanation is the search for iron and other metals. These metals had become an important part of their culture through trading routes originating

Chapter 3: *Migration in the Canadian North: An Introduction*

in China during the Han Empire. Indeed, McGhee suggests that the control of the trade in metals formed an important part of the 'Old Bering Sea culture' of the early Inuit. Interaction with the Tuniit who were then occupying the Canadian Arctic, introduced them to possible new sources of iron and metals. While the Tuniit exploited their own native copper sites, their relations with the Greenlandic Norse provided an important potential source for metals. McGhee suggests that this source motivated the Inuit to move into the Canadian Arctic:

> ...Such sources, in the hands of a relatively small, scattered, and poorly armed population, may have been attractive enough to motivate Inuit adventurers on journeys of exploration across the barren channels of the Central Arctic. These voyages would have provided the information that the Eastern Arctic had animal resources similar to those of Alaska; that the Cape York meteorites were a source of iron that was available for the taking; and also that the area was visited by *qadlunaat*, blue-eyed strangers from whom smelted metal could be obtained either by trading or through attack. This knowledge may have been the trigger that launched the Inuit migration to the Eastern Arctic (McGhee 2005:123).

The evidence points out that starting about 1,000 years ago, the Thule Inuit spread rapidly throughout the High Arctic, displacing the Tuniit and establishing permanent winter villages similar to those in Alaska. Where possible, they continued to develop a lifestyle dependent on the harvesting of bowhead whales. About 400 years ago, this lifestyle started to change quite radically. The permanent whale hunting-based winter villages in the High Arctic islands were abandoned and the Inuit developed the more southern, small group migratory settlement patterns that the Europeans encountered in the 18th and 19th century and that are associated with pre-contact Inuit settlement. Several explanations have been given for this change. These include climatic cooling, the depletion of the whaling stock by the Basque whaling operations of the 16th century, disease, and the attraction of new European sources of metal to replace the Norse (McGhee 2005:127).

It is these migration patterns that have received the most attention from anthropologists and ethnographers. While Boas, Stephansson, Jenness, Rasmussen and later researchers noted the common seasonal migrations of these people within a set territory, they also noted other migration patterns that Rowley (1985) calls historical migrations (1985). In her 1985 article she summarized the evidence of these migrations and isolated 27 major Inuit migrations during the period 1750 to 1930. She noted that for 17 of these migrations, causes could be suggested from the archeological evidence and oral histories. Of the 17 migrations she determined that seven were due to environmental variables such as the depletion of a food source, but that social factors were needed to explain more than half of the migration events. These social factors were dominated by internal community conflicts. For Rowley, mobility was seen as necessary for survival.

> Mobility played a crucial role in Inuit survival. Not only in the seasonal rounds and trading voyages but also as a means of escape from a region when resources became scarce or as a method of ridding the community of an undesirable individual or group of individuals (Rowley 1985:17).

More recently, Fossett (2001) re-examined the issue of pre-contact and early contact Inuit migrations in the Canadian Arctic. She notes the usual importance placed on the physical environment as a source of change. Given the extreme physical conditions, the emphasis on geographical and environmental determinism is quite understandable. Indeed, the Arctic environment sets definite limits on the possibilities of human action. She stresses, however, that these environmental limitations did not mean that the Inuit did not have the freedom to choose between different options, and notes that migrations during the period of 1550 to 1940 should be studied as the result of rational choices on the part of the Inuit.

> ...Even when the forcing factors for response appear to be the same, societies are free to make different choices appropriate to the physical circumstances, suited to their ideological systems, and logical in the light of their past experiences (Fossett 2001:20).

While a certain amount of freedom of choice existed prior to World War II, research during the 1990s created the perception that post-war Inuit migration patterns were largely determined by state coercion. Much attention has been devoted to the relocation initiatives of the Federal Government (Tester and Kulchyski 1994; Marcus 1995), but this perspective has recently been countered by Damas (2002), who contends that the shift from small dispersed all-native hunting–trapping based camps to larger centralized ethnically-mixed villages during the 1950s and 1960s was largely voluntary. Inuit migrants made a reasoned choice to move to these communities for a variety of reasons, including such pull enticements as employment, trading opportunities, access to services, and push factors such as the collapse of the fur trade and the depletion of wildlife (Damas 2002).

Damas notes that until the 1950s, the Inuit population of the Central Arctic maintained a pattern of settlement based on smaller dispersed

Chapter 3: *Migration in the Canadian North: An Introduction*

communities similar to the pattern existing during the period of initial contact. He terms this period the 'contact–traditional era,' and states that this pattern of settlement was supported by both the Federal Government and the fur trade—the main southern economic activity operating in the region. The fur trade saw this pattern of settlement as being essential to their interests; the Inuit needed to be dispersed in order to access furs. The Hudson's Bay Company complained that one of their biggest problems in the region was to break the habit the Inuit had of congregating in large camps—a habit blamed on the previous whaling economy (Damas 2002:30). Until the 1940s, the major external power influencing migration patterns was the Hudson's Bay Company. Relocations by the company undoubtedly took place during this period; however, it is impossible to determine both the extent of these relocations when compared to other migration patterns and what negotiations took place with the Inuit concerned.

The Federal Government largely supported the position of the fur traders on migration patterns of the Inuit until the 1950s. Reasons for this varied. The policy of dispersal helped reaffirm Canadian sovereignty over the region. In addition, it was seen as favourable to try and keep the Inuit in their natural state as much as possible. This was seen for paternalistic as well as for health reasons related to the supposed healthier conditions existing in the natural environment (Damas 2002:46). This position began to change in the 1950s. Famine in the Keewatin region led to relocations to larger settlements on humanitarian grounds. The establishment of nickel mining operations at Rankin Inlet led to new thinking of possible economic opportunities in larger communities.

It was during the 1960s that most Inuit experienced the shift to village life. During this decade, the economic operations of the Hudson's Bay Company shifted to retail and as such reduced the need for a dispersed population. The Federal Government's attention also shifted—from 'preservationalism' to humanitarianism—as it sought to implement the new 'Welfare State Policy' (Damas 2002:191). The provision of new health care and educational services, and new housing during this decade led to increased centralization of the indigenous population in villages. While according to Damas the reasons for Inuit to move into the villages were diverse and varied by region, it is generally explained by "the gradual acquisition of urban preferences…" (Vallee *et al.,* cited in Damas 2002:191). This settlement process was more or less complete by the early 1970s.

Migration of the Non-Indigenous Population

Discussion of non-indigenous migration patterns has been primarily the work of historians (Zaslow 1971, 1988; Coates 1985; Coates and Morrison 2005).[2] Until recently, these patterns were relatively simple to portray and understand. Non-indigenous populations appeared intermittently in the Canadian Arctic from the 1500s to the end of the 19th century. Whaling and the fur trade did not result in large-scale permanent settlement, although their movements did have an impact on the indigenous populations. Non-indigenous populations arrived in small numbers to exploit a particular resource. Their presence in the region would end as soon as their economic goals were achieved. The first large-scale movement of non-indigenous populations started with the Yukon gold rush of the late 1890s. This resulted in a rapid migration of primarily single working-age males into the Dawson area gold fields from 1898 to 1901. The in-migration was short-lived with many migrating out of the region after a short period of time (Coates and Morrison 2005).

This gold rush in-migration of non-indigenous populations into the Yukon was unique as a pattern, in that the migrants arrived as individual entrepreneurs and risk-takers rather than employees. The dream of adventure and quick wealth, combined with the romantic lure of gold mining that had developed in the American west in the second half of the 19th century, created unique conditions to attract thousands to the gold fields with little assurance of the utility of this migration. Americans constituted a major part of the Yukon gold rush. The 1901 census records the population of the Yukon as 27,219. Of this number, 6,720 are described as Americans, representing 35% of the total non-indigenous, declared population. Within ten years of the initial discovery of gold in the Dawson area, a shift in the economic structure of the gold mining industry had already occurred. A rationalization of the industry resulted in its transformation from one based on individual risk-takers to industrial wage-workers.

From a symbolic perspective, the Klondike gold rush is probably the most well-known mining development in Canada's north. At the beginning, it certainly followed Frederick Jackson Turner's frontier model of development. When gold was discovered in the Dawson area of the Yukon in 1896 it brought a rush of at least 30,000 non-indigenous people in the

---

[2] In this chapter we use the term non-indigenous rather than the more common term 'settler.' While the term 'settler' may be appropriate in the American west, the western Canadian provinces, and possibly Alaska where the non-indigenous population actually arrived in the region with the intention of 'settling' for the rest of their lives, this was rarely the case in the Canadian North. Most came to work for a short period of time and, as a result, makes it problematic to use the term settler when referring to them.

Chapter 3: *Migration in the Canadian North: An Introduction*

region in the space of a few years. What Canadian historians have tended to highlight in this development was not the mining of the gold itself but the attempts by the Canadian Government to control what was essentially an American development. According to Zaslow,

...In the Yukon Territory, we see the interaction between official Canadian policies and Canadian institutions and a community largely comprised of (sic) Americans and expressing the American frontier ideology... (Zaslow 1989:134).

While the rush resulted in short-term mining development based on individually owned stakes, after a few years this initial 'American frontier' situation had changed considerably.

By 1900 Dawson was a suitable place for orderly family living, and by 1902 it was reported to be as Canadian as Toronto (Zaslow 1989:147).

While Zaslow and other historians refer to the changes after the initial gold rush as the Canadian Government's attempt to Canadian-ize the Yukon, Zaslow (1989:16) also points out that little effort was expended to keep international capital out of the region. American corporations built and controlled the White Pass and Yukon Railway and American capital financed the rationalization of the Dawson gold fields at the start of the 20th century. Indeed, the Yukon gold rush can be seen as a good example of the inefficiencies of a frontier-type of industrial development in the north. Coates and Morrison describe how the Yukon gold fields had started to change in the first decade of the 20th century:

...(By 1909) The days of the individual prospector and the mining methods that produced the gold rush were finished as an important economic force... Now the symbol of the goldfields was not the pan but the dredge... Dredges processed tons of gold-bearing gravel each day and could make a profit on a trace of gold in each cubic yard—pay dirt that could not support a miner working with simpler techniques... (2005:157).

This need for new technology to rationalize the production process meant that the government had to work closely with American and British investors who had the capital to purchase and utilize this technology, to ensure that conditions would allow them to make a sufficient return on their investments. This meant granting a 'virtual monopoly' over many of the resources to run their operations (Coates and Morrison 2005:158). Less than ten years after the initial discovery of gold, industrial activity in the Canadian north was dominated by a new logic based on close cooperation and planning between the national government and international capital. The distances and conditions in the north meant that the long-term interests of both investors and the government could only be met by long-term planning and a rationalistic exploitation of natural resources.

This was the logic followed in later industrial developments in the Canadian north, such as silver and lead mining in the Mayo–Keno region of the Yukon starting in 1906, radium mining in the Great Bear Lake area in the 1930s, and gold mining in the Yellowknife area starting in the 1930s. This logic became even more prevalent following World War II when American government actions (with some help from Canada), had rapidly established new transportation systems in the Canadian north such as the Alaska Highway, and a series of northern landing strips and airbases. These developments legitimized, in the eyes of many, the superior nature of industrial developments planned by both government officials and large industrial interests. Following the war, industrial activity in the territorial north became almost entirely controlled by the Federal Government as the region became the 'bureaucrat's north' (Coates 1985:1910). The 1950s and early 1960s saw an increase in the pace of highway construction, a railway to Great Slave Lake, the opening up a new lead/zinc mine at Pine Point, and several other mining developments. In the 1960s, when it became apparent that large oil and gas deposits existed in the Mackenzie Delta region, the government ensured that development would be largely controlled from Ottawa, which led to an increased migration of a non-indigenous population into the North.

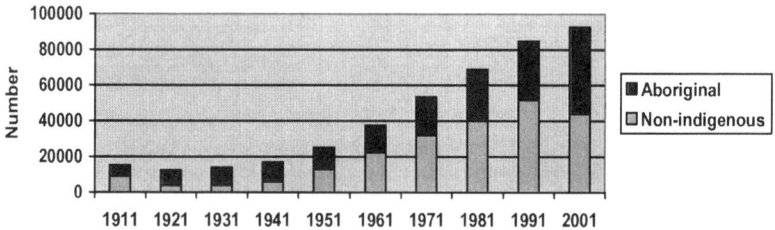

Figure 1: *Combined population of the Canadian Territories. Source: Census of Canada 1911 to 2001.*

Recent Migration Trends
As pointed out above, the two main patterns of migration in Northern Canada in the immediate post-war years involved a process of centralization into villages by the indigenous population (more or less complete by the early 1970s); and the movement of a non-indigenous population into the

Chapter 3: *Migration in the Canadian North: An Introduction*

region to work on natural resource exploitation projects and to provide increased government services to the regional population. Since the 1970s, new economic and social transformations have occurred that would presumably have an impact on these postwar migration patterns. In 1990, Stabler and Howe pointed out that the abandonment of welfare state policies so important in the 1960s was having an important impact on the territories. The decrease in federal transfer payments and a retreat of the state from economic and social policies meant increased hardships in the smaller villages. As the private sector increasingly replaced the public sector, the only way to sustain the people was to concentrate the population in larger communities and abandon the smaller villages (Coates 1985:279).

This policy of increased centralization was highly criticized. Gardiner (1994) pointed out that the indigenous people of the North prefer to live in their smaller communities where they have readier access to the resources of their traditional economic activities. Movement into larger centres would reduce this access and as such increase their dependence on a private sector wage economy that has never been sufficient to meet their needs. Gardiner's research indicated that, left to their own preferences, the indigenous peoples of the North would choose to leave their own smaller villages only if forced to by government policies.

Apart from the 'further centralization' debate of the 1990s, very little has been written about new migration trends in the Canadian North. Substantial research has been done in Canada on interprovincial migration but the Territories are rarely mentioned (*see* Courchene 1974; Grant and Vanderkamp 1976; Finnie 1998a,b). A few studies concerning rural migration patterns appeared at the beginning of this decade (*see* Dupuy *et al*. 2000; Rothwell *et al*. 2002; Tremblay 2001; R.A. Malatest & Associates Ltd. 2002). Although this research is not directly focused on the situation of Northern Canada, the fact that much of Northern Canada falls within the official Statistics Canada definition of 'rural and small town' means that this rural–urban research is a good place to begin to look for migration patterns in Canada that are relevant to the North (Rothwell *et al*. 2002:3).

In a report using 1996 and earlier census data, Rothwell *et al*. (2002) noted that rural and small-town Canada experienced a net out-migration at the end of the 1960s. During the 1970s, however, this situation was reversed with lower levels of out-migration and higher levels of in-migration.

Through the 1980s this trend reversed again. This decade saw a net out-migration from rural and small town Canada due largely to a decrease in the numbers of in-migrants. Finally, from 1991 to 1996 the trend again reversed with a return to a net in-migration due to lower levels of out-migration. The research also showed that from 1971 to 1996, the percentage of in-migrants for rural and small town Canada for each five year census period remained fairly stable at or around 10% of the population. More recently, out-migration rates for these areas have increased (*see* Ferguson *et al*. 2007; Finnie 2004).

Research indicates, therefore, that migration rates for rural Canada vary considerably, and that while more recent trends show increased out-migration, there is no evidence of a continuous trend over the last 30 years. The next section will examine whether this has also been the case in Northern Canada.

Contemporary Migration in Northern Canada

Taxfiler Data

Information on migration in Northern Canada is derived from several main sources. The most reliable is the data provided by the census conducted every five years. Linked to this is the Aboriginal Peoples Survey undertaken in 1991 and 2001 in conjunction with the census. Another source is migration data from taxpayer files. The collection of annual inter-provincial migration data is a legislated requirement to provide population estimates to the Federal Government. The migration estimates are derived from a comparison of addresses from individual income tax returns for two consecutive years. The taxation records are obtained from the Canada Revenue Agency. While less precise than census files, the benefit of taxpayer files is that they are available on an annual basis.

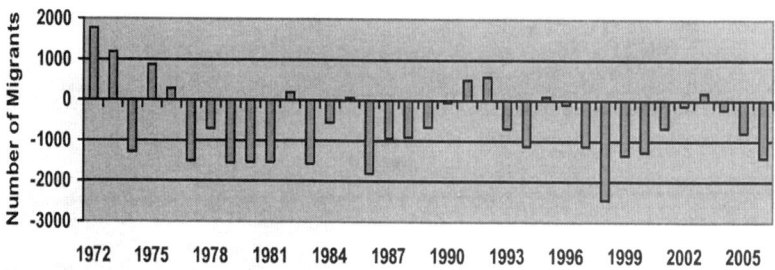

Figure 2: *Net migration in the Canadian Territorial North. Annual Migration Estimates, CANSIM Table 051-0018.* Source: Statistics Canada.

Figure 2 shows the net migration numbers for all territories combined from 1971 to 2006. It is readily apparent that, according to the taxfiler data, there has been greater out-migration than in-migration over this period. It should be noted that this does not exactly agree with the census figures for this period that show less out-migration than that seen in the taxfiler data.[3]

---

[3] One of several limitations of taxfiler data is that it only applies to individuals who file a tax return. Youth, indigenous people, and low income earners are less likely to file a tax return than the

Chapter 3: *Migration in the Canadian North: An Introduction*

Another tendency shown by Figure 2 is the large yearly fluctuations that seem to support the notion that the north is extremely vulnerable to resource industry boom and bust.

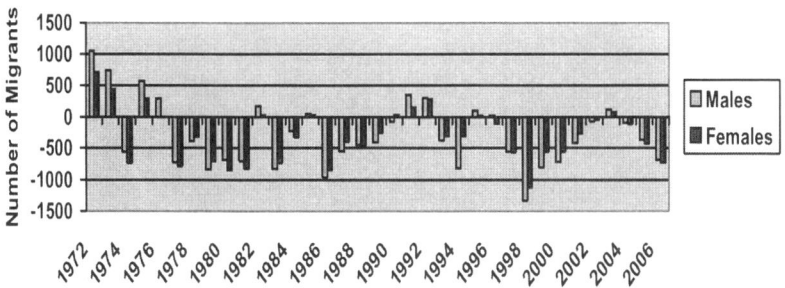

Figure 3: *Net migration in the Canadian Territorial North. Annual Migration Estimates, CANSIM Table 051-0012.* Source: Statistics Canada

Migration differences based on sex are indicated in the taxfiler data for intra-provincial migration. Male net migration rates tend to fluctuate to a greater extent than that of females as shown in Figure 3. The yearly standard deviation for males is 526 and that of females is 421. Differences between age groups were also analyzed. Although the taxfiler data does not allow us to make reliable observations about which age group is most likely to migrate in a given year, the data does indicate that those between the ages of 25 to 44 have the greatest variability in migration rates from year to year; those 65 years of age and over have the least.

The 2001 Census
The most reliable source of data on migration in Canada's North is the census. Many of the questions regarding migration patterns in Canada's north as compared to patterns in other areas of the Circumpolar North can be answered by an in-depth analysis of census data from the region. This analysis will, however, restrict itself to the publicly available data on migration. This is problematic, however, in that this data refers primarily to migrants living in the territories. While some information is available on the destinations of people who have migrated out of the territories, little information is available on the characteristics of these out-migrants.

Table 1 lists the migration data from the 2001 Census for the three Canadian territories and the two largest urban areas in Northern Canada. For comparative purposes, it also lists national averages. Statistics Canada refers to 'migrants' as those people who have moved to a new community

---

general population. For this reason the usefulness of taxfiler data in Northern Canada is extremely limited.

over the previous five years. This differs from Statistics Canada's definition of 'movers' who include migrants and those who have simply moved to a new address in the same community over the previous five years.

Table 1: Migration Data from the 2001 Census.

2001		Canada	Yukon	Whitehorse	Northwest Territories	Yellowknife	Nunavut
Total—Mobility Status 5 years ago		27,932,590	26,795	20,000	34,080	15,205	23,285
As % of population	Migrants	19.5	21.5	21.0	24.9	30.2	19.4
	Internal migrants	16.0	19.9	19.4	23.4	27.6	18.9
	Intra-provincial/ territorial migrants	12.8	5.9	4.9	6.6	4.6	8.1
	Inter-provincial/ territorial migrants	3.2	14.0	14.5	168	23.0	10.8
	External migrants	3.5	1.6	1.6	1.5	2.6	0.5

Source: Statistics Canada, 2001 Census

In terms of migrants as a percentage of the total population, Table 1 shows that, generally speaking, the territories have slightly higher percentages than the national average. They also show considerable variation, however, with the Northwest Territories having 25% of their population as migrants compared to 19.4% for Nunavut and 21.5% for the Yukon. The table also indicates that the Canadian North has significantly lower percentages of intra-territorial migrants than the Canadian average of 12.8%. This varies from 8.1% in Nunavut to 5.9% in the Yukon. The north has a significantly higher percentage of people moving from other provinces or territories into the region. The average of inter-provincial/territorial migrants in Canada is only 3.2%, while in the north it ranges from 16.8% in the Northwest Territories to 10.8% in Nunavut. Finally, Table 1 shows that the Canadian Territories have a significantly lower percentage of migrants coming from outside Canada. Nationally, 3.5% of all migrants into a community over the previous five years came from outside the country. In the north, this ranged from 1.6% in the Yukon to 0.5% in Nunavut.

Table 2. Net Migrants[1] and Net Migration Rates: Provinces and Territories[2] —1976 to 2001.

Province or Territory	1976-1981		1981-1986		1986-1991		1991-1996		1996-2001	
	Number	%	Number	%	Number	%	Number	%	Number	%
Newfoundland and Labrador	-19,860	-3.7	-16,650	-3.1	-13,945	-2.6	-23,240	-4.3	-31,055	-6.1
Prince Edward Island	-15	0.0	1,540	1.4	-850	-0.7	1,455	1.2	135	0.1
Nova Scotia	-8,420	-1.1	6,275	0.8	-4,885	-0.6	-6,450	-0.8	-1,275	-0.2
New Brunswick	-8,505	-1.3	-1,370	-0.2	-6,060	-0.9	-1,950	-0.3	-8,425	-1.2
Quebec	-141,725	-2.4	-63,295	-1.1	-25,560	-0.4	-37,430	-0.6	-57,315	-0.9
Ontario	-78,070	-1.0	99,355	1.2	46,965	0.5	-47,025	-0.5	51,905	0.5
Manitoba	-43,600	-4.6	-1,555	-0.2	-35,260	-3.5	-19,390	-1.9	-18,560	-1.8
Saskatchewan	-5,820	-0.7	-2,830	-0.3	-60,365	-6.4	-19,780	-2.1	-24,940	-2.7
Alberta	197,645	11.3	-27,675	-1.3	-25,005	-1.1	3,575	0.1	119,420	4.7
British Columbia	110,930	4.8	9,515	0.4	125,870	4.6	149,935	4.5	-23,630	-0.7
Yukon	-545	-2.6	-2,655	-11.4	790	3.4	685	2.5	-2,760	-9.5
Northwest Territories	-2,015	-5.0	-755	-1.6	-1,695	-3.4	-465	-1.3	-3,170	-8.6
Nunavut							80	0.4	-330	-1.4

[1] Difference between the number of incoming and outgoing migrants.
[2] These numbers are for internal migration only. They do not include the number of people who were outside Canada in 1996 and entered Canada between 1996 and 2001.

Source: Statistics Canada (2002). Profile of the Canadian Population by Mobility Status: Canada, a Nation on the Move. Ottawa, December, p.20.

Table 3: Top Five Places of Origin and Destination for Northern Canadian Migrants.

Largest Inflows—Net Migrants*	Number	Percent	Largest Outflows	Number	Percent
Yukon Territory					
B.C. non-metro areas	940	25.1	B.C. non-metro areas	1,570	24.2
Vancouver	445	11.9	Alberta non-metro areas	1,145	17.6
Edmonton	220	5.9	Vancouver	635	9.8
Alberta non-metor areas	215	5.7	Edmonton	550	8.5
Northwest Territories	185	4.9	Calgary	435	6.7
Total Inflow	**3,730**		**Total Outflow**	**6,490**	
Northwest Territories					
Edmonton	650	11.3	Alberta non-metro areas	1,705	19.2
Alberta non-metro areas	625	10.9	Edmonton	1,530	17.2
B.C. non-metro areas	550	9.6	B.C. non-metro areas	900	10.1
Nunavut non-metro areas	415	7.2	Calgary	865	9.7
Nfld/Labrador non-metro areas	365	6.4	Ontario non-metro areas	500	5.6
Total Inflow	**5,740**		**Total Outflow**	**8,910**	
Nunavut Territory					
Northwest Territories	300	11.9	Northwest Territories	415	14.6
Nfld/Labrador non-metro areas	220	8.7	Ottawa-Hull	245	8.6
Ottawa-Hull	200	7.9	Edmonton	195	6.9
Ontario non-metro areas	160	6.3	Alberta non-metro areas	185	6.5
Nova Scotia non-metro areas	160	6.3	B.C. non-metro areas	180	6.3
Total Inflow	**2,510**		**Total Outflow**	**2,840**	

*Difference beweeen the number of incoming and outgoing migrants from internal migration

Source: Statistics Canada, 2001 Census, Retrieved June 1, 2007 from www12.statcan.ca/english/census01/Products/Analytic/companion/mob

Analyses of census migration data between 1976 and 2001 confirm the observations suggested by the taxfiler data about a large degree of variability in migration rates from year to year (Table 2). While the region saw a net loss of immigrants from 1976 to 1981 and from 1981 to 1986, the Yukon saw a net gain in migrants from 1986 to 1991 and from 1991 to 1996. Nunavut experienced a slight net gain from 1991 to 1996.

Table 4: Migration Rates According to Age Group.

Age Group	In-Migrants	Out-Migrants	Number of Net Migrants	Rate (%)
Yukon				
5-14	525	945	-420	-8.9
15-29	1,165	1,660	-495	-8.2
30-44	1,370	2,120	-750	-9
45-64	590	1,590	-1,000	-11.9
65 and over	95	160	-65	-3.9
TOTAL	**3,730**	**6,490**	**-2,760**	**-9.5**
Northwest Territories				
5-14	915	1,815	-900	-11.3
15-29	1,785	1,905	-120	-1.4
30-44	2,000	3,320	-1,320	-12
45-64	960	1,695	-735	-9.5
65 and over	70	165	-95	-5.8
TOTAL	**5,740**	**8,910**	**-3,170**	**-8.6**
Nunavut				
5-14	330	640	-310	-4.5
15-29	790	495	295	4.5
30-44	800	1,200	-400	-6.6
45-64	560	475	85	2.5
65 and over	40	35	5	0.7
TOTAL	**2,510**	**2,840**	**-330**	**-1.4**

Source: Statistics Canada, 2001 Census, Retrieved June 1, 2007 from www12.statcan.ca/english/census01/Products/Analytic/companion/mob

Characteristics of Migrants

While available data on the characteristics of migrants in Northern Canada is limited, there are some indicators that provide a starting point for discussions, primarily age, gender, and ethnic differences. Table 4 compares migration rates according to age groups. Previous studies in the Canadian provincial norths have indicated that youth is an important determinant of a propensity to migrate (Southcott 2006). The situation in the Territorial North is more complex. In all territories, the net migration rates for those 15 to 29 years of age are lower than the territorial average. In the Yukon, the net out-migration rate is 8.2% compared to a territorial average of 9.5%. In the Northwest Territories, the net youth out-migration rate is only 1.4% compared to a regional average of 8.6%. In Nunavut we see a net youth in-migration rate of 4.5% compared to a territorial out-migration rate of 1.4%. The age group with the highest net out-migration rates in both the Yukon and Nunavut were those between the ages of 30 and 44. In the Northwest Territories, the age group with the highest net out-migration rate was those between the ages of 5 and 14.

While these differences exist in terms of net migration, Table 4 also indicates that the age groups with the highest number of total migrants, either in or out, is always that of 30 to 44 year olds. This is the age group with the highest propensity to migrate in Northern Canada. In all territories, those 65 years of age and older are the least likely to migrate.

Table 5: Migrants as a Percentage of the Population by Gender.

	Total Migrants	Intra-Provincial Migrants	Inter-Provincial Migrants	External Migrants
Male				
Canada	19.6	12.8	3.3	3.5
Yukon Territory	20.6	6.0	13.2	1.5
Whitehorse	20.2	4.9	13.9	1.4
Northwest Territories	24.6	6.3	16.9	1.3
Yellowknife	30.2	4.4	23.4	2.4
Nunavut	18.8	7.7	10.7	0.4
Female				
Canada	19.5	12.9	3.2	3.5
Yukon Territory	22.3	5.9	14.7	1.7
Whitehorse	21.7	4.9	15.1	1.7
Northwest Territories	25.3	6.9	16.7	1.7
Yellowknife	30.3	4.9	22.5	2.8
Nunavut	20.0	8.6	11.0	0.5

Source: Statistics Canada, 2001 Census

As noted in our discussion of taxfiler migration data, gender can be considered an explanatory factor of migration in the Canadian North. Analysis of data from the 2001 Census confirms this relationship, although it does not appear to be strong. Table 5 shows the percentage of migrants as a percentage of the population by gender. An analysis of these percentages show that women living in the Territorial norths are more likely to have migrated over the past five years, but the differences with men are not great. The relationship is stronger in the Yukon than in the Northwest Territories or Nunavut. In the Yukon 22.3% migrants are women and 20.6% are men. Figures for the Northwest Territories are 25.3% women and 24.6% men. In Nunavut 20% of migrants are women and 18.8% are men.

Chapter 3: *Migration in the Canadian North: An Introduction*

In the Yukon, the difference is largely explained by the higher number of women migrating in from outside the territory. The percentage of intra-provincial migrants is almost identical for men and women. In the Northwest Territories and Nunavut the reverse is true. Most of the difference is explained by higher numbers of female intra-provincial migrants.

The literature on migration in Northern Canada shows that the non-aboriginal population has a much higher migration rate than the Aboriginal population. In most cases, the non-indigenous population moves to the North to exploit the local natural resources. Given these justifications, it is likely they will leave as soon as the exploitation of these resources is no longer profitable. Mobility is intensified by the boom and bust cycles of resource development in the region. The Aboriginal population is less likely to migrate in that they see the North as a homeland. The importance of traditional activities such as hunting and fishing keeps them close to their traditional land base.

Table 6: Rates of Aboriginal Migration.

	Total Population 5 Years and Over	Percent of Migrants	Percent of Internal Migrants	Percent of External Migrants
Yukon				
Total Population	26,795	21.5	5.9	15.6
Aboriginal Population	5,910	20.6	10.7	9.9
Northwest Territories				
Total Population	34,080	24.9	6.6	18.3
Aboriginal Population	16,850	16.4	9.7	6.7
Nunavut				
Total Population	23,285	19.4	8.1	11.3
Aboriginal Population	19,585	11.7	8.6	3.1

Source: Statistics Canada, 2001 Census

Yet Table 6 shows that this situation varies by territory. In the Yukon, the migration rates for the Aboriginal population are lower than that of the population as a whole, but only slightly. What is evident, however, is that the Aboriginal population is more likely to migrate within the Yukon than outside the territory. In the Northwest Territories and Nunavut, the relationship is much more evident with the Aboriginal population in these territories having significantly lower migration rates than the population as a whole. As was the case for the Yukon, when the Aboriginal population does migrate, they are much more likely to migrate within the territory.

Conclusions

Although the publicly available data on migration in Northern Canada is limited, there is enough to allow us to make several observations about the issue. Taxfiler data shows that out-migrants have outnumbered in-migrants since the late 1970s. At the same time, the data shows that there is considerable fluctuation from year to year, indicating that the boom and bust cycles characteristic of resource-based economies continues to affect migration rates in Northern Canada. The taxfiler data also indicates differences based on sex, in that male net migration rates tend to fluctuate to a greater extent than that of females. Differences between age groups indicate that those between the ages of 25 to 44 have the greatest variability in migration rates from year to year and that those 65 years of age and over have the least variability in migration rates.

Census data gives us more reliable data on migration in the Canadian North but analysis is restricted to publicly available data. Such data gives us very limited information on the characteristics of northern migrants. Analyses of migration data from the 2001 and earlier censuses confirm that there is a large degree of variability in migration rates from year to year and that there have been more out-migrants than in-migrants since the 1970s. Data from the 2001 Census also show that, in terms of migrants as a percentage of the total population, the territories have slightly higher percentages than that of Canada. There is also a considerable amount of variation, however, between the territories with the Northwest Territories having higher rates than the Yukon or Nunavut. The Canadian North has a significantly lower percentage of intra-territorial migrants than Canada as a whole and has a significantly higher percentage of people moving from other provinces or territories into the region. The Canadian North has a significantly lower percentage of migrants coming from outside Canada.

An analysis of the origins of migrants to and the destinations of migrants from the Canadian North shows that these vary by territory. Alberta and British Columbia are the largest singe sources and destinations of migrants to and from the Yukon and the Northwest Territories. For Nunavut, the Northwest Territories is the most important source and destination followed by locations in Eastern Canada.

Data from the 2001 Census allow us to make some initial observations about the characteristics of northern migrants. Age is a factor in determining the likelihood of a person to migrate, in that youth are less likely to migrate than in other areas of the country. The elderly are the least likely to migrate, and those between the ages of 30 and 44 years of age are most likely to migrate. Analyses of data from the 2001 Census confirm

Chapter 3: *Migration in the Canadian North: An Introduction*

there is a relationship between migration rates and gender, although it does not appear to be strong. An analysis of these percentages shows that women living in the Territorial North are more likely to have migrated over the past five years, but the differences with men are not great. The relationship is stronger in the Yukon than in the Northwest Territories or Nunavut. The hypothesis that Aboriginal populations are less likely to migrate is confirmed by the census data, but in the Yukon the differences are not very great. The relationship is much clearer in the Northwest Territories and Nunavut where migration rates for the Aboriginal population are much lower than for the population as a whole. In all the territories of Canada, when the Aboriginal population does migrate, they are more likely than the rest of the population to migrate within the territory.

While this introductory survey of the available material relating to migration in the Canadian North does show us some initial tendencies, it is apparent that much less information is available than for other regions of the Circumpolar North. More detailed research is required to better understand the essential characteristics of northern migrants, including the existing push and pull factors, who is most likely to migrate, and why certain locations are popular sources and destinations of migrants.

References

Arctic Council (2004). *The Arctic Human Development Report*. Akureyri: Stefansson Arctic Institute.
Courchene, T. (1974). *Migration, Income and Employment*. Toronto: C.D. Howe Institute,
Coates, K. (1985). *Canada's Colonies: A History of the Yukon and Northwest Territories*. Toronto: James Lorimer.
Coates, K. and W. Morrison (2005). *Land of the Midnight Sun: A History of the Yukon*. Kingston and Montreal: McGill-Queen's Press.
Damas, D. (2002). *Arctic Migrants/Arctic Villagers: The Transformation of Inuit Settlement in the Central Arctic*. Kingston and Montreal: McGill-Queen's University Press.
Dupuy, R., F. Mayer, and R. Morissette (2000). *Rural Youth: Stayers, Leavers and Return Migrants*. Canadian Rural Partnership.
Ferguson, M., K. Ali, M. R. Olfert, and M. Partridge (2007). Voting with their feet: Jobs versus amenities. *Growth and Change* 38(1): 77-110.
Finnie, R. (2004). Who moves? A logit model analysis of inter-provincial migration in Canada. *Applied Economics* 36(16): 1759-1779.
Finnie, R. (1998). Interprovincial Mobility in Canada: A Longitudinal Analysis. Working Paper W-98-5E.a. Ottawa: Applied Research Branch, Human Resources Development Canada.
Finnie, R. (1998a). *Interprovincial Mobility in Canada: Who Moves? A Panel Logit Model Analysis*. Working Paper W-98-5E.b. Ottawa: Applied Research Branch, Human Resources Development Canada.
Fossett, R. (2001). *In Order to Live Untroubled: Inuit of the Central Arctic, 1550-1940*. Winnipeg: University of Manitoba Press.
Gardner, P. (1994) Aboriginal community incomes and migration in the NWT: Policy issues and alternatives. *Canadian Public Policy/Analyse De Politiques* 20(3): 297-317.
Grant, K.E. and Vanderkamp, J. (1976). *The Economic Causes and Effects of Migration: Canada, 1965-71*. Ottawa: Economic Council of Canada.
Malatest, R.A. & Associates Ltd. (2002). *Rural Youth Migration: Exploring the Reality Behind the Myths*. Canadian Rural Partnership.
Marcus, A.R. (1995). *Relocating Eden: The Image and Politics of Inuit Exile in the Canadian Arctic*. Hanover, NH: Dartmouth College, University Press of New England.
McGhee, R. (2005). *The Last Imaginary Place: A Human History of the Arctic World*. London: Oxford University Press.
Rothwell, N., R. Bollman, J. Tremblay, and J. Marshall (2002). 'Recent Migration Patterns in Rural and Small Town Canada,' Agriculture and Rural Working Paper Series Working Paper No. 55, Agriculture Division, Statistics Canada.
Rowley, S. (1985). Population Movements in the Canadian Arctic. *Etudes/Inuit/Studies* 9(1): 3-21.
Southcott, C. (2006). *The North in Numbers: A Demographic Analysis of Social and Economic Change in Northern Ontario*, Thunder Bay: Centre for Northern Studies Press.
Stabler, J. and E. Howe (1990). Native participation in Northern development: the impending crisis in the NWT. *Canadian Public Policy* 16(13): 263-283

Chapter 3: *Migration in the Canadian North: An Introduction*

Statistics Canada (annual). Annual Migration Estimates, CANSIM Table 051-0012 and CANSIM Table 051-0018. Ottawa: Statistics Canada.

Statistics Canada (2002). *Profile of the Canadian Population by Mobility Status: Canada, a Nation on the Move.* Ottawa: Statistics Canada.

Statistics Canada (2001). Census

Statistics Canada (annual). 1901 Census to 1991 Census. Ottawa: Statistics Canada

Tester, F. J. and P.K. Kulchyski (1994). *Tammarniit (Mistakes): Inuit Relocation in the Eastern Arctic, 1939-63.* Vancouver: UBC Press.

Tremblay, J. (2001). Rural youth migration between 1971 and 1996. Working Paper# 44. Ottawa: Agriculture Division, Statistics Canada.

Zaslow, M. (1971). *The Opening of the Canadian North: 1870-1914.* Toronto: McClelland and Stewart.

Zaslow, M. (1988). *The Northward Expansion of Canada 1914-1967.* Toronto: McClelland and Stewart.

Zaslow, M. (1989). 'The Yukon: Northern Development in a Canadian-American Context,' in Kenneth S. Coates and William R. Morrison (eds.), *Interpreting Canada's North: Selected Readings.* Toronto: Copp Clark Pitman Ltd.

Migration in the Circumpolar North

4

Migration and Population Change in the Russian Far North in the 1990s

Timothy Heleniak[1]

Introduction

The two decades since the breakup of the Soviet Union and the introduction of a market economy has been a period of enormous transition for the Russian North. The development practices of the Soviet Union with regard to the resources of its northern and Arctic regions differed considerably from that of other northern countries and a transition away from central planning toward a market economy has impacted the migration patterns in the region and between the Russian North and the rest of the country. This chapter analyzes patterns of migration in the region and compares changes in the population of Siberia and the North between the last Soviet census of 1989 and the first Russian census conducted in 2002.

The chapter begins with an overview of Soviet and Russian northern development practices, a summary of the main factors driving migration in the region, and a brief summary of the data used in the analysis. This is followed by the main section of the paper which describes migration and population change in the Russian North by region and by age, sex, educational level, and nationality. The final section examines the implications of population movements in the Russian North for the future of the region.

---

[1] Research Associate, Department of Geography, University of Maryland. The research presented here is part of a project of the European Science Foundation (ESF EUROCORES Programme BOREAS) called *Moved by the State: Perspectives on Relocation and Resettlement in the Circumpolar North* (MOVE). The US portion of this project was funded by the National Science Foundation, Office of Polar Programs, Arctic Social Sciences Program (award # ARC-0705654). MOVE is an endorsed International Polar Year 2007-2008 project (IPY project No. 436).

Brief Overview of Soviet and Russian Northern Development Policy
Some background comparing Soviet versus Russian policy toward the North will be helpful to understanding the analysis of migration and population change that follows. According to Bradshaw (1995:199), "the Soviet Union promoted a scale of development [of the North] that would not have been possible in a more open market-oriented society". Much of this policy toward the North stemmed from Soviet Marxism which was not in awe of the natural environmental and were based on the premise that the problems of industrialization in the high-latitude regions of the Russian Arctic could be overcome (Honneland and Jorgensen 2006:144). In their development of the North, Soviet policy-makers actively challenged the cold and harsh climatic conditions (Hill and Gaddy 2003:34). This included development of an infrastructure and population levels unlike volumes elsewhere in the circumpolar world. Securing this larger population base was initiated with forced labor and later with various wage and other incentives to retain a permanent population (Bond 1985). It is the transition from this Soviet system of northern development to one based more on market principles that caused the population changes and migration movements described here.

There are three major reasons behind the post-Soviet migration patterns in evidence in the Russian North. The first are changes in the economic geography of the region that caused a restructuring of space and economic linkages. The artificial pricing of industrial inputs and outputs under central planning affected the distant north more than most other regions in Russia because it was transport prices that were most under-valued (Blakkisrud 2006:29). For example, when the subsidies were removed in 1992, the cost of flying across Russia from Moscow to Magadan rose by 1,500 percent (Round 2005:712). While the removal of subsides and allowing prices to be determined by the market affected most northern regions negatively in terms of enterprise profitability and cost of living, it benefited some whose outputs had been undervalued under central-planning against the market. As will be shown here, the oil and gas regions of Khanty-Mansiy and Yamal-Nenets have benefited tremendously from being able to sell their output at world prices and have become the economic engines of the North, if not of all of Russia.

The second reason relates to changes in government finance of and policy toward the North. The levers the Russian Government has at its disposal which allow it to dictate development of its northern periphery are far fewer than those of the Soviet Government. There was a revival of the State Committee on the North in the 1990s, but it has since been abolished and there is now no single body responsible for northern policy (Blakkisrud 2006:30). Government policy has devolved to several entities and local northern governments. While the government still partially funds shipments of food and fuel to the North, it is at but a fraction of the level of support

Chapter 4: *Migration and Population Change in the Russian Far North in the 1990s*

provided during the Soviet period; federal financing of shipments fell from 1.58% of GDP in 1992 to just 0.12% in 1997 (World Bank 1998).

A final reason relates more directly to factors that impact peoples' migration cost–benefit equations. Under Soviet central planning, the regional wage gap was rather compressed and the North was one of the few places were people could legitimately earn high incomes. With the increase in prices and wages set by the market, real incomes in the North have plummeted. Real income in Murmansk fell from 139% of the Russian average in 1990 (Russia=100) to 56% of the national average in 2002. Over the same period, incomes in Yakutia went from 165% of the national average to 62%, Kamchatka from 187% to 51%, and Magadan from 212% to 57%. Simply put, after liberalization of the labor market, the North lost a great deal of its attraction as a place to quickly earn money (Blakkisrud and Honneland 2006a:195). Since migrants are favorably selected against those who do not migrate, it was the best and brightest who left the North in the largest numbers when economic conditions deteriorated. It was many of these recent migrans who arrived to make their fortunes in the North who had fewer ties to the region.

There is no uniform definition of the 'North' or the 'Russian North' (Armstrong 1965; Blakkisrud and Honneland 2006b:8-9). For planning, economic development, statistical and other purposes, the Russian Government defines two different types of northern regions—*Kraynyy Sever* (the Far North) and *mestnosti priravnennyye k rayonam Kraynego Severa* (regions equivalent to the Far North) (Heleniak 1999:204-205). The classification of regions as 'northern' is based on a combination of geographic, economic, and climatic characteristics. As of January 1, 2006, twenty-seven regions fell either completely or partially into one of these two groups (Rosstat 2006c:5-8). The entire territory of ten regions are classified as being in the Far North—Nenets Autonomous Okrug, Murmansk Oblast, Yamal-Nenets Autonomous Okrug, Taymyr Autonomous Okrug, Evenki Autonomous Okrug, Sakha Republic, Chukotka Autonomous Okrug, Kamchatka Oblast, Koryak Autonomous Okrug, and Magadan Oblast.

The Russian Government classifies sixteen regions as belonging to the Far North on the basis that all or a majority of their territory is classified as being in the Far North (Rosstat 2006c:215). In addition to the ten regions listed above, the following are also classified as the Far North—Karelian Republic, Komi Republic, Arkhangel'sk Oblast, Khanty-Mansiy Autonomous Okrug, Tuva Republic, and Sakhalin Oblast. It seems a bit absurd to include Tuva, located on the *southern* border of Russia with Mongolia, in the North, and as will be seen, Tuva is very much an outlier in terms of many northern migration trends. The inclusion of Tuva in the North points to the somewhat political nature of this designation.

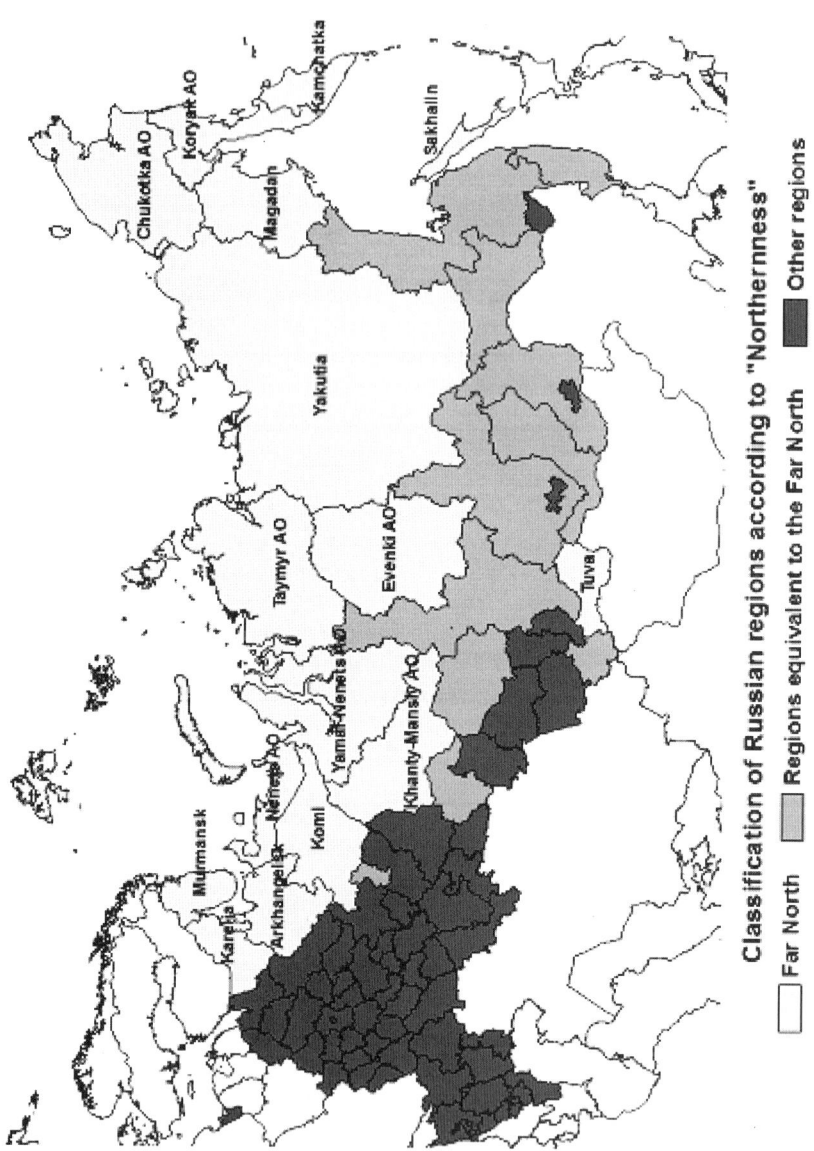

Figure 1. *Regions of the Russian Far North.*

Chapter 4: *Migration and Population Change in theRussian Far North in the 1990s*

Most Russian economic, social, and demographic data are given at the geographic level of the 89 subjects of the federation (often termed the oblast level) and little is available at the next lowest geographic level, the rayon. Because of this, the analysis of population change contained here will be for these sixteen regions, hereafter refered to as the 'Russian North' or simply the 'North' (Fig. 1). The city of Norilsk, which is administratively part of the Krasnoyark Kray but physically located in the Taymyr Autonomous Okrug, is also included in the Far North, although there is not a great deal of separate data on Norilsk.

Population and Migration Data
Two main statistical sources are used for the description and analysis of migration and population change in the Russian North. The first are the most recent population censuses conducted in Russia. The last Soviet census was conducted in 1989 just prior to the breakup of the country, and Russia's first census was carried out in 2002. The questions asked in the two censuses were broadly similar, with some changes in the 2002 Russian census included to capture the new economic and social realities. The question related to social group which was asked in 1989 was dropped. The questions on occupation and employment were changed, including the possibility to declare that the respondent was unemployed. A question on citizenship was added, along with a series of questions about persons in the country temporarily.

The Soviet Union dissolved before the full results of the 1989 census could be published according to plan. However, Russia separately published a number of volumes of results and a western company was able to collaborate with the CIS Statistical Committee and publish results for the entire USSR (Publications 1996). From the 2002 Russian census, 14 printed volumes were published, along with substantial results in electronic form (Rosstat). The next Russian census is scheduled for 2010 (Rosstat).

The second statistical sources used are migration flow statistics, which are somewhat a remnant from the Soviet period when individuals were required to seek permission when migrating within the country. Permission is no longer required, but registration is still required upon arrival in a new location in order to access services. Data from this system are published on age, sex, level of education, and origin and destination of migrants. While the system may not completely capture all movements in Russia, it does include most, and thus provides a good source of information about migration. Data from this source are published in the annual demographic yearbook and in a small tirzah publication titled 'Numbers and Migration of the Population of the Russian Federation,' which includes a special section on migration and population in the Far North (Rosstat 2006a,b).

Migration Trends in the Russian North

This description and analysis of migration in the Russian North during the 1990s begins with a brief overview of migration patterns during the 20th century, to provide some historical context as to how the population and settlement patterns in the region came to be. Next will be an analysis of regional migration and mobility patterns across Russia and in particular, in the Russian North, followed by disaggregations of migration and population change in the northern regions by sex, age, educational level, and ethnicity.

Historical Migration Trends in the Russian North

While the regions that make up the North have been under Russian control and their resources have been exploited for centuries, it was not until the Soviet period that large-scale settlement and migration into the region took place. In 1926 (the time of the first Soviet census), the Russian North had a population of 1.8 million, less than two percent of the Russian population (Rossii 1998:0-53). Half of this total was in the old Russian settlement of Arkhangelsk (Blakkisrud and Honneland 2006b:11) and three-quarters were in the northern European regions of Archangelsk, Komi, and Karelia (Rossii 1998). Much of northern Siberia and the Far East remained sparsely populated.

The first five-year plan launched in 1928 marked the beginning of the push to industrialize the Soviet Union as quickly as possible. Part of this effort included *Osvoenie Severa* (the conquest of the North), which had as its underpinnings the Marxist principle that nature should be subjected to the benefits of man. This was manifested across the Russian North by the establishment and building of large settlements in distant, climatically-harsh regions and the creation of a massive logistical supply effort across vast distances to maintain these settlements and transport from them the resources needed for Soviet industrialization.

Many of the large northern settlements upon which resource extraction were based were founded during the 1920s and 1930s, quickly developed and populated, and as a result, the northern population more than doubled to 3.6 million by 1950. The population continued to grow rapidly, first through forced labor and later through various wage incentive schemes, until it peaked at 9.8 million in 1989. At that time, just prior to the breakup of the Soviet Union and the onset of economic reforms, this represented 6.6 percent of the Russian population.

Chapter 4: *Migration and Population Change in theRussian Far North in the 1990s*

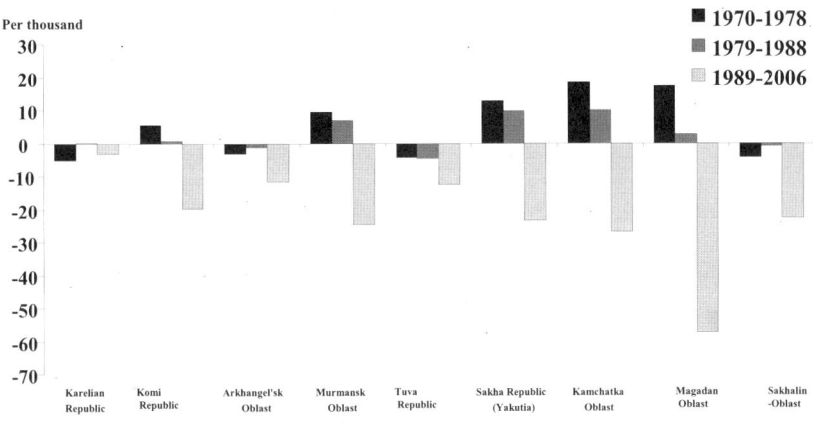

Figure 2. *Net migration in selected northern regions, 1970-2006 (per thousand).*

Migration by Region in Russia

Though there continued to be net in-migration to the North until the late 1980s, migration began to slow in the early part of the decade, especially to regions in Siberia (Fig. 2). The late 1980s was the period of Gorbachev's *perestroika*, where limited forms of private enterprise were allowed, providing an alternative legal source of high incomes. The policy of *khozrashchet* (self-financing) was also introduced, where enterprises had to cover their costs in a manner more similar to that in market economies. It was also the period of *glasnost* where issues such as the wastefulness of the Soviet Union's northern development policy began to be openly debated. Northern regions that continued to have more people arriving than leaving reversed to net out-migration at some point between 1986 and 1989. By 1990, all northern regions had more people leaving than coming. As a result of these changes, migration to the North as a whole switched from net in-migration to net out-migration in 1989, a situation that has remained ever since (*see* Fig. 3).

The year of the greatest out-migration was 1992, the first year of economic reforms and the year that prices were liberalized when the true cost of living in the northern periphery began to be felt. Migration has been the main driver of population change in the Russian North over the period, with a net out-migration of 17 percent of the 1989 population (Table 1), causing the population to fall from 9.8 million to 8.3 million currently. In terms of percentage, this represents 5.8 percent of the total Russian population, about the same share as in 1979 but a still much larger share than in pre-Soviet times. By 1990, all northern regions had more people

63

leaving than arriving and this trend has continued, albeit at much lower rates than the early 1990s.

In 1993, investment in the oil and gas sectors in Khanty-Mansiy and Yamal-Nenets caused economic growth in these regions, which spurred migration into them. Over the entire period, all northern regions except for the Khanty-Mansiy Autonomous Okrug have experienced net out-migration. Ten of the sixteen northern regions have had one-quarter or more of their populations migrate out since 1989. At the extreme are Magadan which saw an out-migration of 57 percent of its population, and Chukotka from which nearly three of every four persons migrated out causing the population to fall from 164,000 in 1989 to just 51,000 currently. Figure 4 clearly shows the regional patterns of migration out of Siberia and the Russian North toward central Russia over the transition period. As mentioned above, this represents a reversal of the regional migration patterns of the 1980s and earlier.

The migration figures used above are based on the 'residual method.' Migration trends based on the *propiska* (migration registration) data are also available from 1993 onward. These data show less out-migration from the North than that based on the residual-method data, as the latter were corrected based on the 2002 population census.

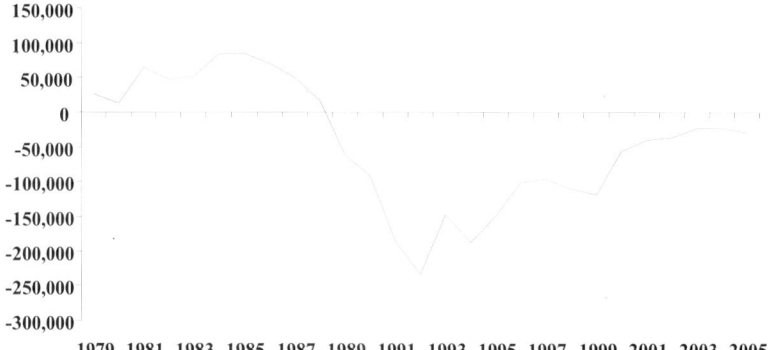

Source: Goskomstat, selected publications

Figure 3. *Net migration in the Russian North, 1979 to 2005. Source: Goskomstat, selected publications.*

Chapter 4: *Migration and Population Change in theRussian Far North in the 1990s*

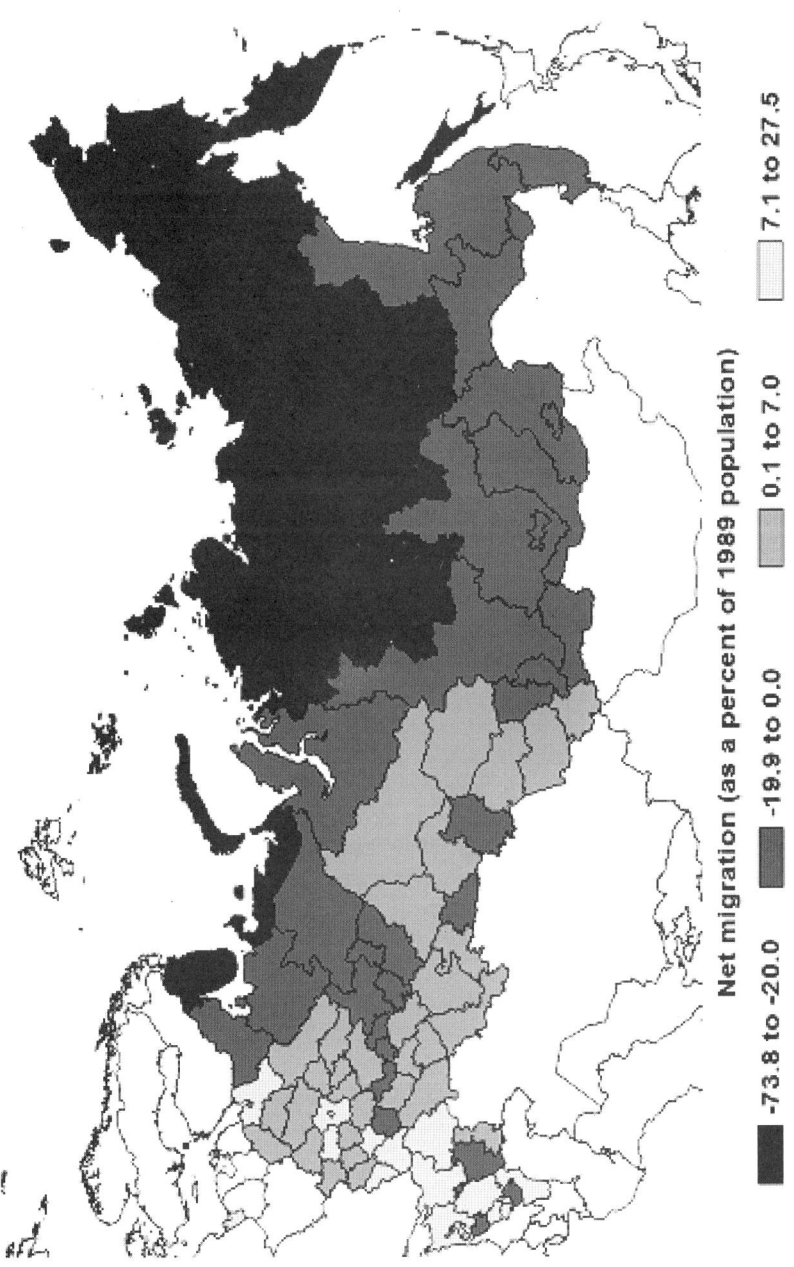

Figure 4. *Net migration by region in Russia, 1989 to 2006.*

The data show that gross migration (the sum of in-migration and out-migration) in the North peaked in 1994, when 575,000 persons migrated to or from a northern region and declined significantly to just 188,000 in 2005 (Rosstat 2006a, annual editions). Both the in-migration and out-migration rates in the North have fallen since the early 1990s, though out-migration rates have fallen more drastically, resulting in a more balanced migration exchange in the North currently. The trend in the North of declining turnover rates is similar to that of the rest of Russia. The early 1990s, just after the breakup of the Soviet Union and start of economic reforms, was a period of significant economic, social, and political restructuring causing many people to migrate as a strategy of adaptation. Now that conditions have stabilized somewhat, migration rates are lower.

The two northern regions of Khanty-Manisy and Yamal-Nenets stand out in terms of how much they influence overall trends for the North. Since the mid-1990s, they have, together, received about 45 percent of all migrants. These two regions are also responsible for one-quarter of out-migration from the region, which indicates that while there is some churning in their labor markets, they manage to retain a large percentage of migrants for work in the oil and gas sectors.

While the North has generally been a region of net out-migration to the rest of the country, it has been a net recipient of migrants from outside of Russia. The overall out-migration in the North from 1993 to 2005 of 821,040 has consisted of a loss to the rest of Russia of 915,029 and a gain from abroad of 93,989. Many regions of the North are economically depressed relative to the rest of Russia but are much better off when compared to the rest of the former Soviet Union. However, the trend has been of declining migration exchange with foreign countries. The percent of in-migration to the North from foreign countries declined from 48.1 percent in 1993 to 13.1 percent in 2005, while over the same period the percent of out-migrants going to foreign countries declined from 34.1 to 6.5 percent. Migration into Russia has become more restrictive over time and those who do come are choosing locations other than the North. Because of the occupational composition of industry in the North, there were large numbers of Ukrainians and Belarussians working and many migrated to their homelands with the breakup of the Soviet Union, but this flow has exhausted itself.

Demographic effectiveness (net migration divided by total migration) measures the extent to which migration turnover affects population change. The measure varies from -100 when there are only out-migrants from a region to 100 when there are only in-migrants, and is 0 when in-migrants equal out-migrants. For the North, the measure has been negative since the mid-1990s but less so over time—from -27 in 1993 to -17 in 2005—indicating that migration has become somewhat less unidirectional.

Table 1: Population Trends in the Russian North, 1989-2006 (Beginning of year; in thousands).

Region	Total Population		Percent Change, 1989-2006			Absolute Change, 1989-2006		
	1989	2006	Total	Natural Increase	Migration	Total	Natural Increase	Migration
RUSSIAN FEDERATION	147,022	142,754	-2.9	-6.9	4.0	-4,268	-10,165	5,897
The North	9,774	8,260	-15.5	1.8	-17.3	-1,514	174	-1,688
Karelian Republic	790	698	-11.7	-8.3	-3.4	-92	-66	-27
Komi Republic	1,251	985	-21.3	-1.3	-19.9	-266	-16	-249
Arkhangel'sk Oblast	1,570	1,291	-17.7	-6.2	-11.6	-279	-97	-182
Nenets Autonomous Okrug*	54	42	-22.2	5.4	-27.6	-12	3	-15
Murmansk Oblast	1,165	865	-25.8	-1.3	-24.5	-300	-15	-286
Khanty-Mansiy Aut. Okrug	1,282	1,478	15.3	11.6	3.7	196	149	48
Yamal-Nenets Aut. Okrug	495	531	7.2	13.9	-6.7	36	69	-33
Tuva Republic	308	308	0.2	12.6	-12.5	0	39	-38
Taymyr Auronomous Okrug	56	39	-30.4	5.7	-36.1	-17	3	-20
Evenki Autonomous Okrug	25	17	-30.9	5.8	-36.6	-8	1	-9
Sakha Republic (Yakutia)	1,094	950	-13.2	10.4	-23.5	-144	114	-258
Chukotka Autonomous Okrug	164	51	-69.2	4.6	-73.8	-113	8	-121
Kamchatka Oblast	472	349	-26.0	0.9	-26.9	-123	4	-127
Koryak Autonomous Okrug*	40	23	-42.0	0.5	-42.5	-17	0	-17
Magadan Oblast	392	172	-56.2	1.2	-57.4	-220	5	-225
Sakhalin Oblast	710	526	-25.9	-3.3	-22.6	-184	-23	-161

Notes: 'The North' as defined here are the sixteen regions designated as such in the study. * Data for these areas are also included in the larger geographic unit of which they are a part. Sources: 1991-1994, 1996-1999: Goskom stat website (www.gks.ru accessed 12 May 2006). These data have been revised based on corrections from the census. —1990, 1995, 2000-2002: Goskom stat Rossii, Demographic Yearbook 2005 (www.gks.ru accessed 3 March 2006). —1989 population totals: Goskom stat Rossii, Demograficheskiy yezhegodnik 2002. —2005 population totals: Goskom stat website www.gks.ru accessed 14 January 2007). —1990-1993 births, deaths, and natural increase: Goskomstat Rossii, Demograficheskiy yezhegodnik Rossiyakoy Federatsii 1993, 1994. —1994 births, deaths, and natural increase: Goskom stat Rossii, Sotsial'no-ekonomicheskoye polozheniye Rossii 1993-1994 gg. —1996 births and deaths: Goskom stat Rossii, Sotsial'no-ekonomicheskoye polozheniye Rossii 1996 g., 1997. —1997-98 births and death rates in Goskom stat Rossii, Regiony Rossii, 1999, p. -54-57: Birth and death rates from this source are multiplied by mid-year population. The published number of births and deaths are used for the national totals. —1999 births and deaths: Goskom stat Rossii, Sotsial-ekonomichekoye polozhenite Rossii v yanvarye 2001 g. pp. 385-387. —2000-2001 births and deaths: Goskom stat Rossii, Demograficheskiy yezhegodnik 2002. —2002-2004 births and deallhs: Goskom stat website (www.gks.ru accessed 15 February 2006). —2005 births and deaths: Goskom stat website (www.gks.ru accessed 14 January 2007). —1989-2006 net migration: Based on residual method. Data for 2002 implicitly include any census adjustments.

Several groups of northern regions can be identified according to this measure. The Khanty-Mansiy and Yamanal-Nents okrugs are the only two that have consistently had positive demographic effectiveness measures, although it has fallen for both in recent years so that in-migration and out-migration are currently roughly balanced. Karelia has had a measure of near 0 since the mid-1990s. Most other northern regions have highly negative demographic effectiveness measures of between -30 and -60, indicating that while there are some people migrating to the region, the predominate trend has been out-migration and in some regions in some years, quite uni-directional, with measures lower than -60. At the onset of the transition period, many northern regions were populated by large numbers of highly-mobile persons in the young working ages and found it hard to retain them when economic conditions worsened.

Brief Demographic Profile of the Russian North
This section provides a brief overview of the demographic trends and profile of the population of the North in order to better understand migration trends and changes in the population structure. Selected demographic indicators for the northern regions and Russia are given in Tables 2a and b.

The fertility decline in Russia from an approximate replacement level in 1989 of 2.1 children per woman to a low of 1.16 in 1999 (before a slight rebound to 1.34 in 2004) is the major reason behind Russia's overall population decline—a trend that is expected to continue well into the future. In 1989, some northern regions had higher total fertility rates (TFRs) than the Russian average, and some lower. However, by 2004, all northern regions, with the exception of Karelia and Murmansk, had higher TFRs than the Russian average. This was driven, in part, by women in all ethnic groups residing predominantly in the North having more children than Russian women. However, despite these higher fertility rates, all regions essentially are at or below replacement level, which will lead to population decline if the trend continues.

The declines in life expectancy in Russia have been well-documented. Life expectancy for both sexes declined from a high of 69.9 years in 1988 to a low of 63.9 in 1994 before a slight increase to 65.3 in 2005. This level remains far below that of countries at comparable levels of income and the male–female life expectancy gap is the largest in the world at 13.5 years. In 1989, all but two of the nine northern regions for which data were available had lower levels of life expectancy than Russia as a whole. In 2004, all but two of 16 northern regions had lower life expectancies with some such as Tuva, Chukotka, and the Koryak Okrug being 8 to 12 years lower than the pitifully low Russian average.

Chapter 4: *Migration and Population Change in the Russian Far North in the 1990s*

Table 2a: Selected Demographic Indicators for the Russian North, 1989-2004.

REGION	Total Fertility Rate		Life Expectancy					
			1989-1990			2004		
	1989	2004	Both Sexes	Males	Females	Both Sexes	Males	Females
RUSSIAN FEDERATION	1.950	1.340	69.38	63.99	74.37	65.27	58.89	72.30
Karelian Republic	1.943	1.310	69.29	63.75	74.23	61.58	54.80	69.57
Komi Republic	1.878	1.397	68.52	63.35	73.62	62.21	56.09	69.28
Arkhangel'sk Oblast	2.049	1.400	69.50	63.99	74.68	62.33	55.59	70.49
Nenets Autonomous Okrug	----	1.877		----	----	62.13	55.36	70.91
Murmansk Oblast	1.598	1.293	70.27	65.34	74.41	63.59	57.14	70.66
Khanty-Mansiy Aut. Okrug	----	1.590		----	----	68.15	62.59	74.04
Yamal-Nenets Aut. Okrug*	----	1.674		----	----	67.87	62.95	73.17
Tuva Republic	3.223	2.186	62.43	57.33	67.75	56.49	51.09	62.40
Taymyr Autonomous Okrug	----	2.001		----	----	63.20	57.13	70.29
Evenkii Autonomous Okrug	----	2.118		----	----	60.13	57.11	63.14
Sakha Republic (Yakutia)	2.450	1.907	66.92	62.49	71.54	64.21	58.48	70.67
Chukotka Autonomous Okrug	----	2.170		----	----	57.45	54.00	61.66
Kamchatka Oblast	1.678	1.409	66.08	60.43	70.98	63.60	57.99	70.32
Koryak Autonomous Okrug	----	2.164		----	----	53.07	46.40	62.08
Magadan Oblast	1.854	1.436	67.04	62.23	71.52	62.44	56.84	69.08
Sakhalin Oblast	1.997	1.448	67.27	62.19	72.41	61.49	55.32	69.02

Sources and Notes: 1989 total fertility rates: Goskomstat Rossii, Demograficheskiy uyezhegodnik Rossiyskoy Federatsii 1993. —2004 fertility rates: Goskomstat Rossii, Demograficheskiy Rossiyskoy Federatsii 2005, pp. 109. —1989-90, 1995 life expectancies: Goskomstat Rossii, Demograficheskiy yezhegodnik Rossiyskoy Federatsii 1997, pp. 102-11—2004, 2001 life expectancies: Goskomstat Rossii, Demograficheskiy yezhegodnik Rtossiyskoy Federatsii 2005, pp. 121.

69

Table 2b: Selected Demographic Indicators for the Russian North, 1989-2004.

REGION	Below Working Ages		Age Structure Working Ages		Above Working Ages		Median Ages	
	1990	2004	1990	2004	1990	2004	1989	2002
RUSSIAN FEDERATION	24.3	16.8	56.7	62.9	19.0	20.3	32.8	37.1
Karelian Republic	25.4	16.5	57.8	64.4	16.8	19.1	31.7	37.1
Komi Republic	27.7	18.2	61.6	67.6	10.7	14.2	29.4	34.5
Arkhangel'sk Oblast	26.4	17.2	57.7	64.3	15.9	18.5	31.2	36.5
Nenets Autonomous Okrug*	31.4	23.5	61.1	64.8	7.5	11.7	28.3	31.5
Murmansk Oblast	26.1	16.6	64.5	69.4	20.6	22.6	29.9	34.4
Khanty-Mansiy Aut. Okrug	33.5	20.9	62.9	71.7	3.6	7.4	27.3	31.4
Yamal-Nenets Aut. Okrug*	32.3	22.7	65.3	71.8	2.4	5.5	27.4	31.0
Tuva Republic	37.1	30.2	54.4	60.6	8.5	9.2	23.2	25.5
Taymyr Autonomous Okrug	31.8	24.0	63.3	68.7	4.9	7.3	28.1	30.6
Evenki Autonomous Okrug	33.0	25.1	62.0	65.2	5.0	9.7	27.5	31.4
Sakha Republic (Yakutia)	32.2	24.9	60.8	64.9	7.0	10.2	27.5	30.0
Chukotka Autonomous Okrug	29.6	22.2	67.7	70.9	2.7	6.9	29.3	32.6
Kamchatka Oblast	27.2	17.4	66.8	69.4	6.0	13.2	28.7	33.4
Koryak Autonomous Okrug*	32.4	22.9	62.5	65.9	5.1	11.2	29.0	33.6
Magadan Oblast	28.0	17.7	66.8	70.2	5.2	12.1	29.6	35.2
Sakhalin Oblast	26.6	17.2	62.7	67.4	10.7	15.4	30.3	35.5

Sources and Notes: Age structure: Rosstat, Regiony Rossii: Sotsial'no-ekonomicheskiye pokazateli 2005, Moscow: 2006, pp. 44. —Median Age: Rosstat, Vserossiyskaya perepisi naseleniya 2002 goda, vol. 14, no. 9. Below working ages are 0 to 15, working ages are males 16 to 59, and females 16 to 54, pension ages are males 60 and older, and females 55 and older.

In 1990, all northern regions had larger youth population shares than Russia and in 2004, all but two still did. The statement that "the distinctiveness of northern population as a whole with lower average age, higher fertility, is gradually disappearing" is confirmed by statistics (Blakkisrud and Honneland 2006b:11). Of course, the Russian North has been and continues to be a place of work and thus all northern regions except one (Tuva), had and continue to have higher shares of their populations in the working ages.

The most important change in the age structure in the North has been an increase in the elderly shares of the population. In 1990 and in 2004, only Murmansk had a larger pension-age population than Russia. While the elderly population increased only moderately in Russia from 19.0 to 20.3 percent of the population, it increased rather significantly in most northern regions. While the population of Russia is affected by the general aging trends of its population, northern regions have also been affected by age-specific migration of the young adult population and the lack of ability of many pension-age persons to be able to migrate out of the North. While still younger, the median age of the northern population is reaching that of the Russian average.

For Russia, the sum result of these trends of continued low fertility, low life expectancy and an aging population is that deaths began to exceed births in 1992, a trend that is expected to continue into the foreseeable future. While there was a slight surplus of births over deaths in the North for the period 1989 to 2006, deaths began to exceed births in 1993 and has continued to since then. In 2005, only some of the smaller ethnic homelands in the North continued to show natural increase. Thus, in addition to the expected continued trend of out-migration from the North, population decline is expected to accelerate for the bulk of northern regions because of an excess of deaths over births.

Regional Population Change by Sex
Russia has long had very low sex ratios (number of males per 100 females). Males suffered the brunt of the devastating losses during WWII and at the end of the war, there were only 74.7 males per 100 females (Heleniak 2008). As cohorts with more balanced sex ratios replaced those with deficits of males, the ratio gradually increased to a peak of 88.4 males to 100 females in 1995, before beginning to decline again. Russia's sex ratio in 2002 of 87.2 males to 100 females was among the lowest in the world because of high male mortality due mainly to lifestyle causes of death resulting in the widest male:female gap in life expectancy in the world. On a global scale, there are 101 males to 100 females (Population Division 2005). However, an analysis of regional and northern sex ratios must be seen relative to Russia and not to those of a normal population with more equal sex ratios.

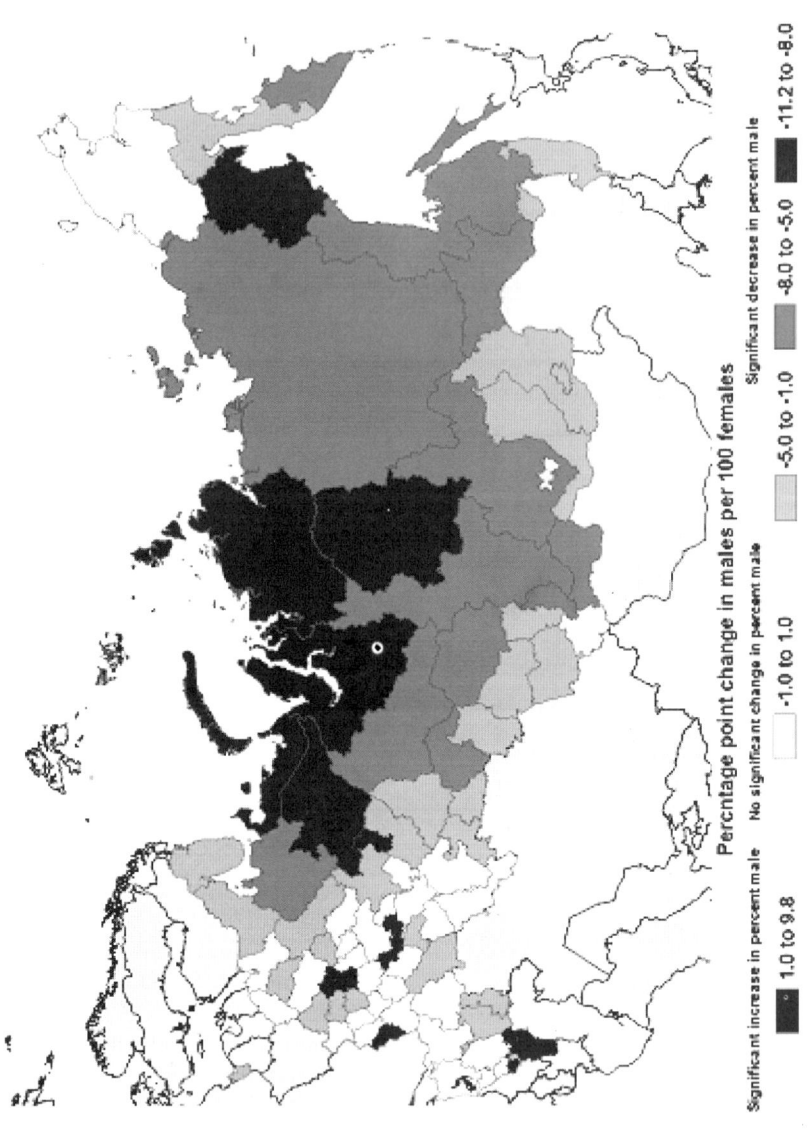

Figure 5. *Change in the sex ration by region in Russia, 1989 to 2002.*

Given the sectoral and occupational structure of the North, these regions tended to attract more males. Young males were most often single and did not migrate with families. The sex ratio for the 16 northern regions in 1989 was 100.7 males to 100 females. All of the northern regions had sex ratios well above the national average and the few regions with more males than females were all located in the North. This included the region with the highest sex ratio, Chukotka at 111 males:100 females.

For Russia, the sex ratio in 2002 of 87.2 males per 100 females was a slight decrease from 1989 when there were 87.7 males per 100 females. This was largely attributable to the increasing male–female life expectancy gap during the transition period. For the North, the sex ratio fell from 100.7 in 1989 to 94.3 in 2002. The sex ratio fell in every northern region, although in all but one the ratio remained above the national average.

Because males constituted the majority of migrants, migration was the main factor explaining changes in sex ratios among regions. Regions with large in-migrations experienced large increases in the ratio of males to females while those with large percentages of out-migration experienced the opposite. In Moscow—the prime destination of both internal and international migrants—the sex ratio increased from 81.4 in 1989 to 91.2 in 2002. Many northern regions that experienced a large exodus had among the largest percentage point declines in their sex ratios (Fig. 5).

At the national level, higher male mortality can explain much of the decrease in the sex ratio between censuses. While most northern regions have lower life expectancies than Russia as a whole, the female advantage is smaller, indicating that natural increase differences were less of a factor in explaining changes in the sex ratios. As illustrated in Figure 6, which compares sex ratios by age in the North in 1989 and 2002, the largest declines were at the most mobile ages (15 to 34), indicating that it was out-migration that drove much of declining sex ratio in the North.

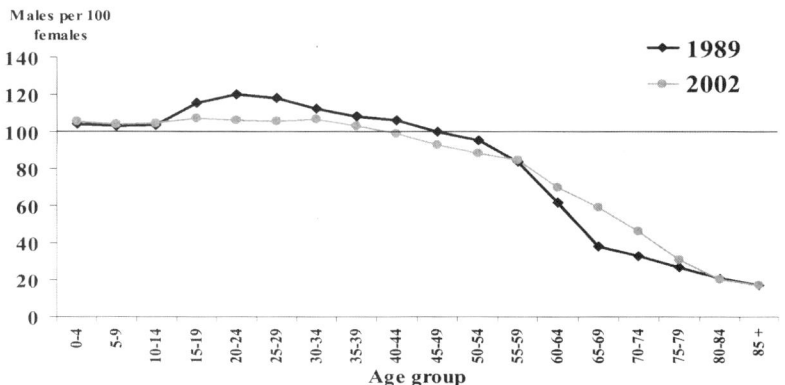

Figure 6. *Sex ratio by age in the Russian North, 1989 and 2002.*

Despite the decline in the sex ratio across the North, the region remains predominantly male compared to the rest of the country, simply because it had such an excess of males to begin with (*see* Fig. 7). Across the North, there is a distinct trend by size of settlement. The larger cities in the Russian North have lower male sex ratios than the northern average. This is indicative of more diversified economies, including service sectors which predominantly employ females. Smaller northern settlements with limited economies and employment in resource extraction industries tend to have large excesses of males. This is a pattern similar to Alaska, Greenland, Norway, and Iceland where small northern settlements based on either resource extraction or hunting and fishing tend to be predominantly male (Hamilton and Seyfrit 1994).

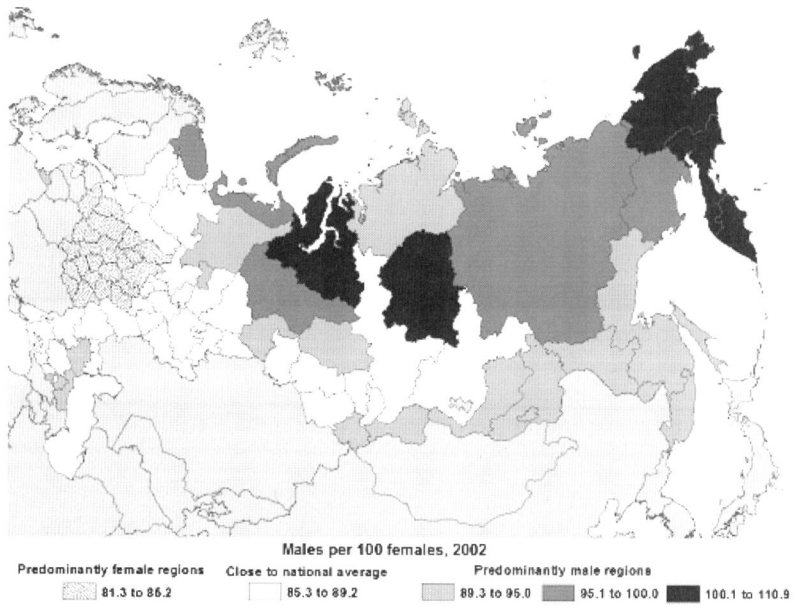

Figure 7. *Sex ratio by region in Russia, 2002.*

Regional Population Change by Age

The age of a person is one of the most important characteristics influencing the likelihood that they will migrate (Plane and Rogerson 1994:107). There are well-documented probabilities of movement across the life course, with the highest occurring in young adulthood. Because the Russian North was a region of in-migration for a long period of time until the end of the Soviet period, the region had developed a much younger age structure than the rest of Russia. With most of the regions of the North now experiencing out-migration, it is among the mobile, young-adult portions of their populations that declines are the largest.

The three components of population change—fertility, mortality, and migration—contribute to changes in the age structure of any country or region. Like other countries, Russia has been undergoing a long-term aging of its population, mainly as a result of declines in fertility. This trend accelerated with the steep decline in fertility during the post-Soviet period. The median age of the Russian population increased from 32.8 in 1989 to 37.1 in 2002, an increase of 4.3 years, which is rather large in such a short time. In 1992, the number of deaths in Russia began to exceed to the number of births (a situation referred to as negative natural increase or natural decrease). This trend is expected to continue into the foreseeable future, leading to a continued aging of the population. Nearly all Russian regions, including nearly all in the North, currently experience more deaths than births.

Because of the age selectivity of migration, the age structure of regions experiencing larger amounts of in-migration or out-migration will be significantly affected by this component. Because of these past demographic trends, there are distinct regional differences in age structure. Russia can be characterized as having an elderly core and a young periphery. Several regions in central Russia surrounding Moscow have the oldest age structures, all having median ages over 40 years in 2002. Moving out from this older core are regions with slightly younger age structures but still with median ages above the national average. The populations of the regions get progressively younger further to the south and east. Regions with the youngest median age are ethnic regions in the Caucasus and Siberia. This is due in part to many of the non-Russian ethnic groups having younger age structures and higher fertility rates than ethnic Russians. The much younger average age of northern natives was also a factor contributing to the younger age structure of many northern regions (Overland and Blakkisrud 2006:181). Other non-ethnic regions in Siberia and the Far East that were primary migration destinations during most of the Soviet period, also have younger age structures. This is a pattern not unlike northern peripheries elsewhere.

The largest differences in age structure between Russia and the North was in the population of young working ages of 20 to 39. In 1989, this cohort comprised 32 percent of the population of Russia, but 39 percent of the population in the North (Heleniak 1999:159). Many were lured to the northern region for the high wages offered during the Soviet period, but most returned to the *materik* (mainland) before retirement. Pension-aged persons comprised only 8.8 percent of the population of the North in 1989 while they accounted for 18.5 percent of Russia's population. The population in all northern regions had lower median ages than the Russian average, with the youngest populations being in those northern regions furthest from central Russia in northern Siberia and the Far East.

Figure 8 shows changes in the age structure of the population of the Russian North between the 1989 and 2002 censuses. Several factors contributed to these changes, including the steep decline in fertility, age-selective migration, and the echoes of Russia's peculiar age structure. Overall, the population of the North declined by 15.5 percent over this period, while the population of those under age 10 declined by half as a result of fertility declines combined with out-migration of young-adult parents. There was an increase among those aged 15 to 19, in part because of a short-lived fertility boom in the late 1980s. Those in the prime working ages of 25 to 39 years declined by 38 percent, due largely to this cohort also being among the most mobile and those who left the North in the largest numbers during the transition period. There were increases in all ages above 40 as result of population aging and lower mobility rates, except among those at retirement age 55 to 59.[2]

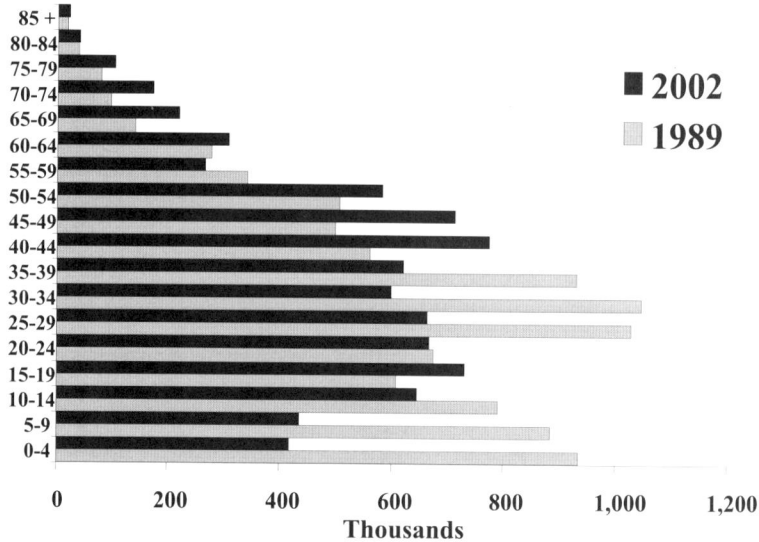

Figure 8. *Age structure of the Russian North, 1989 and 2002.*

---

[2] Officially, retirement ages are 55 for females and 60 for males. However, many in the North are able to retire early because of service in the region and persons in many occupations found in the North are also eligible for early retirement.

Chapter 4: *Migration and Population Change in theRussian Far North in the 1990s*

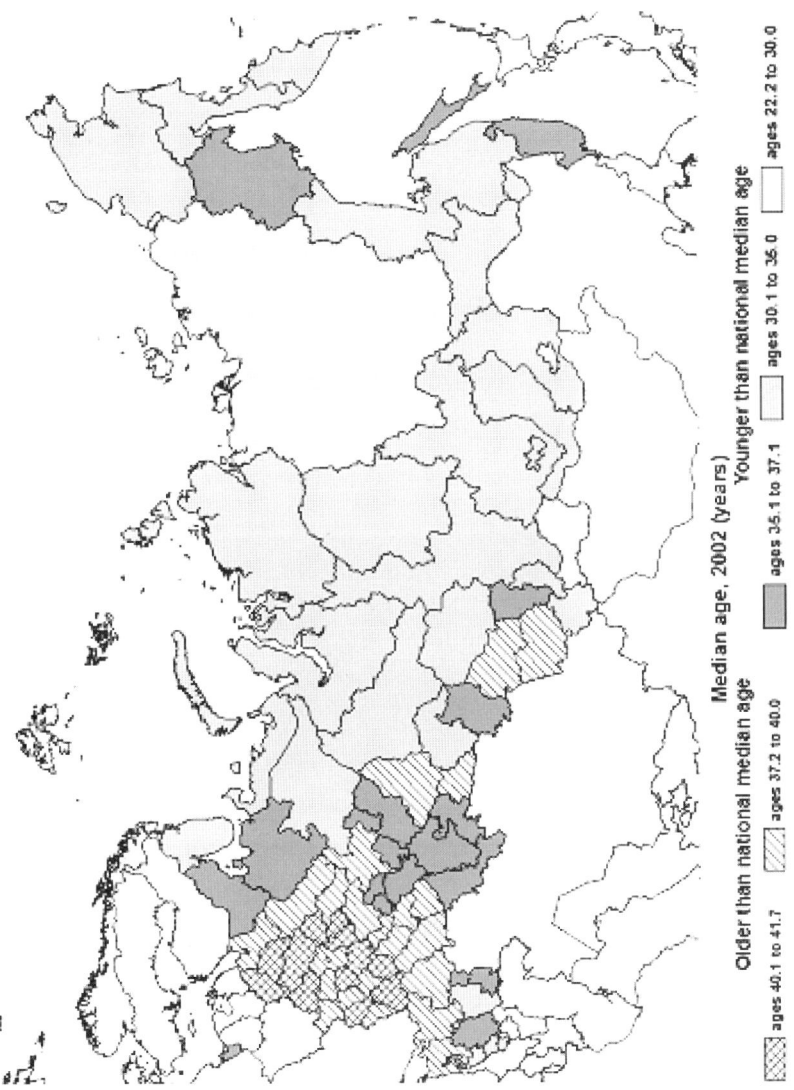

Figure 9. *Median age by region in Russia, 2002.*

Between 1989 and 2002, all regions in Russia had an increase in their median ages. Those with the largest increases were concentrated in the Central and Northwest Federal Okrugs. The regions with the smallest increases were those with the youngest populations in Siberia and the Caucasus. In 1989, all northern regions had younger median ages than the national level, and while all still do, most have moved closer to the Russian average. The elderly core and young periphery remains in Russia with Siberia and the Russian North being regions with larger than average young and working-age populations and smaller than average pension-age populations (see Fig. 9).

There are several implications of the changing age structure for Russia and the northern regions. The relative dependency ratio in each region also has an impact on the public spending mix. At both the national and regional levels, this will require a shift in spending away from education toward pensions and health care. While there has been considerable out-migration from the North during the period between the censuses, much of this is of the able-bodied portions of the population, leaving many elderly 'stuck' in the region without the resources to move. It is for this reason that there are several regional and federal programs to assist pensioners and others who wish to migrate from the North. Magadan, Vorkutka (Komi Region), and Norilsk (Krasnoyrask Kray) are included in the $80 million *Northern Restructuring Project* which is supported by a loan from the World Bank, to help assist persons who wish to voluntarily leave (see www.worldbank.org for more details).

Regional Population Change by Educational Level
Prior to the economic transition, the population of the northern regions of Russia were all more educated than the rest of the country. This was partially due to an economic structure that required a more educated workforce. A related factor was that with limitations on mobility and many northern regions restricting entry even to Soviet citizens, enterprises in the North could be quite selective in whom they hired.

The large-scale social and economic transformation that Russia underwent in the decade and a half after the last census had an enormous impact on its educational system and on the supply and demand for human capital at the individual, national, and regional levels. According to theory, migration tends to be quite selective toward more educated persons. This led the Russian North, a region of continued in-migration during the Soviet period, to develop a much more educated population than the Russian average. But as a region of large-scale out-migration during the post-Soviet period, it also lost its more educated segments in disproportionate numbers.

There has been a decreased demand for technical training in vocational schools and engineering at higher levels and an increased demand for courses in the humanities, economics, finance, languages, and other skills needed for the new labor market. More importance is being placed on business education, such as MBAs, and other skills needed for the market economy. The wage structure under the Soviet economic system was rather narrow but has widened considerably under market conditions. One consequence of this has been a large increase in returns to education (Gorodnichenko and Peter 2004). At the national level, the trend toward a much more educated population is clearly evident. In 1959, over sixty percent of the population had but a primary education or less and less than 3 percent had a higher education. By 2002, less than 9 percent of the population had only a primary education or less and 16 percent possessed a completed higher education.

The 2002 census offers insight into changes in human capital as measured by educational attainment at both the national and regional levels, and a more quantitative than qualitative snapshot of changes to the Russian education system. Both the devolution of financial responsibility to lower levels and privatization have led to some disparities in access and quality, as well as perhaps educational outcomes.

There were three questions asked in the census about education, with several sub-questions, depending on initial answers. The first question realted to persons six years and older and asked whether they were in school or not, and if so, what type of educational institution they were attending. The second question asked whether children ages 3 to 9 were in a preschool or primary school. The third asked about highest level of education attained. The question was asked of persons 10 years and older, but the results were compiled for those 15 and older. The first three choices were primary general education, basic general education (incomplete secondary), or secondary general (completed). Those possessing a general secondary education or less were asked if they had completed a primary professional or professional–technical education.

One factor that can explain some of the differences in levels of education at the regional level are differences in attainment by nationality. This is especially true in non-Russian regions of the country, where the differences in educational levels between Russians and the titular groups can be quite large. For instance, among the Chukchi only 4.9 percent have completed higher education versus 15.7 percent of the total population; 15.4 percent have a secondary professional education against 27.1 percent of all people in Russia. At the other end of the spectrum, 2.4 percent have less than a primary education (1.0 percent nationally) and 1.8 percent are considered illiterate (0.6 percent nationally).

For Chukotka and many other Siberian and northern ethnic homelands, the lack of education of the native groups is partly due to a lack of local infrastructure, especially of higher education facilities. Like many ethnic groups, the Chukchi are concentrated in and near their homeland. With decentralization of the funding of education, disparities in the availability and quality of educational facilities have become even greater (Canning *et al.* 1999). If differences in educational attainment persist or widen, this could exacerbate variances in economic growth rates across regions. But also with decentralization, some ethnic regions have begun to base curriculum and teaching methods on national and historical traditions, which could have a positive effect.

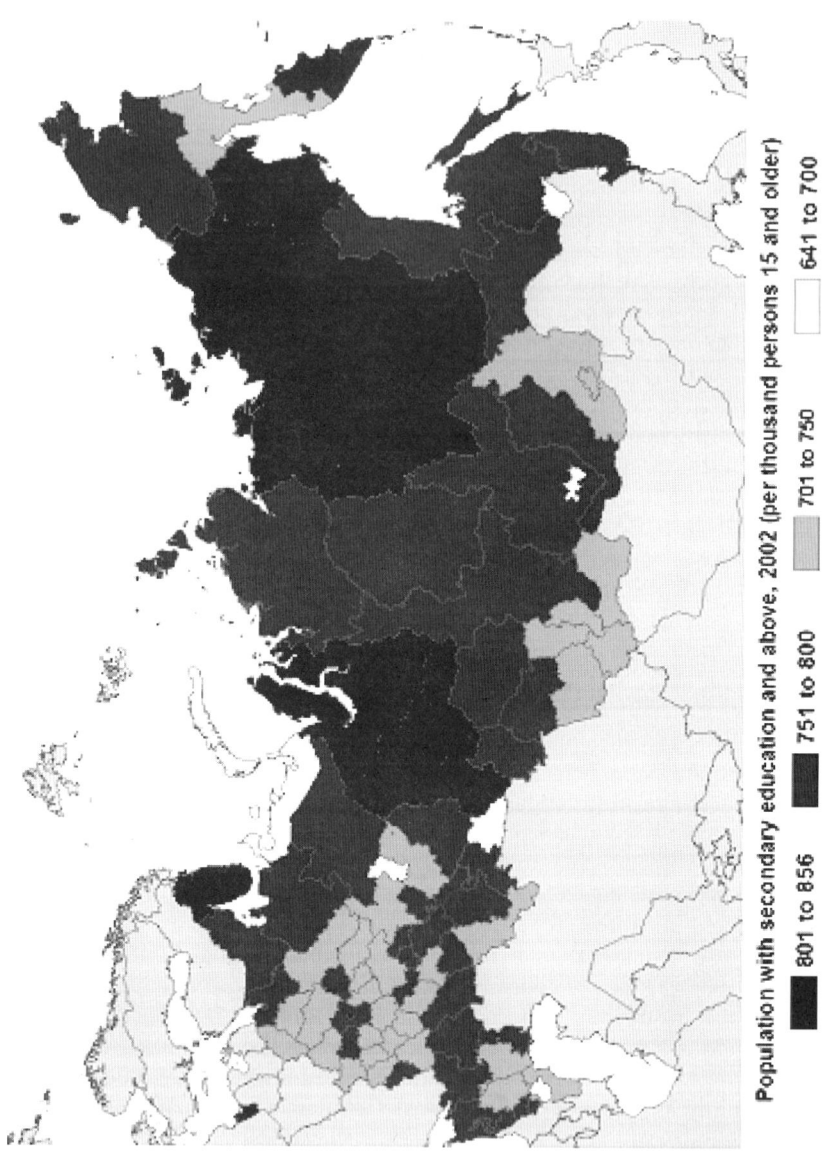

Figure 10. *Population with secondary education and above by region in Russia, 2002.*

Chapter 4: *Migration and Population Change in theRussian Far North in the 1990s*

There are two major education issues of importance at the regional level in Russia. The first is growing disparities in access to the education system among regions in Russia and the increased differences in the quality of education among regions brought about by the decentralization of education expenditures. The second is the possibly wide and growing gaps in human capital which could be playing a role in regional economic disparities. A major issue in regional development in Russia is the role that migration has played, as migration tends to be very age and skill-level selective.

Figure 10 shows the regional pattern of educational attainment, in 2002. This includes all persons with a completed secondary education or higher, that is all persons with a post-graduate, higher education, incomplete higher, secondary professional, vocational, and completed secondary education. In United States' terms, it basically equates to the percent of persons who had at least graduated from high school. The share of regional populations who had this level of education or higher ranged from 86 to 64 percent. Regions with high shares included Moscow city, St. Petersburg, and a number of northern and Siberian regions—Murmansk, the Khanty-Mansiy and Yamal-Nenets okrugs, Tyumen' Yakutia, Magadan, and Kamchatka.

Those regions that were in the top ten in 1989 but fell out in 2002 were all regions in the Russian Far East, from which there was considerable overall out-migration and obviously disproportionate out-migration of more highly educated persons, as predicted. Chukotka, which experienced a population decline of nearly two-thirds of its 1989 population during the inter-census period, was one of the very few regions of Russia to have a decline in the share of the population with a higher education.

Figure 11 shows changes according to those with completed secondary and higher education. The regional pattern of change by level of education is broadly similar to the overall patterns of net migration by region during the inter-census period. The change in the educational levels by region broadly followed this pattern, with those regions that had large amounts of out-migration also being those that had the smallest increases or decreases in the percent of the population with secondary or higher education. There were actually only three small homelands of Siberian ethnic groups that experienced decreases in the shares of their populations with secondary education: the Koryak, Taymyr, and Chukotka autonomous okrugs.

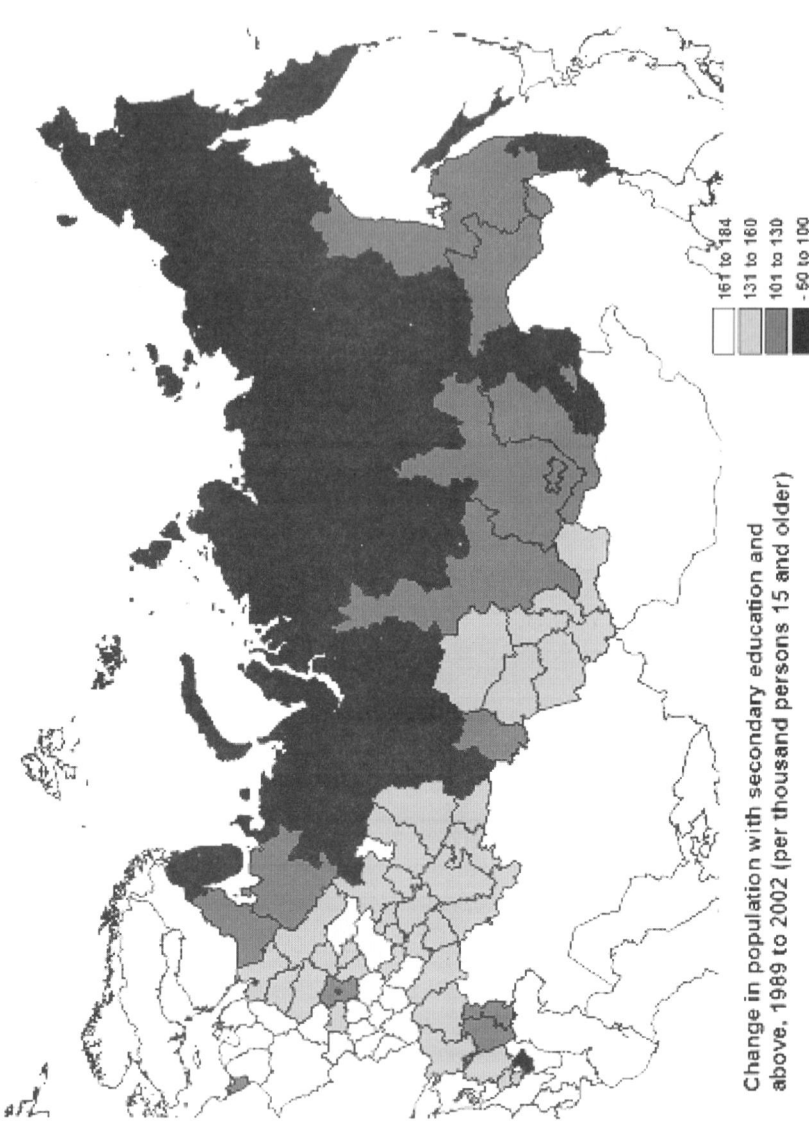

Figure 11. *Change in population with secondary education and above by region in Russia, 1989 to 2002.*

Chapter 4: *Migration and Population Change in the Russian Far North in the 1990s*

The important implication of the regional migration patterns that have characterized Russia since 1990 is that because migration is so education-selective, those regions that have lost people in large numbers due to out-migration have lost them disproportionally among their most educated segments. Conversely, those regions that have gained have disproportionally gained more educated members. Since more educated people tend to be more productive and more innovative, this has important implications for regional economic growth. Thus, the 72 percent population decline from migration that Chukotka experienced during the inter-census period will have a drastic impact on economic growth because it was the best and brightest that left. Similarly, the 26 percent increase in Moscow's population from migration should provide a boost to growth and productivity in that region because so many of the newcomers were highly educated. This correlation between net migration and change in percent of population with higher and post-graduate degrees can be seen in Figure 12.

Changes in the Ethnic Composition of the Russian North

The in-migration of non-native groups to the Russian North during the Soviet period caused rather significant changes in the ethnic composition, dropping natives to rather miniscule shares in some regions. Out-migration during the post-Soviet period reversed some of the demographic superiority of Russians and Russian-speakers, but they remain a significant presence. The Soviet Union had a rather complex and overlapping ethnic geography that included 53 ethnic homelands, 31 of these are in Russia. Fifteen of these homelands became successor states to the Soviet Union. Eleven of the 16 regions defined as the Far North here are territorially-defined ethnic homelands.

There are three ways in which the ethnic composition of a region can change between censuses—different rates of natural increase, net migration, or ethnic re-identification. All Siberian and northern native ethnic groups have higher fertility rates than Russians, and despite often higher mortality rates, when combined with younger age structures, they grew faster than the national average. An undetermined percentage of the change in the ethnic comparison of the North over the inter-census period is attributable to persons identifying themselves as belonging to one ethnic group in the 1989 census and another in the 2002 census. The out-migration that consisted primarily of Russians and other groups not indigenous to the North seems to have been the main cause of the changing ethnic composition.

Another set of factors that contributed to changes in the ethnic composition were differences in the manner in which the data on nationality was compiled and presented in the two censuses and the number of ethnic groups identified in each. In 1989, data were only presented for the largest few ethnic groups in each region, thus it was not possible to identify the entire composition of many northern regions or the location of all members of many groups (SSSR 1991). In the Soviet period, there was a general trend toward consolidation of ethnic groups, and in 1989 data were presented for 128 different groups, plus a total for the Small-Numbered Peoples of the North (*malochislenny narod severa*), and 'other nationalities,' thus for 130 categories.This was especially problematic for some of the smaller Siberian groups. In 2002, data were published for all ethnic groups to the last person for all 89 regions of Russia. For the latter census, the number of ethnic groups had expanded to 184.

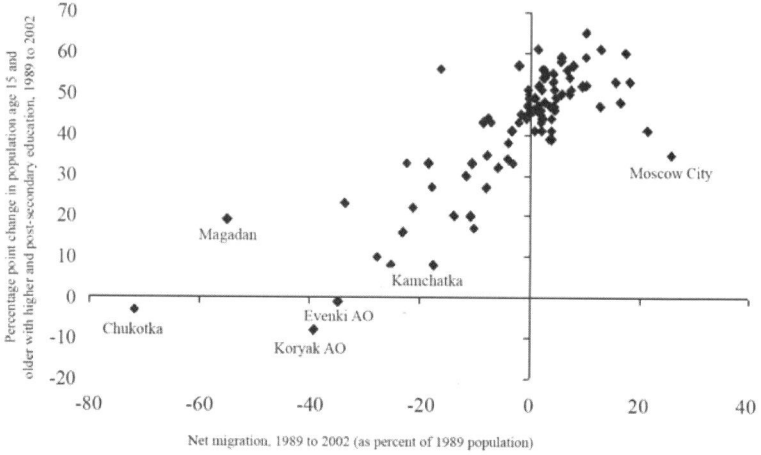

Figure 12. *Relationship between net migration and change in share of population with higher education by region in Russia, 1989 to 2002.*

The categorization of peoples as indigenous or small-numbered is more political than scientific (Overland and Blakkisrud 2006:163). For most of the Soviet period, there were 26 groups identified as belonging to the Small-Numbered Peoples of the North. Because of the numerical threshold of 50,000, this did not include such larger groups found primarily in Siberia and the North as Yakuts, Komi, and Karelians. In 2000, this list was expanded to 45 groups, including some not indigenous to the North (Overland and Blakkisrud 2006:172-173).

Thus, in the 2002 census, there were 38 ethnic groups identified as belonging to the Small-Numbered Peoples of the North. Obviously, many of these groups were identified separately for the first time and this was partially the reason for the increase in their numbers from 181,517 in 1989 to 249,572 in 2002.

Chapter 4: *Migration and Population Change in theRussian Far North in the 1990s*

Table 3 shows the ethnic composition of the Russian North in 1989 and 2002. Over this period, there was an overall population decline in the North of 1.4 million and a decline in the Slavic population of 1.5 million, with increases in other groups. The absolute number of Russians declined in all northern regions except the Khanty-Mansiy and Yamal-Nenets okrugs where there had been recent in-migration. It was Russians and other Russian-speakers who were leaving the North in the largest numbers when economic conditions changed rapidly. Despite this out-migration, the Russian percent of the northern population declined only moderately from 70.9 to 69.8 percent of the population, and Russians remain the majority population in all but two northern regions.

The percentage of Russians increased in the European North as well as Magadan and Sakhalin. This was due in part to a larger exodus of Ukrainans and Belarussians who had staffed many of the northern enterprises in large numbers. The largest Russian declines were in the ethnic regions of Tuva, Chukotka, and the Koryak Okrug. Partly as a result of re-identification, the absolute numbers of persons identifying themselves as belonging to one of the groups of Small-Numbered Peoples of the North increased in every northern region in both absolute and percentage terms. In Chukotka, which had such a dramatic out-migration over the period, the Russian share fell from 66.1 to 51.9 percent, while the indigenous share increased from 9.6 to 31.3 percent. The percent that the Koryaks make up of the Koryak Okrug increased from 24.8 to 40.7 percent with the out-migration of non-titular groups. This is the closest that any small-numbered group comes to being a plurality in its homeland. Of the three larger northern groups with homelands, Yakuts supplanted Russians as the largest ethnic group in Yakutia. In the Komi republic, both Komis and Russians increased their shares. In Karelia, the Russian share increased while the Karelian share decreased, in part because of a demographic profile closer to that of Russians after having lived in proximity to them for centuries.

Of the 31 homelands in Russia, the majority had increases in the titular share (Fig. 13). This was due to a combination of out-migration of Russians, higher rates of natural increase of the non-Russian groups, and ethnic re-identification, in most cases away from Russian and toward the titular group. The largest increases in titular shares in their homelands were in several regions in the north Caucasus and Siberia. This could also be attributable to in-migration of persons living outside their homeland, so-called diaspora migration. With the breakup of the Soviet Union, in some cases there was a pattern of ethnic segregation toward one's ethnic homeland. Of the ethnic groups with homelands in the North, there was a universal pattern of increased shares of ethnic group members residing in their homelands.

Table 3: Ethnic Composition of the Russian North, 1989 and 2002 (percent).

1989	All Nationalities	Russian	Ukrainian	Belarussian	Other FSU State Titular Nationalities	Yakuts	Komi	Karelians	Small-Numbered Peoples of the North	Other Nationalities
RUSSIAN FEDERATION	100.0	81.5	3.0	0.8	1.5	0.3	0.2	0.1	0.1	12.5
The North	100.0	70.9	8.0	2.3	0.8	3.7	3.2	0.8	1.3	9.0
Karelian Republic	100.0	73.6	3.6	7.0	0.2	0.0	0.0	10.0	0.0	5.6
Komi Republic	100.0	57.7	8.3	2.1	1.4	0.0	23.3	0.0	0.0	7.1
Arkhangel'sk Oblast	100.0	92.1	3.4	1.3	0.3	0.0	0.5	0.0	0.5	1.9
Nenets Autonomous Okrug*	100.0	65.8	6.9	1.9	0.0	0.0	9.5	0.0	11.9	3.9
Murmansk Oblast	100.0	82.9	9.0	3.3	0.5	0.0	0.2	0.3	0.1	3.6
Khanty-Mansiy Aut. Okrug*	100.0	66.3	11.6	2.2	1.8	0.0	0.3	0.0	1.4	16.4
Yamal-Nenets Aut. Okrug*	100.0	59.2	17.2	2.5	2.4	0.0	1.2	0.0	6.0	11.6
Tuva Republic	100.0	32.0	0.7	0.0	0.0	0.0	0.0	0.0	0.0	67.3
Taymyr Autonomous Okrug*	100.0	67.1	8.6	1.3	0.4	0.0	0.0	0.0	15.5	7.1
Evenki Autonomous Okrug*	100.0	67.5	5.3	0.0	0.0	3.8	0.0	0.0	14.0	9.4
Sakha Republic (Yakutia)	100.0	50.3	7.0	0.9	0.3	33.4	0.0	0.0	2.2	5.8
Chukotka Autonomous Okrug	100.0	66.1	16.8	1.9	0.4	0.0	0.0	0.0	9.5	5.3
Kamchatka Oblast	100.0	81.0	9.1	1.6	0.3	0.0	0.0	0.0	2.6	5.5
Koryak Autonomous Okrug*	100.0	62.0	7.3	1.0	0.0	0.0	0.0	0.0	24.8	4.9
Magadan Oblast	100.0	75.2	14.9	1.9	0.4	0.0	0.0	0.0	1.3	6.4
Sakhalin Oblast	100.0	81.6	6.5	1.6	0.4	0.0	0.0	0.0	0.4	9.5

Source: *East View Publications and CIS Statistical Committee, 1989 USSR Census (CD-ROM), 1996.*
Note: Komi are the sum of Komi, Komi-Izhems, and Komi-Permyaks.

Chapter 4: *Migration and Population Change in the Russian Far North in the 1990s*

2002	All Nationalities	Russian	Ukrainian	Belarrsian	Other FSU State Titular Nationalities	Yakuts	Komi	Karelians	Small-Numbered Peoples of the North	Other Nationalities
RUSSIAN FEDERATION	100.0	79.8	2.0	0.6	2.2	0.3	0.3	0.1	0.2	14.5
The North	100.0	69.8	5.5	1.6	1.8	5.2	3.5	0.8	2.1	9.7
Karelian Republic	100.0	76.6	2.7	5.3	1.0	0.0	0.0	9.2	0.7	4.6
Komi Republic	100.0	59.6	6.1	1.5	1.7	0.0	26.5	0.0	0.1	4.5
Arkhangel'sk Oblast	100.0	94.2	2.1	0.8	0.6	0.0	0.4	0.0	0.6	1.3
Nenets Autonomous Okrug*	100.0	62.4	3.2	1.0	0.5	0.0	10.9	0.0	18.7	3.3
Murmansk Oblast	100.0	85.2	6.4	2.3	1.3	0.0	0.4	0.2	0.2	3.9
Khanty-Mansiy Aut. Okrug*	100.0	66.1	8.6	1.4	4.3	0.0	0.5	0.0	2.0	17.1
Yamal-Nenets Aut. Okrug*	100.0	58.8	13.0	1.8	3.9	0.0	1.5	0.0	7.4	13.6
Tuva Republic	100.0	20.1	0.3	0.1	0.6	0.0	0.5	0.0	1.5	76.9
Taymyr Autonomous Okrug*	100.0	58.6	6.1	0.7	2.1	0.1	0.1	0.0	24.8	7.5
Evenki Autonomous Okrug*	100.0	61.9	3.1	0.6	1.2	5.6	0.1	0.0	23.1	4.4
Sakha Republic (Yakutia)	100.0	41.2	3.6	0.4	1.4	45.5	0.0	0.0	3.5	4.3
Chukotka Autonomous Okrug	100.0	51.9	9.2	1.0	1.0	0.1	0.0	0.0	31.3	5.4
Kamchatka Oblast	100.0	80.9	5.8	1.0	1.2	0.0	0.0	0.0	4.3	6.8
Koryak Autonomous Okrug*	100.0	50.6	4.1	0.6	0.6	0.1	0.0	0.0	40.7	3.4
Magadan Oblast	100.0	80.2	9.9	1.2	1.3	0.3	0.0	0.0	2.7	4.4
Sakhalin Oblast	100.0	84.3	4.0	1.0	0.9	0.0	0.0	0.0	0.6	9.2

Source: *Goskomstat Rossi, 2004, "Osnovnyi Itogi Vserossiyskaya perepisi Naseleniya 2002."*
Note: Komi are the sum of Komi, Komi-Izhems, and Komi-Permyaks.

Migration in the Circumpolar North

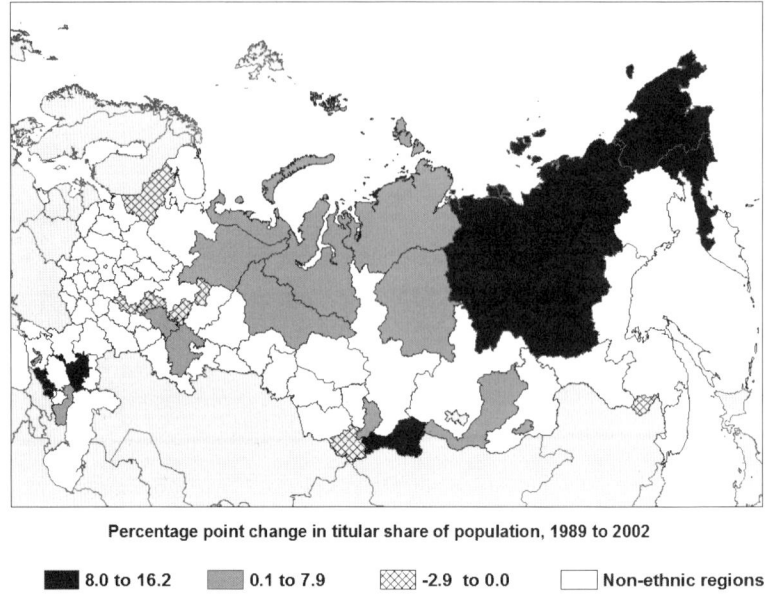

Percentage point change in titular share of population, 1989 to 2002

■ 8.0 to 16.2   ■ 0.1 to 7.9   ▨ -2.9 to 0.0   ☐ Non-ethnic regions

Figure 13. *Percentage point change in the titular share of total population in the homelands within Russia from 1989 to 2002.*

One factor that will certainly affect development and migration patterns in these Siberian homelands, albeit in an uncertain manner, is that many are in the process of being abolished and merged with other units. This is reflective of a general effort of consolidation of regions, ostensibly with the goal of making administration of Russia's federal structure more efficient. This battle of consolidation of homelands and other regions is being fought at several levels—between the Federal Government and the regions and among regions themselves—with both political and economic agendas at work.

As a result of this consolidation process, many of the northern homelands are likely to disappear as independent entities (Blakkisrud and Honneland 2006b:15). It is possible that all ethnic regions might disappear in the future and that the number of regions might decrease from 89 to 28 (Yasmann 2006).

As of this writing, in the North and Siberia, the Komi-Permiak Okrug has merged with Perm Oblast (Blakkisrud 2006:36), the Ust-Ordyn Buryat Okrug has merged with the Irkutsk oblast, the Taimyr and Evenk okrugs have joined the Krasnoyrask Kray, and the Koryak Okrug has been subsumed into the Kamchatka Oblast (Dmitriyev 2007). There are other proposals to eliminate or consolidate the northern ethnic regions, including one to create a 'Tyumen energy territory' by merging the Khanty-Mansiy and Yamal-Nenets Okrugs with the Tyumen Oblast, although this is being opposed by the heads of the okrugs.

In many cases, these consolidations represent the merge of a prosperous ethnic region (often with substantial natural resources), with a poorer Russian one. At issue is control over financial assets, taxes, and revenue from natural resources. There is an obvious political element as mergers eliminate the position of head of the region and the accompanying bureaucracy and increases the clout of the newly-created region. For the homelands of the smaller northern groups, this process seems to have a negative effect, as they lose control over their homeland or area of traditional settlement and lose a voice in national politics. Often the loss of a territorial homeland is the beginning of a process of eventual assimilation.

Conclusions

While there has been considerable out-migration and population change from the Russian North, the path dependency of decades of Soviet development policy toward the region seems to indicate that it will not return to its pre-Soviet population levels nor will it begin to resemble the settlement patterns of other northern regions. The resources of the region, combined with the infrastructure and the attachment to place of the population mean any dramatic downsizing of the population has already taken place. The small indigenous population retains its attachment to the land and doesn't wish to move (Poppel *et al*. 2007:10). Many members of the non-indigenous population retain an attachment to the mines and other enterprises of the North. There have been considerable social costs associated with the transition; the migration assistance programs of the federal and local northern governments have played but a minor role in overcoming these.

The most recent set of regional population projections conducted by the Russian statistical office point toward a continued out-migration from the region, causing the population to further decline from 8.3 million in 2006 to 7.8 million in 2026 (Rossii 2005). This would be roughly the same number of persons in the Russian North as in 1979 and would represent roughly the same portion of the total Russian population at 5.8 percent. This is lower than its peak just prior to the transition in 1989 when 6.6 percent of the Russian population lived in the North but still higher than prior to the industrialization of Russia and the North in the 1920s when only 1.9 percent of Russia's population lived in the region.

Like other population projections, these were undertaken in rather mechanical fashion, a method that doesn't easily incorporate the impact of economic development at the national or regional level, nor exogenous events. The most critical future trend for the Russian North is likely to be global warming as,

The Soviet Union is a high-latitude country, much of it deep within the largest country. No other country has so much land in arctic regions, or is so remote from oceans. ... This landlocked interior position is a constant, but its significance changes with developments in transportation and strategy. (Cressey 1962)

However, the impact that climate change might have on the population and settlement patterns in the Russian North is the subject of a separate enquiry.

References

Armstrong, T. (1965). *Russian Settlement in the North*. Cambridge: Cambridge University Press.
Blakkisrud, H. (2006). What is to be done with the North?,' pp. 25-51 in H. a. G. H. Blakkisrud (ed.), *Tackling Space: Federal Politics and the Russian North*. Lanham: University Press of America.
Blakkisrud, H. and G. Honneland (2006a). 'The Burden and Blessing of Space,' pp. 193-203 in H. a. G. H. Blakkisrud (ed.), *Tackling Space: Federal Politics and the Russian North*. Lanham: University Press of America.
Blakkisrud, H. and G. Honneland (2006b). 'The Russian North—An Introduction,' pp. 1-24 in H. a. G. H. Blakkisrud (ed.), *Tackling Space: Federal Politics and the Russian North*. Lanham: University Press of America.
Bond, A.R. (1985). Northern Settlement Family-Style: Labor Planning and Population Policy in Norilsk. *Soviet Geography* 26(1): 26-47.
Bradshaw, M.J. (1995). The Russian North: General Introduction. *Post-Soviet Geography* 36(4): 195-203.
Canning, M., P. Moock, and T. Heleniak (1999). *Reforming Education in the Regions of Russia* Washington, DC: The World Bank.
Cressey, G.B. (1962). *Soviet Potentials: A Geographical Appraisal*. Syracuse: Syracuse University Press.
Dmitriyev, I. (2007, March 30). Federal Misalliance. Robbing Peter to Pay Paul. The Kremlin has begun to consolidate 'non-Russian' lands around Moscow, and in the regions. *Moscow News*.
Gorodnichenko, Y. and K.S. Peter (2004). Returns to Schooling in Russia and Ukraine: A Semiparametric Approach to Cross-Country Comparative Analysis. *IZA Discussion Paper Series* No. 1325.
Hamilton, L.C. and C.L. Seyfrit (1994). Coming Out of the Country: Community Size and Gender Balance Among Alaskan Natives. *Arctic Anthropology* 31(1): 16-25.
Heleniak, T. (1999). Out-Migration and Depopulation of the Russian North During the 1990s. *Post-Soviet Geography and Economics* 40(3): 155-205.
Heleniak, T. (2008). 'Population, Health, and Migration,' in M. Bressler (ed.), *Understanding Contemporary Russia*. Boulder, CO: Lynne Rienner Publishers.
Hill, F. and C..G. Gaddy (2003). *The Siberian Curse: How Communist Planners Left Russia Out in the Cold*. Washington, DC: Brookings Institution Press.

Chapter 4: *Migration and Population Change in theRussian Far North in the 1990s*

Honneland, G. And J.H. Jorgensen (2006). 'The Ups and Downs of Environmental Governance,' pp 143-161 in H. a. G. H. Blakkisrud (ed.), *Tackling Space: Federal Politics and the Russian North*. Lanham: University Press of America.

Overland, I. and H. Blakkisrud (2006). 'The Evolution of Federal Indigenous Policy in the Post-Soviet North,' pp. 163-192 in H. a. G. H. Blakkisrud (ed.), *Tackling Space: Federal Politics and the Russian North*. Lanham: University Press of America.

Plane, D.A. and P.A. Rogerson (1994). *The Geographical Analysis of Population: With Applications to Planning and Business*. New York, Chichester, Brisbane, Toronto, Singapore: John Wiley and Sons, Inc.

Poppel, B., J. Kruse, G. Duhaime, and L. Abryutina (2007). *SLiCA Results*. Anchorage: Institute of Social and Economic Research, University of Alaska Anchorage.

Publications, CIS Statistical Committee and EastView. (1996). *1989 USSR Census* (CD-ROM).

Rossii, G. (1998). *Naseleniye Rossii za 100 let (1897-1997): Statisticheksiy sbornik, (The Population of Russia Over 100 Years: Statistical Handbook)*.

Rossii, G. (2005). *Goskomstat Rossii, Predpolozhitel'naya chislennost' naseleniya Rossiyskoy Federatsii do 2025 goda, 2005* Moscow: Rosstat.

Rosstat (2007). Federal State Statistics Service of the Russian Federation web site Retrieved 25 October, 2007 from http://www.gks.ru/eng/

Rosstat (2006a). *Chislennost' i migratsiya naseleniya Rossiyskoy Federatsii v 2005 godu: Statisticheskiy byulleten' (Number and Migration of the Population of the Russian Federation in 2005: Statistical Bulletin)* Moscow: Federal'naya Sluzhba Gosudarstvennoy Statistiki (Rosstat).

Rosstat (2006b). *The Demographic Yearbook of Russia 2006: Statistical Handbook*. Moscow: Rosstat.

Rosstat (2006c). *Ekonomicheskiye i sotsial'nyye pokazateli rayonov Kraynego Severa i priravnennykh k nim mestnostey v 2005 godu (Economic and social indicators of the Regions of the Far North and Equivalent Regions in 2005)*. Moscow: Federal'naya Sluzhba Gosudarstvennoy Statistiki (Rosstat).

Round, J. (2005). Rescaling Russia's Geography: the Challenges of Depopulating the Northern Periphery. *Europe-Asia Studies* 57(5): 705-727.

SSSR, Goskomstat. (1991). *Natsional'nyy sostav naseleniya SSSR: Po dannymn Vsesoyuznoy perepisi naseleniya 1989 g*.

World Bank (1998). *Policy Note on Migration from the Russian North*. The World Bank.

Yasmann, V. (2006). Analysis: The Future of Russia's 'Ethnic Republics' [Electronic Version]. *Radio Free Europe/Radio Liberty*. Retrieved April 21 from http://www.rferl.org

5

Impacts of Regional Labour Market Changes on Migration Trends: Research Examples from Norway

Lasse Sigbjørn Stambøl

Introduction

This chapter explores some recent migration trends in Norway and the extent to which changes in regional labour markets have affected inter-regional migration, especially for the communities of Northern Norway. First, we present an overview of current internal and international trends, focusing on the capital region and North Norway. We then briefly describe the application of a regional migration sub-model (developed from a regional economic model that features some empirical data), and describe a recent application of the model for analyzing the migration effects of increased economic transfers to municipalities. Finally, we present the results generated on regional labour mobility and job growth.

The results reveal a clear trend toward centralisation of internal migration, where North Norway shows the highest net out-migration. Although the immediate effect of immigration is a more regionally balanced distribution of the population, this effect seems to be temporary. There are observed significant positive relationships between gross in-migration and job growth and negative relationships to out-migration. It would seem that an increase in economic transfers to Norwegian municipalities would have a positive effect on migration to regions outside the capital area, and would be especially effective in bringing migration balances to the northern part of Norway.

Current and Recent Facts About Migration in Norway

Inreased Centralization

The trend in recent years has been increased out-migration from the least central and a noticeable increase in in-migration to the most central municipalities in Norway (*see* Figs. 1 and 2). In 2006, for example, 596,000 domestic relocations were registered in Norway; 202,000 were between municipalities (an increase of 8,400 from 2005), and 394,000 were within municipalities.

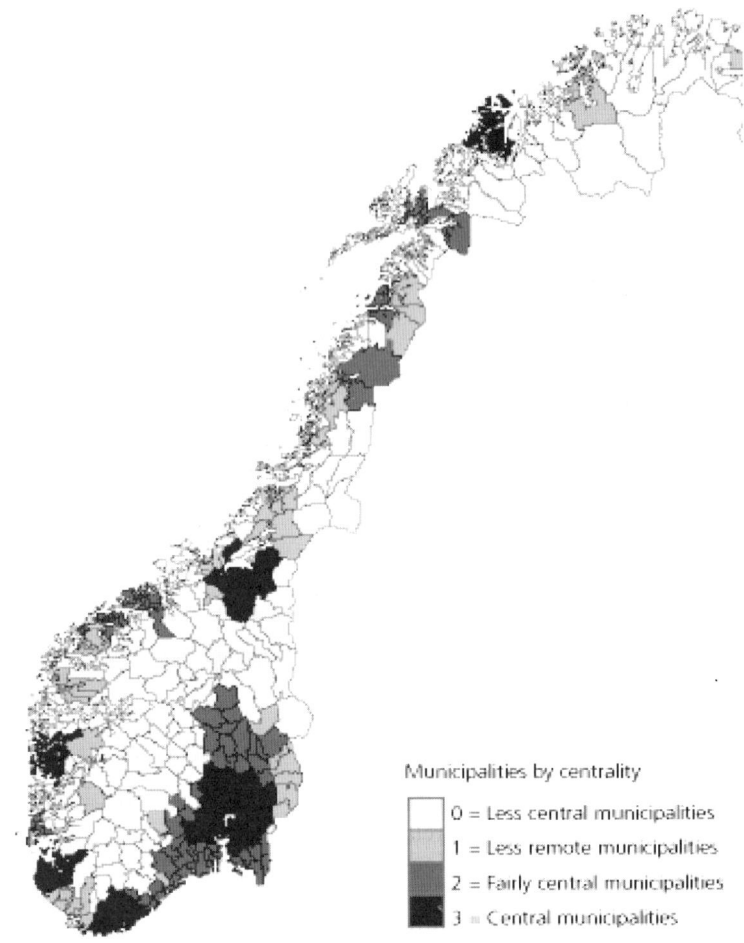

Figure 1. *Norwegian municipalities by centrality.*
Copyright: Norwegian Mapping Authority.

Immigrants tend to be much more mobile than long-term residents, and many move to areas in and around the capital of Oslo. Immigrants and their children accounted for a considerable portion of domestic relocations in 2006, including one third of net relocations from all regions of the country to the most central municipalities, and one fourth of total out-migrations from the least central municipalities.

Chapter 5: *Impacts of Regional Labour Market Changes on Migration Trends: Research Examples from Norway*

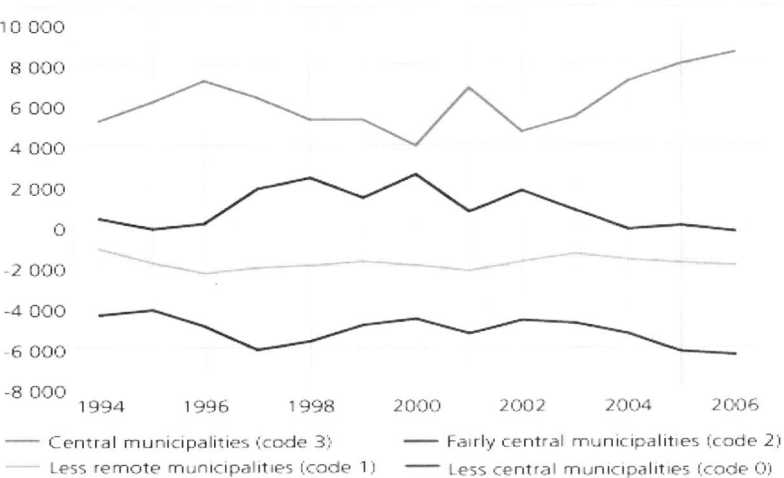

Figure 2. *Internal net migration (no. of individuals) in Norway by centrality, 1994-2006. Source:* Statistics Norway

In Figure 3 the recent internal migration trends are illustrated by the most central region (represented by the capital area of Oslo and Akershus), and the northernmost part of the country (North Norway). With the exception of the year 2000, the capital area experienced a positive migration balance relative to the rest of the country, while North Norway had a negative migration balance.

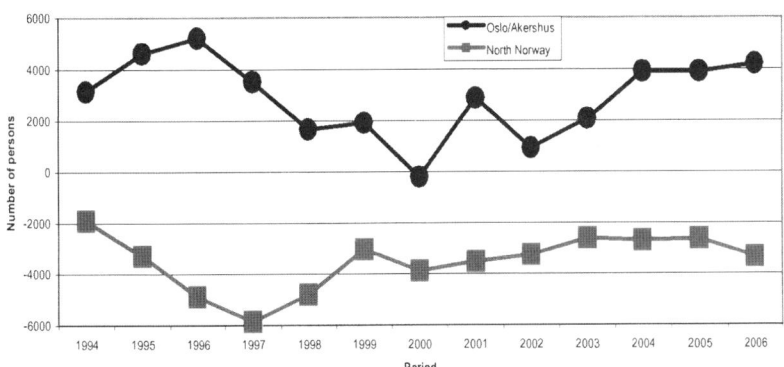

Figure 3. *Net internal migration (no. of individuals) in the capital area of Oslo and Akershus and in North Norway, 1994-2006.* Source: Statistics Norway.

95

There were, however, some year-to-year differences during this period, with strong centralization in the late 1990s after a period of more balanced migration caused by delays in out-migration from many remote regions. The later years again witnessed stronger centralization of internal migration with increased net in-migration to the capital area and somewhat higher net out-migration from North Norway.

Recent High Net Immigration
In 2006, a total of 45,800 immigrations and 22,100 emigrations were registered in Norway; thus net immigration in that year was 23,700—an increase of 5,300 or almost 30 percent from 2005. Average net migration from 2000 to 2006 was 13,000.

Net immigration from European countries made up the largest group, with 15,200 net immigrations, followed by Asia with 6,800. From the 1970s to 2005, net immigration from Europe varied between 2,000 and 5,000, but increased to 9,400 in 2005 and 15,200 in 2006. The increase in net immigration from Poland from 2003 to 2006 was 6,700, and net immigration from Sweden, Lithuania and Germany also increased. On the other hand, net immigration from Russia (and Spain) decreased. High net immigration in earlier years was explained by extraordinary situations in the countrie(s) of origin, resulting in many refugees.

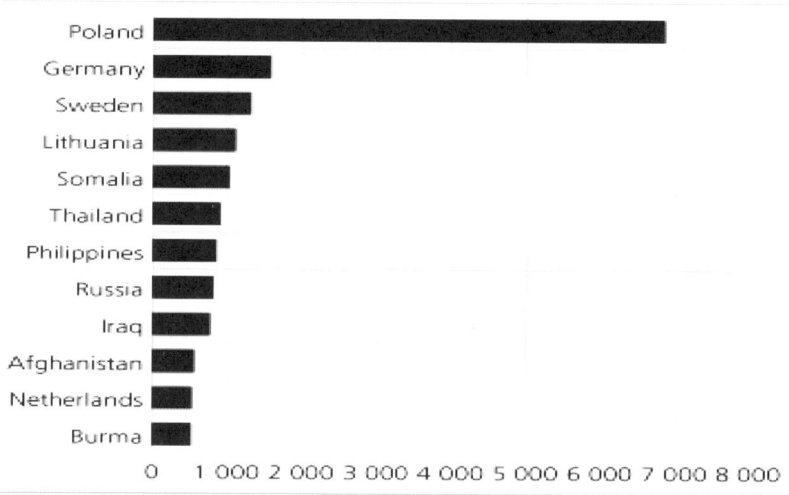

Figure 4. *Net immigration to Norway by foreign citizens in 2006.*
Source: Statistics Norway

Polish Immigrants

Polish citizens made up the largest group of immigrants in 2006 (7,400), followed by Swedes (3,400) and Germans (2,300). In the same year, Swedes made up the largest group of emigrants at 2,100, followed by Danes (1,300), Germans (700), and Poles (600). Polish citizens, therefore, accounted for the largest net immigration with 6,800 (up from 2,900 in 2005), followed by Germans and Swedes at 1,600 and 1,300, respectively (*see* Fig. 4). With the change from refugee-based to labour-based immigration, the share of men increased from 49 to 55 percent in later years, in particular those in the 30-39 year age group.

At the regional level, the capital area municipalities of Oslo and Akershus received the highest number of immigrants in 2006 with 10,800 and 5,600, respectively, followed by the west Norwegian counties of Rogaland and Hordaland. The northernmost county of Finnmark received the lowest number of immigrants.

Oslo's share of net immigration increased from 8 percent of the total in 2003 to 17 percent in 2006. Akershus and Rogaland's share also increased substantially, whereas net immigration decreased for other counties, most markedly for the north Norwegian county of Nordland—a result of the change from refugee to labour-based immigration in later years.

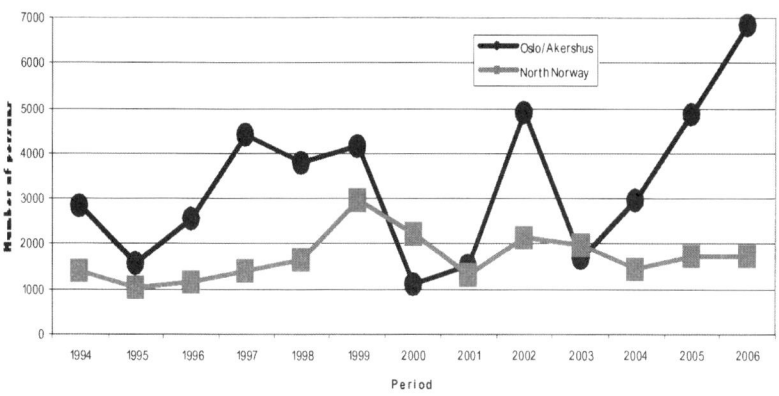

Figure 5. *Net immigration (no. of individuals) to the capital area of Oslo and Akershus and to North Norway, 1994-2006.* Source: Statistics Norway.

Figure 5 shows net immigration to the capital region municipalities of Oslo and Akershus and to the northernmost part of the country, the region of North Norway, over the last decade. The net immigration to the capital region was generally higher compared to the northern part of Norway, and especially during the last few years. It is, however, important to also note that North Norway generally shows positive net immigration from abroad during this period. This net immigration has not been strong enough to counter-balance the high internal net out-migration shown in Figure 2, but it has definitely reduced its negative effects. It is, however, important to note that the positive effect of net immigration to North Norway gradually dissipates because new immigrants, after a while, adopt the migration patterns of native Norwegians and move to more central parts of the country (*see* Stambøl 2005; Edvardsson *et al.* 2007).

Model-Based Migration Analyses: Inter-Regional Gross Migration as a Function of Relative Economic Change Across Regional Labour Markets

As in other countries, there have been several attempts in Norway to investigate and analyze trends to understand the most important driving forces of migration. To follow is an example of such an analysis—a small excerpt linking migration processes to changes in regional labour markets. First, we briefly describe a regional migration sub-model constructed as part of a regional economic model for Norway, showing further top-down connections to the main macroeconomic models at the national level. This system allows us to analyze the implications of a given macroeconomic scenario on regional employment, labour force, and migration. Further, the model can be applied to analyze effects of changes in economic policy on these variables. In this instance, we provide empirical data from migration estimates, and we apply the model using a scenario of changed economic policy concerning transfers to Norwegian municipalities.

At the national level, demand for labour is driven primarily by general macroeconomic development, while the size of the labour force is determined by demographic factors and labour force participation. Advanced methods have been developed to model the demand and supply of labour for the national market (*see* e.g., Boug *et al.* 2002). The national analyses consider the labour market as one single market for all of Norway, while in reality it should be considered a complex of various sub-markets, consisting of different industrial sectors, socio-economic composition of the labour force, and in particular, regional divisions.

In order to analyse the regional implications of macroeconomic development of employment, labour force and unemployment, it is necessary to have appropriate analytic tools. At the same time, the tools used to analyse regional labour markets ought to include mechanisms that are consistent with national models. To this end, we developed a regional model called REGARD (Regional Model for Labour Market and Demography—*see* e.g., Mohn *et al.* 1994, Stambøl *et al.* 1998, Langset and Stambøl 2006).

Chapter 5: *Impacts of Regional Labour Market Changes on Migration Trends: Research Examples from Norway*

The REGARD Model
Figure 6a provides a schematic of the model system. The most central calculations of the REGARD model are projections of employment and labour force in seven Norwegian regions. These two aspects are provided by two sub-models: a sub-model for production describes the demand side of the labour market, while the supply side of the labour market is described by a sub-model for demography, migration, and supply of labour. Internal migration frequencies are calculated as a function of these two sub-models, given that migration in REGARD is dependent both on regional employment and the development of the regional labour force. All regional calculations of labour supply and demand are, however, consistent with similar calculations using national models.

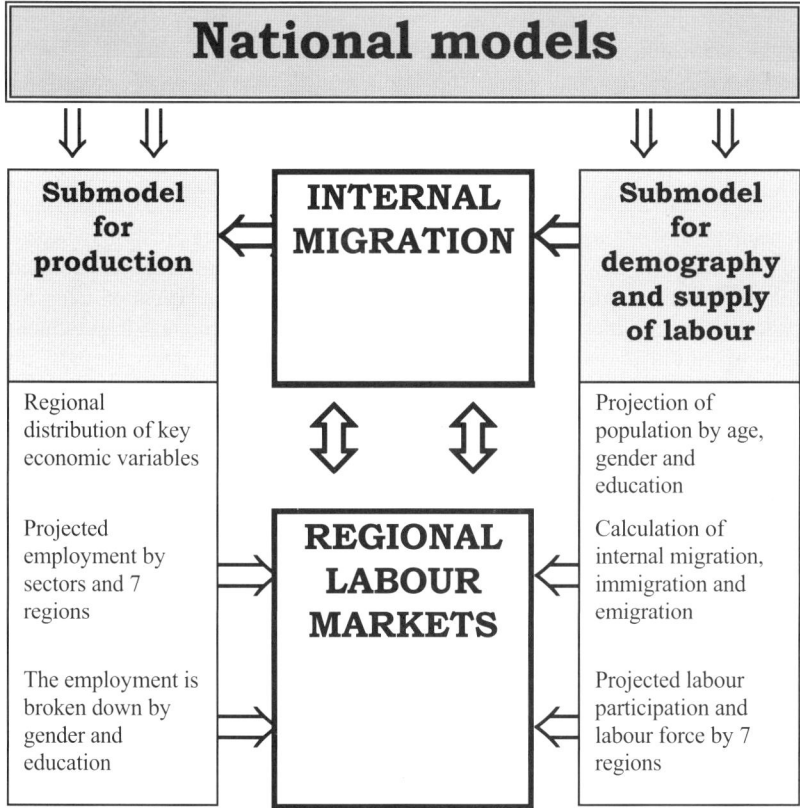

Figure 6a. *The REGARD model—an overview*

The REGARD model operates at an aggregate level of seven Norwegian regions. The sub-model for production uses fixed regional shares of 28 economic sectors derived from the most up-to-date year in the Norwegian Regional Account. The sub-model for demography, migration and labour force participation is based on a projection of the population by one-year age group, gender, and region. The results of these projections are further aggregated to the broader age groups for estimates of changes in educational level of the population, for interregional migration, and for international in- and out-migration. Estimates of changes in educational level, labour force participation, and migration are concentrated in the working-age population; that is, those aged 16 to 74 years.

The regional population projections in REGARD group the active population into three categories based on educational level: primary school, secondary school, and higher education. The regional estimates are based on those obtained for the whole country by means of the national model for labour force and education, MOSART (*cf.* Fredriksen 1998). By means of projections at the national level, rates of change for population groups by education can be constructed by regional level. The implemented changes are corrected for regional variations observed as annual averages for a base period.

A similar method is used to model regional labour force participation. The national econometric models project the total national labour force disaggregated by broad socio-economic groups. Labour force participation rates from the national model show the share of the active population expected to be included in the labour force. Labour force participation rates are adjusted for changes in macroeconomic conditions. Labour force participation rates are endogenous variables, depending on real disposable income and employment rates at the national level. Labour force participation also depends on demographic structure, as reflected by such socio-economic variables as age, gender and marital status of women. To express labour force participation by education, labour force participation rates from MODAG are combined with projections of the labour force by education from MOSART. In the REGARD model, the derived educational-specific labour force participation rates are combined with regional adjusted parameters that consider the regional variation in labour force participation as observed as annual averages during a base period.

The REGARD Migration Sub-Model

In the REGARD model, the rates of inter-regional migration are projected using the share of the population in one region that is expected to migrate to a certain other region during one year. The migration sub-model is formulated as an interactive one, where origin–destination migration flows are used to determine the levels of out- and in-migration (Fig. 6b). Migration rates are also disaggregated by gender, age group, and educational level. In the model, there are estimated relationships between changes in migration frequencies and changes in the regional labour markets for persons aged 16-44 years. The interregional migration patterns for the other age groups are calculated assuming fixed rates of out-migration between the regions as annual averages during a base period. Gross migration of children is assumed to depend on out-migration of women 25 to 44 years of age. This is operationalised by setting the migration rates of children 0-6 years of age as a fixed function of the migration rates of women of 25 to 34 years as observed in a base period, and the migration rates of children 7-15 years of age as a fixed function of the migration rates of women 35 to 44 years of age.

A REGIONAL INTERACTION MODEL	REGIONS OF DESTINATION:						
REGIONS OF ORIGIN	A. Capital region	B. East Norway (South)	C. East Norway (North)	D. South & southwest Norway	E. West Norway	F. Middle Norway	G. North Norway
A. Capital region	(A/A)	A/B	A/C	A/D	A/E	A/F	A/G
B. East Norway (South)	B/A	(B/B)	B/C	B/D	B/E	B/F	B/G
C. East Norway (North)	C/A	C/B	(C/C)	C/D	C/E	C/F	C/G
D. South- & southwest Norway	D/A	D/B	D/C	(D/D)	D/E	D/F	D/G
E. West Norway	E/A	E/B	E/C	E/D	(E/E)	E/F	E/G
F. Middle Norway	F/A	F/B	F/C	F/D	F/E	(F/F)	F/G
G. North Norway	G/A	G/B	G/C	G/D	G/E	G/F	(G/G)

Figure 6b. *The seven regions used in the REGARD model, and how the labour market indicator (A-G) in each region of origin is measured against the corresponding labour market indicator in each region of potential destination.*

The REGARD's migration sub-model is based on interaction theories, where both the origin and destination regions are considered (*cf.* Mohn *et al.* 1994; Stambøl 1994; Stambøl *et al.* 1998; Langset and Stambøl 2006). A change in one region's labour market might affect migration flows between some regions more than others. A hypothesis is that a change in the labour market in one region will primarily affect migration flows between it and other regions with which it has shown a high degree of interaction in the past. When deconstruction has shown strong differences in a region's out-migration rates with regard to destination regions, we expect that changes in a region's total out-migration rates directly relate to those regional labour markets that have changed most drastically.

Migration also depends on socio-economic variables such as gender, age, and the migrant's qualifications measured by highest completed educational level. Classification by education is very important, because migration frequencies increase greatly as educational level increases.

To explain variations in regional out-migration rates, a labour market indicator—defined as the relationship between demand for and supply of labour—is constructed for each region. Demand is defined as employment by place of residence, while supply is the regional labour force defined as employment by place of residence and unemployment. Thus regional commuting is taken into account on the demand as well as on the supply side. The labour market indicator is further disaggregated by gender and three educational levels; i.e., by six sub-markets for each region. For the purpose of estimating the relationship between out-migration rates and regional labour markets, each region's labour market indicators are measured against the corresponding indicators in each of the other regions. Charateristics of regional labour markets is expected to impact the disposition to stay or to migrate.

Figure 6 shows how this labour market indicator in each of the seven Norwegian regions is measured relative to the labour market indicator in the other regions. This relative tightness in each region's labour market is thus used as a right hand side independent variable to explain and decide the level of each region's out-migration rates.

The estimates of the migration sub-model are currently based on data from the 1980s and 1990s. Altogether the REGARD migration sub-model provides estimates for 1008 regional migration rates, organized by gender, four age groups, three educational groups and forty-two regional interactions. The estimates are based on a probability model with discrete choice, and the migration rates are generated by a multinomial logit-model. Each person is given the possibility to choose one of the model's seven regions as residence, which then also includes the region where each person already resides.

Some empirical results
The estimation of the migration sub-model resulted in negative significant estimates for the relationship between out-migration and changes in labour market indicators for all regional interactions and all groups disaggregated by socio-economic status. This is in accordance with our hypotheses, that a relative improvement in a region's labour market will result in a decrease in out-migration frequency; and, correspondingly, that a relative decrease in a region's labour market will lead to an increase in out-migration frequency.

Table 1 shows the effects on out-migration rates for all origin and destination regions as a consequence of an improvement of one percent in the labour market in the origin regions relative to the destination regions. The results show the effects measured per thousand inhabitants based on a

Chapter 5: *Impacts of Regional Labour Market Changes on Migration Trends: Research Examples from Norway*

weighted annual average for all regions. For the age group 16-44 years, the effects on out-migration rates measured in this way are twice as strong for persons with higher education than to those with only primary school. Correspondingly, the strongest effects on out-migration rates are in the 20-24 years and 25-34 years age groups, while the weakest effects are in the youngest and oldest age groups. Overall, there are moderate differences between the genders, although there are tendencies to stronger effects on female out-migration rates in the two youngest age groups and somewhat stronger effects on male out-migration rates in the oldest age groups. When we disaggregate the results in Table 1 at all regional interactions, the variations become somewhat stronger.

Table 1. Changes in Out-migration Rates in the Regions of Origin (calculated from 1 per cent improvement in the regions' relative labour market indicator. Annual average for all regions by gender, age and education. Based on data from the 1980s and 1990s, per 1,000 inhabitants).

Age	MEN			WOMEN		
	Primary School	Secondary School	Higher Education	Primary School	Secondary School	Higher Education
16-19	-0.5	-0.6		-0.7	-1.3	
20-24	-1.3	-1.7	-2.6	-1.9	-2.2	-2.8
25-34	-1.1	-1.4	-2.9	-1.0	-1.3	-2.7
35-44	-0.6	-0.6	-1.1	-0.5	-0.5	-0.9
16-44	-0.7	-1.2	-2.0	-0.8	-1.3	-2.0

Source: Statistics Norway

Table 2 shows the effect on out-migration for males and females 16-44 years old in each region of origin of a relative improvement of one percent in the labour market indicator between the origin and destination regions. There are clear differences in the degree to which changes in a region's labour market will affect out-migration rates. For the capital region of Oslo and Akershus, changes in labour markets relative to other nearby regions of East Norway have a greater effect than the same relative changes in the labour market indicator with the other regions. For all regions outside of Oslo and Akershus, it is changes in their labour market relative to the capital region that have the strongest impact on out-migration rates.

Most noticeable is the impact of the labour market in other regions of East Norway, and especially North-East Norway, where the effect of changes in relation to Oslo/Akershus account for almost half of the impact on out-migration rates caused by regional labour market changes. For regions outside East Norway, the relative labour market indicator in relation to Oslo/Akershus constitutes just under 1/3 of the total effect on out-migration rates, resulting from changes in regional labour markets. As shown in Table 2, there are also several regional interactions where the effects of changes in regional labour markets have almost no impact on the out-migration frequency. The results also show small variations between the genders, namely, a slightly stronger effect on female out-migration rates (see male results in brackets).

It is, however, important to keep in mind that if we consider these results in terms of net migration, the effects are effectively double, because an improvement in one region's labour market, leads not only to a decrease in out-migration from that region but also to an increase in in-migration.

In the next section we describe some results of a recent analysis whereby the impact of changes in regional labour markets is measured as an effect of both out-migration and in-migration, and thus as a function of net-migration and migration balances across regions.

An example of a recent application of the model system:
What would be the impact of increasing national economic transfers to Norwegian municipalities on migration?
There is always strong interest in measuring what effects various policies would have for different regions of Norway, both concerning regional labour markets as well as population development and migration. There has, for several decades, been a strong political goal to maintain the settlement pattern of the country, that is, to keep migration between regions as balanced as possible. As noted in the introduction, there has been a rather clear tendency toward centralisation in the migration pattern over the last decade. One way to address the goal of regional balance is to intervene by introducing policies that will be favourable for most regions of the country.

To this end, we recently conducted a model-based analysis to measure what effect an increase in the public budgets of Norwegian municipalities would have on migration across regions. As a basic condition, we introduced an increase of one percent in the budget in one basic year, in this case, 2003. This scenario was effected by a simple addition to the existing budget without making any claims of any budget balances; in other words, the increase was a straightforward in-sourcing of money into the local public budget.

Local public consumption is an exogenous input into national econometric models for the Norwegian economy. Thus it is possible to operate the models using various levels of input to analyse what effects increases or decreases in the public budgets will have on the level of employment in different sectors. First, we generated a projection using MODAG, a very large and detailed national econometric model that makes a huge number of endogenous calculations for the Norwegian economy based on a numbers of exogenous assumptions. This projection defined the base point reference describing an expected scenario for the Norwegian economy some years into the future.

Table 2. The Effects on Gross Out-migration Rates of 1% Improvement in the Relative Labour Market Development Between the Regions of Origin and the Regions of Destination (Persons 16-44 years by gender, per 1000 inhabitants).

REGIONS OF ORIGIN	REGIONS OF DESTINATION							TOTAL FROM ORIGIN REGION
	Capital Region	East Norway (South)	East Norway (North)	South and Southwest Norway	West Norway	Middle Norway	North Norway	
Capital Region (Oslo/Akershus)		-0.5 (-0.4)	-0.3 (-0.3)	-0.2 (-0.2)	-0.2 (-0.2)	-0.1 (-0.1)	-0.2 (-0.2)	-1.5 (-1.4)
East Norway (South)	-0.5 (-0.5)		-0.1 (-0.1)	-0.1 (-0.1)	-0.1 (-0.1)	-0.1 (-0.1)	-0.1 (-0.1)	-1.1 (-1.1)
East Norway (North)	-0.7 (-0.6)	-0.2 (-0.2)		-0.1 (-0.1)	-0.1 (-0.1)	-0.1 (-0.1)	-0.1 (-0.1)	-1.4 (-1.3)
South and Southwest Norway	-0.3 (-0.3)	-0.2 (-0.2)	-0.1 (-0.1)		-0.3 (-0.2)	-0.1 (-0.1)	-0.1 (-0.1)	-1.0 (-0.9)
West Norway	-0.4 (-0.3)	-0.2 (-0.2)	-0.1 (-0.1)	-0.2 (-0.2)		-0.1 (-0.1)	-0.1 (-0.1)	-1.1 (-1.0)
Middle Norway	-0.4 (-0.4)	-0.2 (-0.2)	-0.1 (-0.1)	-0.1 (-0.1)	-0.2 (-0.2)		-0.3 (-0.2)	-1.3 (-1.2)
North Norway	-0.5 (-0.5)	-0.3 (-0.3)	-0.1 (-0.1)	-0.2 (-0.2)	-0.2 (-0.2)	-0.3 (-0.2)		-1.6 (-1.5)

The effects on men's out-migration rates are in brackets.

The second task was to generate a new projection of the national model by simply increasing the local public consumption by one percent. All other factors and inputs were left the same as for the analysis made in the first. This way, we could measure the isolated effect of one variable, here local public consumption. It is, important to note however, that the one percent increase in local public consumption in one basic year (2003 in our analysis) was maintained for the entire period of the analysis.

We did make some assumptions, however, of local budget behaviour. We considered how Norwegian municipalities might spend the extra grant. One scenario might be that they would distribute the extra money in the same manner as they distribute the usual local budget. But we also suggested three alternatives for spending this extra grant. In the first alternative (nA), we assumed local governments would use the entire extra grant for wages, therefore increasing local public employment. In the second (nB) we assumed they would use the majority of the extra grant for wages but in combination with the purchase and application of products. In the third and last alternative (nC) we assumed they would distribute the the extra grant in a manner more similar to the total budget, by still using the majority for wages, in combination with the purchase and application of products, as well as using part of it for new investments. Thus we made three alternative analyses from the national model in addition to the first basic reference scenario.

The regional model REGARD functions as described—as a drill-down of the national models—which means that the sum of regional results are consistent with results for the entire country as calculated in the national models. We generated analyses by breaking down the results of all four national analyses to the regional level; that is, the reference scenario and the three alternatives for handling the extra grant.

At the regional level, however, we generated three additional drills according to different regional keys for distribution of the extra grant across regions. In the first drill (reg1) we distributed the entire extra grant equally among all inhabitants in Norway—each region received a share of the extra grant proportional to the number of inhabitants. In the second drill (reg2) the distribution of the extra grant was made according to the regional distribution of all free income to municipalities as it was done in 2003. In the final drill (reg3) the regional key was established according to a special calculation based on the cost of basic necessities in the Norwegian municipalities.

In summary, we generated three alternatives on the national level according to assumptions of how the local government would spend the extra grant, and three regional drills according to how the extra grant would be distributed across regions. Altogether then, we have a combination of nine different analyses which all are compared to the basic reference scenario.

The results of the analyses indicate an increase of employment in all nine alternatives. The strongest employment effects were in local public services, and obviously stronger when a higher share of the extra grant is spent on wages. With higher employment in the local public sector, private consumption also increased, resulting in positive employment effects in such sectors as construction and private services. However, because of increased pressure in the economy resulting in higher wages and prices, employment effects in sectors that are vulnerable for international competition, usually the manufacturing sector, were mostly negative. The stronger the positive effects in some service sectors, the stronger the negative effect in the manufacturing sectors. However, in our analyses of a one per cent rise in public expenditure, the positive employment effects in the majority of sectors were significantly higher than the negative effects for the manufacturing sectors, resulting in a total surplus of employment at the national level.

At the regional level, the structure of production is of immense importance to these employment effects. In many small and more remote regions, local public services represent a very important sector, in fact, in many of these regions it has grown to be the most important. In other regions, where the manufacturing sectors represent a more important element of production, obviously less positive employment effects are observed from our analyses. The profile of regional distribution of the extra grant, of course, also impacts regional employment effects.

Our analyses indicated a positive employment effect in all regions. Due to the production structure and variance in importance of different sectors, the strongest employment effects were observed in the regions outside the most central, and the weakest effects were observed in the capital region.

It is, however, important to note that there is a different time dimension in the employment effects. The positive effect for local services seems to appear during the first few years after in-sourcing the extra grant to the budget, while the positive effect, albeit smaller, in private service branches has a somewhat lag in time. The negative employment effect in some of the manufacturing sectors also seemed to increase after some years.

What then is the migration effect of in-sourcing an extra grant to the local public budget?
We have already shown empirically how migration functions in relation to changes in regional labour markets. Using these estimates, the REGARD model can project migration balances across regions. Thus, we also analysed the regional migration effects of all the alternatives described in the former section.

The results indicate a positive migration balance in all but the capital region from an increase of the local public budget. The positive net-migration effect in the other regions, of course, result in a similar, but negative, migration effect in the capital region.

Migration in the Circumpolar North

Figures 7a-c show the estimated migration effects for the seven Norwegian regions. The results are given for the three alternatives at the national level (nA-nC), while we apply the first regional alternative (reg1) in all figures, that is, equal distribution of the extra grant to each person in Norway.

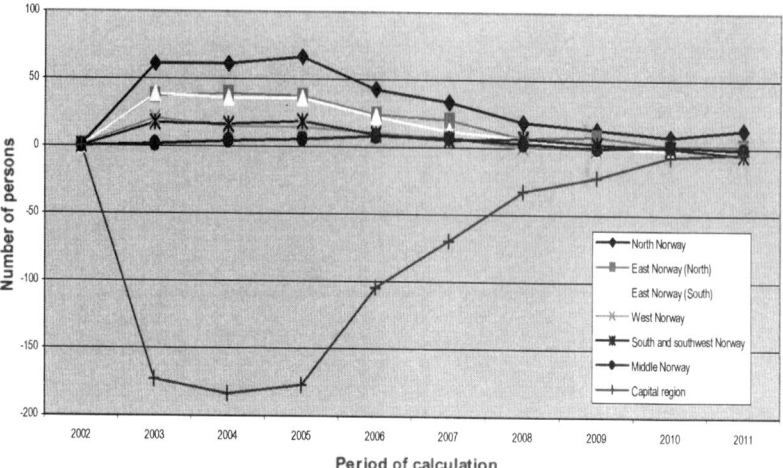

Figure 7a. *Net migration effects of a 1 percent increase in the national economic transfers to Norwegian municipalities. Basic year 2003. National alternative, nA, Regional alternative, reg1. Number of persons*

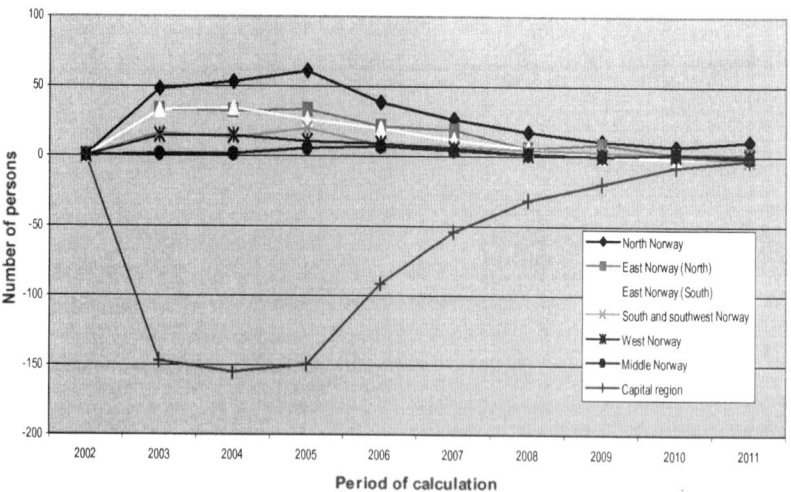

Figure 7b. *Net migration effects of a 1 percent increase in the national economic transfers to Norwegian municipalities. Basic year 2003. National alternative, nB, Regional alternative, reg1. Number of persons.*

Chapter 5: *Impacts of Regional Labour Market Changes on Migration Trends: Research Examples from Norway*

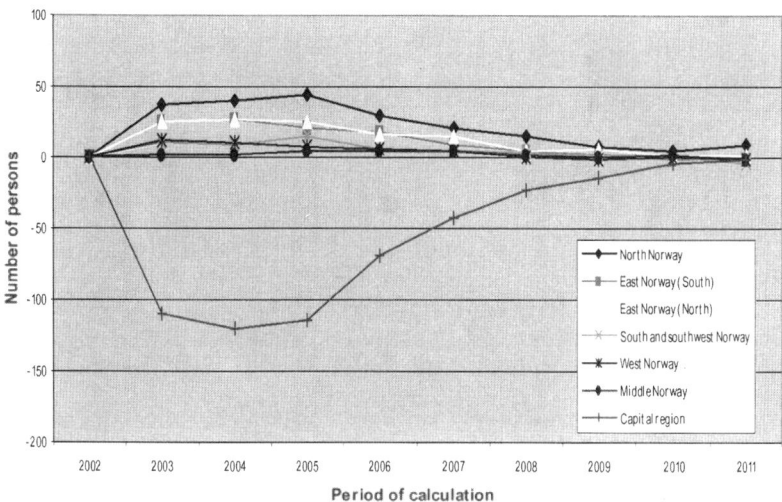

Figure 7c. *Net migration effects (number of persons) of a 1 percent increase in the national economic transfers to Norwegian municipalities. Basic year 2003. National alternative, nC, Regional alternative, reg1.*

The strongest net-migration effect is, as expected, found in the first national alternative (nA), where the entire increase in the local public budget is used for wages. It is also this alternative that gives the strongest employment effect, increasing net migration in North Norway by approximately 60 persons annually in the first three years of the calculation period, while the effect on net migration then gradually decreases when the employment effect also decreases. The net migration effect is also positive for all regions except the capital region of Oslo and Akershus, although the effects in the regions of West Norway and Middle Norway are relatively weak. Since employment effects in the capital region were clearly below the national average, and thus also lower relative to the other regions, the model analyses shows negative effects on net-migration for the capital region. The first alternative results in a net decrease of approximately 170-180 persons annually in the three first years of the calculation period, and then the negative effect decreases with decreasing effect on employment.

Corresponding net-migration effects from the other two national alternatives are provided in the other sections of Figure 7. The regional structure of these effects is similar to that shown in the first alternative, but because of weaker employment effects in alternatives nB and nC, the net-migration effects are somewhat more moderate compared to that for the first alternative.

Migration in the Circumpolar North

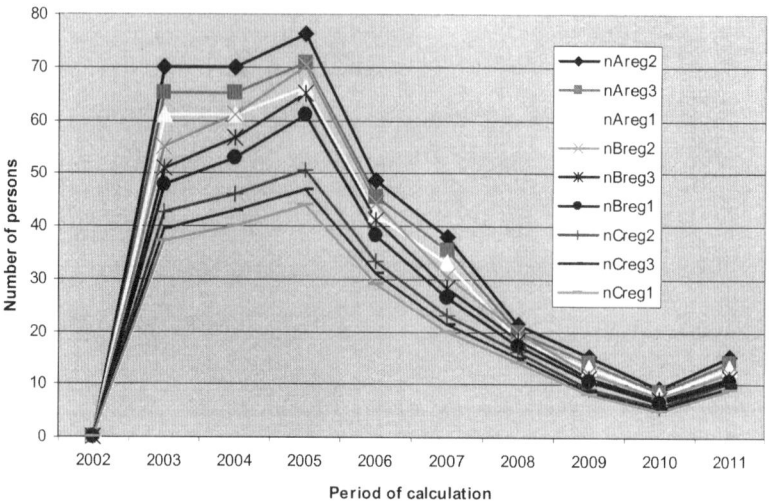

Figure 8a. *Net migration effects of a 1 per cent increase in national economic transfers to Norwegian municipalities. Basic year 2003. National alternatives, nA, nB, nC. Regional alternatives, reg1, reg2, reg3. North Norway.*

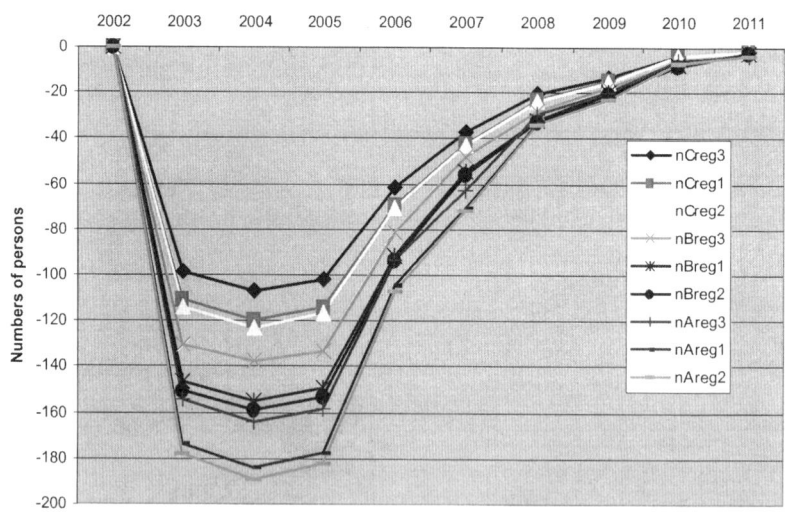

Figure 8b. *Net migration effects of a 1 per cent increase in national economic transfers to Norwegian municipalities. Basic year 2003. National alternatives, nA, nB, nC. Regional alternatives, reg1, reg2, reg3. The capital region of Oslo and Akershus*

Chapter 5: *Impacts of Regional Labour Market Changes on Migration Trends: Research Examples from Norway*

In Figures 8a-b we focused on the net-migration effects in the two regions showing the strongest net-migration effects—North Norway for positive effects, and the capital region of Oslo and Akershus for the negative effects. In this case, we also considered the three regional drills for distribution of the extra grant; therefore, the results of nine alternatives are presented.

Figure 8a shows that the net-migration effects in North Norway vary from about 70-80 persons annually for the first years of the calculation period and then decrease to approximately 40 persons annually in the weakest net migration effect. The relationship between the different alternatives indicates that the national alternatives, showing different ways of spending the extra grant, are of immense importance. The net migration effect of national alternative nA is generally stronger than that of nB that itself generally shows stronger effects compared to nC, independent of the three regional alternatives. However, the net migration effects of the regional alternatives are also consistent, where alternative 2 (reg2), in which the extra grant is distributed according to the observed regional distribution of free incomes to the municipalities, generally gives the strongest net-migration effect within each of the national alternatives. On the other hand, regional alternative 1 (reg1), where the extra grant is distributed equally to each inhabitant in Norway, is showing the weakest net-migration effect within each of the national alternatives. Therefore, when national alternative nA and regional alternative 2 (reg2) result in the strongest positive effects on net migration in North Norway, national alternative nC and regional alternative 1 (reg1) shows the weakest, albeit still positive, effect in the same region.

In the same way we show the net-migration effect in the capital region of Oslo and Akershus (Figure 8b). The effects are, in many ways, opposite that observed for North Norway. The alternatives that cause the strongest positive net-migration effects in North Norway result in the strongest negative net migration effects in the capital region, while the alternatives that caused the weakest positive effects in the north show less negative effects in the capital region.

As shown in the figure, the negative net-migration effects in Oslo/Akershus varies between approximately 180 persons annually the first years of the calculation period, decreasing to about 100 persons. So when the national alternative nA in combination with the regional alternative 2 (reg2) result in the strongest negative effect on migration balances in Oslo and Akershus, the national alternative nC in combination with the regional alternative 1 (reg1) result in the weakest negative effect in the capital region.

The Relationship Between Net Employment Growth and Specific and Total Labour Mobility Rates in Norway

In this final section, we provide some excerpts from an analysis investigating the relationship between labour mobility and job growth in 86 Norwegian regions (see Stambøl 2005). We concentrated the gross flow of persons to and from jobs both within and across local labour markets, thus people who migrate to and from regions without having been employed in or moving to a job are not included. It is expected that increased labour mobility will be important for achieving the targets of employing as much of the work force as possible in regular employment. Furthermore, regional high labour mobility is expected to increase job growth generally, and especially in regions experiencing low mobility rates. We should then expect that regions showing the highest labour mobility also experience the highest net growth of employment. Thus we undertook an analysis to show the relationship between net change of employment and level of gross mobility to job by using an ordinary least square regression model.

Table 3. The Relationship Between Net Employment Growth and Gross Labour Mobility (expressed by mobility rates to and from jobs; by type of mobility and education 1997-1998: Basis: 86 Norwegian regions).

TYPE OF MOBILITY	Low education	Middle education	High education
Still in job locally	0.462***	0.159	0.706***
	(3.48)	(1.23)	(4.30)
To job from education locally	-0.014	0.027	0.133***
	(-0.27)	(0.76)	(4.53)
To job from unemployment locally	0.041	0.077**	0.006
	(1.17)	(2.41)	(0.61)
To job from others outside the labour force locally	0.656***	0.070	0.121***
	(3.79)	(1.24)	(3.77)
To job from internal in-migration	1.388***	0.959***	0.846***
	(4.29)	(4.67)	(6.81)
To job from immigration	0.316*	4.073	0.548
	(1.70)	(1.14)	(0.56)
From job to internal out-migration	-0.717**	-1.051***	-0.843***
	(-2.13)	(-5.06)	(-9.29)
From job to emigration	-2.142**	-0.745	-1.332*
	(-2.52)	(-0.60)	(-1.90)
Adjusted R²	0.88	0.93	0.79

Level of significance: 99%***, 95%**, 90%*. (t-values in brackets). Number of observations=86)

Chapter 5: *Impacts of Regional Labour Market Changes on Migration Trends: Research Examples from Norway*

Table 3 correlates the relationship between net employment growth and different types of gross mobility to and from jobs in 86 Norwegian local labour markets in the strong upswing period of 1997-1998. A strong, positive and highly significant relationship was observed between the ability to stay in a job in a region and employment growth for employed individuals with low and high levels of education. This relationship is positive but not significant for employed individuals with middle levels of education. The relationship between employment growth and mobility as it relates to education is rather weak for low and middle educated persons, but positive and highly significant for persons with higher education. The relationship between net growth and recruitment from the ranks of the unemployed shows some significance only for persons with medium levels of education. The ability to increase the transitions from other persons outside the labour force in an upswing period is definitely stronger for those with low and high levels of education than for those with medium levels of education. Recruitment to jobs from internal in-migration is highly significant for all groups, but strongest for more highly educated employed individuals. Net job growth and immigration show a rather weak correlation with a certain exception of persons with lower levels of education. Out-migration from a job seems to be very sensitive to job growth, and have a high but negative correlation for all educational groups, and especially for highly educated employed, which here shows the highest estimated value of all mobility groups. The highly significant and negative estimates for out-migration and job-growth can be understood in terms of the expectation that employed persons are better informed of the situation in their own local labour market than with all other labour markets, regulating the out-migration processes closer to the regional business cycles than the corresponding in-migration processes. Job leaving through emigration shows certain significance but a negative correlation with the employment growth for employees with lower and higher education.

Conclusion and Perspectives

This chapter shows that there is a clear trend toward centralisation in migration in Norway over the last decade, and that this is still occurring. The capital region and other central areas in South-East Norway are receiving a surplus of migrants through internal migration, while the northern part of the country is losing inhabitants. Direct immigration to Norway shows, however, a somewhat more regionally balanced distribution of immigrants, although immigrants have a clear tendency to move to more central regions after some years of settlement in the country.

The article has further shown that there is a significant relationship between gross migration and regional labour markets in Norway, with clear negative relationship between gross out-migration and job growth on the one hand, and a clear but positive relationship between gross in-migration and job growth on the other hand.

By taking such relationships into consideration, we have constructed regional economic and demographic models for Norway that make regional projections and effect analyses of regional demand and supply of labour and corresponding impacts on regional migration processes.

We presented an example to show what effects an increase in a grant to the local public budget would have on regional migration. In the model-based analyses, we increased national transfers to Norwegian municipalities by one per cent. The results indicate a negative effect on migration balances in the capital region, and positive effects on net-migration in other regions of the country, with the strongest effect in the northernmost region, North Norway. When comparing these effects with recent regional migration figures presented earlier in the chapter, however, the calculated migration effects are small and moderate.

It is, important to keep in mind that the analysis was based on an in-sourcing of an extra grant to Norwegian municipalities without claiming any budget balances. In Norway this would be entirely possible if it was decided that some extra money could be allocated from the large pension fund (former petrol fund). However, claiming a budget balance in the analyses would definitely give different results than those presented above. One way to attain budget balance would be to increase personal taxes to cover the extra grant to local governments. Personal taxes are also treated as exogenous variables in the national models, so we could make this effect analysis for personal taxation as well. Regardless, this is an area for political discussions.

There are, on the other hand, political groups who want to reduce national economic transfers to Norwegian municipalities, and as an alternative allocate the same amount of money directly to the Norwegian population. This could be achieved by reducing personal taxes. Just as we can analyse, an increase in personal taxes with the model so we can analyse a decrease in personal income taxes. One tentative hypothesis is that the results would probably give the strongest employment and highest positive net migration effects in the more central part of the country, because private consumption would increase most where the largest populations with the highest average incomes and wages are concentrated.

On the other hand, reaction to the effect analysis presented have advanced the question: Why increase local public budgets by only one percent? Why not 2, 3 percent or even more? The expectations are obvious—the increase is twice or three times as much, then the effects on regional employment and migration will be twice or three times as strong. However, the fact is that many of the effects in the model analyses are not linear. For example, the negative effects of an increase in public budgets as a result of stronger competition in the labour markets and increased prices and wages may accelerate when these factors cross certain thresholds of the national economy. When we can demonstrate that we can analyse the effects on regional employment and migration of an increase of one percent in the local public budget, we can also generate analyses by increasing the same public budgets by 2 or 3 percent or more.

References

Boug, P., Y. Dyvi, P.R. Johansen, and B.E. Naug (2002). MODAG—En makroøkonomisk modell for norsk økonomi. *Social and Economic Studies* 108. Statistics Norway.
Edvardsson, I.R., E. Heikkilä, H. Johannesson, M. Johansson, D. Rahut, T.D. Schmidt, L.S. Stambøl and S. Wilkman (2007). *Demographic Changes, Labour Migration and EU-enlargement—Relevance for the Nordic Regions.* Report 2 in the Nordic Research Programme 2005-2008: Internationalisation of regional development policies—Needs and demand in the Nordic countries. NORDREGIO, Stockholm.
Fredriksen, D. (1998). Projections of population, education, labour supply and public pension benefits—Analyses with the Dynamic Microsimulation Modell MOSART. *Social and Economic Studies* 101. Statistics Norway.
Langset, B and L.S. Stambøl (2006). *Kommuneoverføringer som regionalpolitisk virkemiddel.* Reports 2006/43, Statistics Norway.
Mohn, K., L.S. Stambøl, and K.Ø. Sørensen (1994). Regional analyse av arbeidsmarked og demografi—Drivkrefter og utviklingstrekk belyst ved modellsystemet REGARD. *Social and Economic Studies* 88. Statistics Norway.
Stambøl, L.S. (1994). *Flytting, utdanning og arbeidsmarked 1986-1990. En interaktiv analyse av sammenhengen mellom endringer i flyttetilbøyelighet og arbeidsmarked.* Reports 94/17. Statistics Norway.
Stambøl, L.S. (2005): Urban and regional labour market mobility in Norway. *Social and Economic Studies* 110, Statistics Norway.
Stambøl, L.S., N.M. Stølen and T.Åvitsland (1998). Regional analyses of labour markets and demography—a model based Norwegian example. *Papers in Regional Science—The Journal of the Regional Science Association International (RSAI)*, Illinois, USA 77(1): 37-62

6

Determinants of Migration in Northern Sweden: Exploring Intra-regional Differences in Migration Processes

Olle Westerlund

Introduction

In this paper, we examine the determinants of migration among residents in northern Sweden for the period 1997 to 2000. It represents a first attempt at a quantitative analysis of modern out-migration trends among all residents in the arctic and the near arctic region, including a specific analysis of migration among individuals active in reindeer husbandry.[1] An overwhelming majority of this group belongs to the Saami minority population in Sweden.

For decades, economic development in northern Sweden has been less favourable than the country average. The coastal region has been relatively well-off in terms of economic growth, and there has been no decrease in the total population. In fact, the coastal area of the two northernmost counties, Västerbotten and Norrbotten, experienced a small increase of about one percent in their population between 1997 and 2007, mainly due to population increases in the two university cities, Umeå (+8.4 percent) and Luleå (+2.3 percent). The other coastal municipalities (here used as a term for local authority regions and fiscal jurisdictions called *kommuner* in Swedish) experienced decreases or only small changes in their population during the last ten years. For these municipalities, the changes range from minus eight to plus one percent of their 1997 populations.

The northern inland has fared worse in economic terms and in terms of population change. In this study, we define the northern inland as the county of Jämtland and the inland regions of the counties of Västerbotten and Norrbotten. The total population of this area decreased by slightly more than eight percent between 1997 and 2007. The only municipality that experienced an increase was the ski resort, Åre, with a population growth of about two percent. All other municipalities experienced a drop in

---

[1] Here proxied by individuals with incomes mainly from reindeer husbandry, according to official registers.

populations, in most cases between ten and twenty percent. This is partially due to falling fertility rates, but also because of out-migration to cities on the coast and central and southern Sweden. Naturally, this development reinforces a long-term trend of an increasing proportion of older people in the northern inland. This region has an extremely low population density, the infrastructure is inferior as compared to the coastal region, employment opportunities are relatively scarce, and the per capita tax base is diminishing.

The differences between the coastal and inland regions in economic development, demographics, and in other characteristics motivate separate analyses of population dynamics for these regions.

Using longitudinal micro data for explorative empirical analysis, we address three questions. First, how do individual socioeconomic factors affect migration in northern Sweden? Second, does the migration process differ between the economically 'depressed' northern inland and the relatively dynamic coastal region? Third, are the determinants of out-migration for the Saami population (with incomes from reindeer husbandry) in the northern inland different from those of the rest of the population in this area?

The next section presents the data and provides definitions of variables and samples. In the subsequent section, the econometric model is specified and the projected estimates presented. The final section provides a summary and a brief discussion.

Data

The statistical analysis is based on population register data collected by various public authorities and administered by Statistics Sweden (SCB). The data used in this study consist of yearly observations pertaining to all individuals aged 19 years or more in 1997 and who, in that year, were registered as a resident in one of the three northernmost counties in Sweden: Jämtland, Västerbotten, or Norrbotten. The total sample amounts to 500,961 individuals, divided into two major sub-samples—people living near the coast (278,354 individuals), and people residing in the inland (210,936 individuals).[2]

We also define a sub-sample of Saamis active in reindeer husbandry as individuals living in the inland in 1997 who, according to the official income registers, derived their *main* income from reindeer husbandry in any

---

[2] A list of municipalities defining the coastal and inland regions is given in Table A1 in the Appendix.

Chapter 6: *Determinants of Migration in Northern Sweden—Exploring Interregional Differences in Migration Processes*

of the years 1995, 1996 or 1997.[3] This sub-sample consists of 794 individuals.

Registration according to ethnicity is forbidden by law and there is no undisputed definition of 'being Saami.' The Saami parliament registers voters for elections and reports a total Saami population in Sweden of about 20,000 people.[4] According to the same source and official statistics, there are about 4,500 owners of reindeer. Almost without exception, they reside in the inland of the three counties mentioned above, with a major concentration in Norrbotten. This is the largest (spatially) and northernmost county in Sweden with a large part of its area located above the Arctic Circle.

Most reindeer owners receive their main income from employment in sectors other than reindeer husbandry; our sample includes not only reindeer owners but also employees in the reindeer husbandry sector. This means that our sub-sample of the Saami population can be perceived as a core group of individuals who are relatively intensively involved in this traditional occupation in an economic sense. In the remainder of this study, this particular population will sometimes be referred to as Saamis, although presumably a very small minority of this sub-sample does not belong to this ethnic group. It is important to keep this particular definition in mind when interpreting the empirical results reported in the next section. The majority of Swedish Saamis are not active in the reindeer sector and live outside the northern inland of Sweden. The empirical results presented in this study cannot be generalized as valid for the entire Saami population.

To increase the sample size, and allowing for sufficient variation in all dimensions of the data, we use a three-year time span (1997-2000) between observations. Migration is recorded if an individual changed municipality of residence between observations on December 31 in respective years.[5] In the empirical models, the dependent variable takes a

---

[3] This definition excludes individuals whose income from reindeer husbandry is less than their income from any other employment activity. It is possible that a very small number of individuals with no or few other connections to the Saami ethnic group or the Saami culture are included in this sample. Given the requirement that the *largest single source* of a person's total earnings must come from reindeer husbandry, this should not be of any practical importance. It is reasonable to categorize these individuals as a sub-sample of the Saami population.

[4] See Hassler *et al.* (2004) on the size and composition of the Saami population in Sweden.

[5] This is according to official registers. These are relatively accurate and, to the best of our knowledge, there is no available information on measurement errors that would substantially affect the results reported in this study.

Migration in the Circumpolar North

value of one if migration is observed between time points of observation, and zero otherwise.

The explanatory variables include a set of individual attributes measured in 1997, i.e., before migration can be observed: individual experience of unemployment (variable labelled as *Unemployed*); participated in labour market policy programmes (*Labormarketpol*); received social welfare benefits (*Socialwelfare*); was a student (*Student*); had children under 18 years of age (*Children*); had children under 7 years of age (*Small children*); level of educational attainment (*Education1* to *Education7*); age (*Age*), and a variable indicating gender (*Female*). We also include the size of the population in the municipality of residence in 1997 (*Population97*), and the percentage change of this population between 1996 and 1997 (*Popchange9697*). All variables except *Age, Population97*, and *Popchange9697* are 'dummy' variables coded as 'one' if the attribute applies and zero otherwise.[6]

Descriptive statistics for non-migrants ('stayers') and migrants in the three samples are given in Table 1. Among those who resided in the coastal region, 16.92 percent of the stayers and 28.27 percent of the migrants had personal experience of unemployment in 1997 (before migration). In all three samples, a much higher proportion of migrants experienced unemployment in 1997 as compared to non-migrants. This is accentuated for the sample of individuals with an income from reindeer husbandry, where fifty percent of the migrants were unemployed before migration. A similar pattern applies for the variables indicating participants in labour market programmes (offered to the unemployed) and recipients of social welfare benefits. Individuals with these attributes are clearly over-represented among the migrants in all three samples. It should be noted that participation in labour market programmes is often preceded by a longer period of unemployment, and also that a large share of the welfare recipients are long-term unemployed. In all, individuals with a less favourable socioeconomic situation, as indicated by these three variables, are strongly over-represented among migrants. This is especially true for those individuals who derived their main income from reindeer husbandry before migration.

---

[6] A full list of variables and definitions is included in the Appendix.

Chapter 6: *Determinants of Migration in Northern Sweden—Exploring Interregional Differences in Migration Processes*

Table 1: Sample Means.

	Coast		Inland		Reindeer Husbandry	
Variable	Stayers	Migrants	Stayers	Migrants	Stayers	Migrants
Unemployed	.17	.28	.18	.31	.23	.50
Labourmarketpol	.09	.15	.10	.20	.21	.31
Social Welfare	.19	.22	.19	.25	.16	.31
Student	.06	.38	.03	.20	.02	.12
RHSB	.0001	.0001	.0026	.0008	1.00	1.00
Children	.34	.25	.31	.31	.34	.38
Small Children	.16	.09	.14	.11	.07	.15
Age	47.97	30.74	50.74	34.39	46.28	30.35
Female	.51	.49	.50	.49	.11	.27
Education 1	.14	.04	.18	.05	.33	.12
Education 2	.08	.07	.09	.11	.26	.19
Education 3	.34	.19	.35	.26	.27	.19
Education 4	.13	.26	.11	.28	.07	.42
Education 5	.13	.32	.09	.18	.03	.04
Education 6	.09	.10	.06	.09	.01	.04
Education 7	.0077	.0097	.0013	.0016	.00	.00
Population 97	63,931	70,571	22,237	25,274	12,389	10,119
Pop Change 96-97	-.24	-.01	-1.21	-1.17	-1.28	-1.46
Jobs	251,306	24,855	180,122	17,630	755	26
Migration Rate		.090		.089		.033

The gender distribution is fairly equal in the coastal and inland samples and there is no evidence of over-representation of males or females among migrants. The percentage of females in our sample of Saamis is generally low and, interestingly, females are clearly overrepresented among migrants in this case. Migrant percentages of total population are about 9 percent for both the coastal and the inland sample. Only 3.3 percent migrated among our sample of Saamis residing in the inland.

As a complementary backdrop to the empirical analysis in the next section, some stylized facts on the aggregate migration flows may be informative. About 55 percent of migrants in our total sample moved out of the northern region (Jämtland, Västerbotten, and Norrbotten) to the rest of Sweden.[7] About 40 percent of this outflow was directed to Stockholm, the capital of Sweden, and about two thirds had as their destination the three metropolitan areas (Stockholm, Göteborg, and Malmö).

---

[7] We have no information on emigrants from Sweden, since missing observations for place of residence in the year 2000 mean that the individual has died or emigrated.

The migration flows, conditional on region of residence in 1997, are summarized in Table 2.

Table 2: Geographical Distribution of Migration Flows (percent).

Region of Residence in 1997	Destination of Migrants		
	The Coast	The Inland	Rest of Sweden
The Coast	31	9	60
The Inland	24	28	48

Approximately 60 percent of those migrating out of the coastal region of northern Sweden moved from the north, 31 percent migrated within the northern coastal region, and only nine percent moved from the northern coast to the northern inland. Migrants starting out in the northern inland had a larger share of internal migration within the three northernmost counties. About 48 percent moved out from the north, 24 percent moved from the northern inland to the northern coast, and 28 percent moved to another municipality within the northern inland. It is striking how disproportionate the flows are from coast to inland and inland to coast, respectively.

Raw sample means, as those in Table 1, provide very useful information, but seemingly large differences between non-migrants and migrants in one attribute may be explained by group-wise differences in other attributes. In the next section, a multivariate migration model is used to generate information on partial associations between specific attributes and migration, while heterogeneity in other characteristics is taken into account.

Empirical Model, Method and Estimation Results

Model and Method

Out-migration from a municipality of residence is assumed to be a function of an individual's attributes and regional characteristics. Most of the variables included in the empirical model to be generated can be motivated by the implications of the human capital theory (Becker 1964; Sjaastad 1962; Schultz 1960) or economic job-search theory (*see* Rogerson *et al.* 2005 for an overview).[8] Based on theoretical considerations and empirical

---

[8] They can also be motivated from the results of previous empirical research and other theoretical perspectives. The empirical model is a single equation representing a so-called reduced form. The estimated effect of, for example, education on migration in this model may, in reality, work through several channels in an underlying structural system of high complexity. The projected estimates should thus be interpreted with some caution.

Chapter 6: *Determinants of Migration in Northern Sweden—Exploring Interregional Differences in Migration Processes*

results from previous studies (*see* e.g., Greenwood 1985, 1997), we expect unemployment and education to increase the probability of migration. Increasing age is expected to have the opposite effect. Previous empirical studies on geographical mobility in Sweden have found evidence of a regional 'locking-in effect' of labour as a result of of labour market programmes; *see* e.g., Fredriksson (1999) and Westerlund (1997).

In the basic specification of the model, we estimate the probability of migration as a function of the variables presented in the previous section describing the data. We allow for an additional non-linear effect of age by including the square of age as a regressor.[9] The variable indicating individuals who derive their main income from reindeer husbandry does not figure in the estimates for the coastal region because of an insufficient number of observations with this attribute in this sample. The probability of migration is estimated as a logistic regression-model by the method of maximum likelihood.

The migration model is estimated separately for the coastal sample, the inland sample, and the sub-sample of Saamis. Potential differences in parameters between samples are tested by the following procedure. The samples, henceforth also referred to as 'groups,' are merged into one set of observations. The migration model is enhanced with group-wise interaction variables allowing a group-wise difference in partial 'effects' of each explanatory variable (on the probability of migration). Statistically significant estimates of the parameters on the interaction variables indicate differences between samples.

Results

The projected estimates of the basic specification of the migration model are presented in Table 3. We begin by commenting on the results related to labour market attributes and the coastal region sample. This is followed by comments on the corresponding results for the two other samples. The last part of this section presents the outcomes of the tests of group-wise differences in the determinants of migration.

For individuals who resided in the coastal regions in 1997, individual experience of unemployment seems to increase the probability of migration (Table 3).

---

[9] The logistic regression model, *de facto*, allows for non-linear effects of explanatory variables on the probability of migration.

Migration in the Circumpolar North

Table 3: Estimation Results, Logistic Regression Model for the Probability of Out-migration.

Variable	Coast		Inland		Reindeer Husbandy	
	Coefficient	Odds Ratio	Coefficient	Odds Ratio	Coefficient	Odds Ratio
Unemployed	.039**	1.04	-.054**	.95	1.30**	3.66
Labourmarketpol	.155***	1.17	.185***	1.20	-.529	.59
Social Welfare	.285***	1.33	.374***	1.45	.617	1.85
Student	.967***	2.63	.869***	2.38	.224	1.25
RHSB			-1.12***	.33		
Children	-.488***	.64	-.334***	.72	-.224	.80
Small Children	-.457***	.63	-.472***	.62	.675	1.96
Age	-.126***	.88	-.141***	.87	-.095	.91
Agesq	.001***	1.00	.001***	1.00	.000	1.00
Female	.014	1.01	.046***	1.05	.666	1.95
Education 3	-.131***	.88	-.058***	.94	-.720	.49
Education 4	.179***	1.20	.354***	1.42	1.06*	2.89
Education 5	.643***	1.90	.673***	1.96	.414	1.51
Education 6	.83***	2.30	1.036***	2.82	1.14	3.14
Education 7	1.49***	4.43	1.605***	4.98		
Population 97	.000***	1.00	.000***	1.00	.000	1.00
Pop Change 96-97	.338***	1,402	.006	1.01	-.822**	.44
Nagelkerke R²	.27		.23		.28	
Correct Predictions of Migration	72.2		67.8		80.8	
Obervations	268,971		203.609		781	

Note: Levels of statistical significance: one percent (***), five percent (**), ten percent (*). Estimates of constants are omitted from the table. Because of too few or no observations, RSHB is not included in the coastal sample and the dummy indicating a PhD as educational attainment is not included in the sample of individuals with income from reindeer husbandry. Predictions pertain to the number of correctly predicted observations of migration in percent of the total number of actual migrants. The cut off level used for predictions is equal to the migration rate .09 for the coastal and inland samples, .03 for our sample of Saamis.

The estimated coefficient on this variable is positive and the odds ratio (1.04) indicates that the probability of migration among unemployed individuals is 1.04 times that for other individuals in the sample. This applies when controls are applied to other explanatory variables. The results also indicate higher probabilities of migration among participants in labour market programmes and social welfare recipients. The locking-in effect of labour market programmes found in previous studies is not corroborated by the data in this case.

Turning to the sample that includes all residents in the northern inland, we find an unexpected negative and statistically significant coefficient on the variable for unemployment, where, in contrast to the coastal region, individual experience of unemployment seems to be associated with a lower probability of out-migration. For this sample, the seemingly positive relationship between unemployment and migration indicated by the descriptive statistics (Table 1) is reversed when the other explanatory factors are taken into account. Merging the coastal and the inland sample in a joint estimation of the migration equation, we find no significant effect at all of individual unemployment on migration.[10] In this case, the very small point estimate and large standard errors obscure the interesting difference between the coastal and the inland region in terms of labour market adjustment via migration.

The results for the variables indicating participation in labour market programmes and social welfare are similar to the results for the coastal sample. Controlling for the other attributes in the empirical model, migration probabilities are higher among programme participants and welfare recipients.

The results for the inland sample also indicate a lower probability of out-migration among individuals whose main incomes are derived from reindeer husbandry in 1997. Judging from the odds ratio, this group seems to have a considerably lower probability of out-migration as compared to other residents in the northern inland when other explanatory variables are controlled for.

Using the sub-sample of individuals who derive their incomes mainly from reindeer husbandry (the last two columns on the right-hand side of Table 3), the migration model yields few significant estimates. This is not unexpected, given that there are only 25 observations of migration in this sample. However, the results indicate a higher probability of migration among individuals who were unemployed some time during 1997. The implied odds ratio indicates a relatively strong effect in this case. The estimates for the covariates indicating participation in labour market programmes and individuals with welfare benefits are not significant. This is also the case with the coefficient on *FEMALE*. The point estimate and the implied log-odds ratio imply a considerably higher probability of migration of females in our sample of Saamis, which is in accordance with the over-representation of female migrants in the Saami sample indicated in the descriptive statistics. However, the standard error is too large, therefore, a hypothesis stating that there is no difference between the sexes cannot be rejected in this case.

It is interesting to compare the results for the whole inland sample with the results for the sub-sample of inland residents whose incomes fare rom reindeer husbandry. The latter sample has a generally lower probability

---

[10] Results not reported here, available from the author upon request.

of migration (the estimated coefficient on *RSHB* in Table 3) and the effect of unemployment on migration seems to differ between the two groups. Having been unemployed in 1997 is associated with a decreased probability of migration among 'inlanders' in general. For our sub-sample of Saamis, the estimates indicate the opposite, i.e., unemployment means a higher probability of migration.

Briefly, other results for the coastal and inland samples found that students have a substantially higher probability of migration. Also in line with *a priori* expectations, the estimates indicate negative effects of increasing age on migration and having children also decreases mobility. Moreover, the higher the education, the higher the probability of migration. Interestingly, we find that females from the inland have, *ceteris paribus*, a higher probability of migration, while the results indicate no significant difference in mobility between males and females among residents in the coastal regions. This is in line with 'popular' perceptions of women fleeing the sparsely populated northern inland for the 'bright lights' of the medium-sized cities on the northern coast or metropolitan areas further south.

The results are not sensitive to changes in specifications or the definition of individuals attached to reindeer husbandry. The estimated parameters on variables indicating unemployment, participation in labour market programmes and social welfare benefits almost remain unchanged when dropping one or two of these variables from the migration equation. Omitting population size and regional population change, or using alternative criteria of dummy variables for levels of education, is also of importance for the main results and conclusions. Restricting our definition of individuals with incomes from reindeer husbandry to include only those with their main income from this source in 1997 does not yield any major changes in the results.

Testing Groupwise Differences

Table 2 illustrates the differences in migration processes when comparing the estimates for the coastal sample with estimates for the inland sample. Are these differences then statistically significant? For all parameters, the answer is positive. Using all observations in the two samples, we have estimated an extended migration model allowing different parameters for the two samples on all explanatory variables in the migration equation.[11]

---

[11] Including different estimates of the constant. In other words, we add a set of interaction variables to the basic specification. In principle, the interaction variables are computed as: *Coast97*X*, where *Coast97* takes the value of one if the individual resided in the coastal region in 1997 and zero otherwise and *X* is an explanatory variable. Interaction effects for all explanatory variables included in the basic specification are allowed in this extended model.

Chapter 6: *Determinants of Migration in Northern Sweden—Exploring Interregional Differences in Migration Processes*

The results confirm the levels of estimated parameters and the differences in estimates between the coastal and the inland samples implied by the results in Table 3. The effect of unemployment on migration is negative for the inland sample but not for the coastal sample. The estimated effect of social welfare on migration is also higher for the inland as compared to the coast. This is also the case for educational attainment; the effects of increased educational attainment on migration are significantly larger for the inland than for the coastal sample. The results confirm that the probabilitites of migration are larger for females residing in the inland, not only as compared to males, but also as compared to females living in the coastal region. The size of the regional population is positively correlated with out-migration, more strongly in the costal region than in the inland. The recent increase in the regional population is also associated with a higher probability of migration. Once more, this is accentuated for the coastal sample. We find statistically insignificant differences between the two samples in only three cases: the estimated effects of participation in labour market programmes, having small children, and an educational attainment equal to a university education of less than three years.

Overall, the results imply statistical differences in the migration processes when comparing the populations residing on the northern coast with inland residents. The differences are throughout in accordance with the estimates presented in Table 3.

Some additional experimentation with the data yields two interesting findings. Using all observations and the basic specification of the migration model (without interaction variables), we find no significant effect of unemployment on migration. Thus, estimates of the 'average' effect of unemployment on migration based on all residents could lead to erroneous conclusions regarding the migration processes, regional labour market adjustment, and the evolution of regional populations. The second finding is that the negative relationship between individual experience of unemployment and migration indicated for the inland sample seems to be valid only for the young, say 25 years or younger.

Testing whether the migration process for individuals with their main income from reindeer husbandry is different from other individuals in the inland sample, we use the same interaction-variable approach as before. Allowing for interaction effects between *RSHB* and all explanatory variables in the migration equation, the estimates indicate significant differences in two cases. Unemployment increases the probability of migration among the Saamis in our data set. Moreover, a decline in the regional population during the previous year is associated with a higher probability of out-migration among the Saamis. These results are in line with the estimates for the inland sample and for the sample of people with incomes from reindeer husbandry in Table 3. Females have a higher probability of out-migration than males in the inland sample. The estimates of interaction effects indicate no significant differences between the Saamis and other residents in the northern inland in this respect.

Summary and Discussion

This exploratory study of human migration in northern Sweden examines three questions: (i) How do various socioeconomic factors affect migration?; (ii) does the migration process differ between the economically 'depressed' northern inland and the relatively dynamic coastal region?; and (iii) are the determinants of out-migration among the Saami population (active in reindeer husbandry) in the northern inland different than for the rest of the population in this area?

As regards the first question, the effects of several attributes on migration, such as age, education, and having children were expected. Generally, the findings were in line with previous studies of internal migration in Sweden and other developed economies.

When exploring the second question, migration processes seemed to differ substantially when the populations residing in the coastal region and the inland areas were compared. Some of the differences have potentially important implications relative to regional labour market adjustments and regional demographics. Individual experience of unemployment increases the probability of migration among coastal residents. The opposite applies to residents of the inland. This fundamental difference averages out to an insignificant relationship between unemployment and migration when estimating 'average' behaviour for all of northern Sweden. In accordance with virtually all earlier studies, we find higher probabilities of migration among the well-educated. In northern Sweden, this relationship is stronger for residents of the inland as compared to those living in the relatively more prosperous and urbanised coastal region. We also find that the probability of out-migration is positively correlated with increases in the regional population on the coast, while this is not the case for the interior of northern Sweden.

As for the third question, the lower probability of migration among the unemployed in the northern inland does not apply to the sample of Saamis. Individual experience of unemployment increases out-migration in our sample of Saamis. Finally, females have a higher probability of out-migration than males among residents in the northern inland. This also seems to apply to Saamis with incomes from reindeer husbandry; the estimates indicate no significant difference *vis-à-vis* the whole sample of inland residents in this respect.

The negative relationship between individual experience of unemployment and migration in the inland sample should be subject to further research. According to some indications, this unexpected result

Chapter 6: *Determinants of Migration in Northern Sweden—Exploring Interregional Differences in Migration Processes*

predominantly applies to young residents of the inland. This, together with other results, such as the increased high probability of out-migration among university-educated in the inland, and the higher migration rates among females than males, may indicate serious long term impacts in the future composition of the labour force and population structure in the inland of northern Sweden.

References

Becker, G.S. (1964). *Human Capital: A Theoretical Analysis with Special Reference to Education*. New York: Columbia University Press.

Fredriksson, P. (1999) The Dynamics of Regional Labor Markets and Active Labor Market Policy: Swedish Evidence. *Oxford Economic Papers* 51: 623–648

Greenwood, M. (1985) Human Migration: Theory, Models, and Empirical Studies. *Journal of Regional Science* 25: 521–44

Greenwood, M. (1997). 'Internal Migration in Developed Countries,' pp. 647-711 in MR Rosenweig and O Stark (eds.), *Handbook of Population and Family Economics*. Elsevier Science B. V.

Hassler, S., P. Sjölander, and A. Ericsson (2004). Construction of a database on health and living conditions of the Swedish Sami population (in English), in P. Lantto and P. Sköld (eds), *Befolkning och bosättning I norr—Etnicitet, identitet och gränser i historiens sken*. Umeå: Center for Sami Research, Umeå University, Nyheternas Tryckeri.

Rogerson, R., R. Shimer, and R. Wright (2005). Search–Theoretic Models of the Labour Market: A Survey, *Journal of Economic Literature* 43: 959-988

Schultz, T.W. (1960) Capital Formation by Education. *Journal of Political Economy* 68: 571-583

Sjaastad, L.A. (1962). The Costs and Returns of Human Migration. *The Journal of Political Economy* 79: 80-93

Westerlund, O. (1997). Employment Opportunities, Wages and Interregional Migration in Sweden 1970–1989. *Journal of Regional Science* 37: 55-73

Appendix: Table A1: List of Municipalities (kommuner)

Coastal Region	Population in 1997
Nordmaling	7,934
Robertsfors	7,559
Vännäs	8,667
Umeå	103,151
Skellefteå	74,122
Kalix	18,557
Älvsbyn	9,277
Luleå	71,491
Piteå	40,553
Boden	29,415
Haparanda	10,617

Inland Region	Population in 1997
Ragunda	6,598
Bräcke	7,990
Krokom	14,558
Strömsund	14,825
Åre	9,930
Berg	8,364
Härjedalen	11,790
Östersund	59,088
Bjurholm	2,813
Vindeln	6,289
Norsjö	4,960
Malå	3,866
Storuman	7,314
Sorsele	3,323
Dorotea	3,492
Vilhelmina	8,279
Åsele	3,845
Lycksele	13,549
Arvidsjaur	7,546
Arjeplog	3 575
Jokkmokk	6 412
Överkalix	4 419
Övertorneå	5 962
Pajala	7 848
Gällivare	21 376
Kiruna	25 269

Appendix. Table A2: Definitions of Variables

Variable	Definition
Unemployed	Dummy variable = 1 if individual received unemployment benefit
Labormarketpol	Dummy variable = 1 if individual received compensation for participation in labour market programs
Socialwelfare	Dummy variable = 1 if individual received social welfare benefits.
Student	Dummy variable = 1 if individual participated in education (all levels included).
RHSB	Dummy variable = 1 if individual derived main income from reindeer husbandry in any of the years 1995, 1996, or 1997.
Children	Dummy variable = 1 if individual had children under 18 residing at home.
Smallchildren	Dummy variable = 1 if individual had received parental leave benefits.
Age	Individual's age, in years.
Agesq	*Age* squared.
Female	Dummy variable = 1 if individual is a female.
Education1	Dummy variable = 1 if individual's educational level is six years of primary school.
Education2	Dummy variable = 1 if individual's educational level is seven to nine years of primary school.
Education3	Dummy variable = 1 if individual's educational level is two years of upper secondary school.
Education4	Dummy variable = 1 if individual's educational level is three years of upper secondary school.
Education5	Dummy variable = 1 if individual's educational level is post secondary school education $\leq$ 3 years.
Education6	Dummy variable = 1 if individual's educational level is university graduate.
Education7	Dummy variable = 1 if individual's highest educational level is Ph.D.
Population7	Total population in individual's local authority region of residence in 1997.
Popchange9697	Percentage change in total population 1996-1997 in individual's local authority region of residence in 1997.

Note: *Variables measured in 1997 if not otherwise stated.*

7

Migration and Population Dynamics in the Regions of Finland: Special Analysis of Lapland[1]

Elli Heikkilä and Maria Pikkarainen

Introduction

Finnish society has undergone vast structural changes since the Second World War. Its impact is reflected in the nature of regional development that has taken place. In this context, migration has played an important role in shaping the areal patterns of settlement. The rapid change in occupational structure and the associated process of urbanization led to an orientation of migration away from the countryside into the cities and towns and from rural districts into the urbanized areas. This trend is also manifest in a retraction of population toward Southern and South-Western Finland (Karjalainen 1989:11) .

An aging population is becoming increasingly detrimental in terms of Finnish society's future development. According to projections, the percentage of elderly will grow in all regions of Finland. This growth will be greatest in the capital area, where the number of elderly is expected to double by 2030. In rural areas, the population is already quite old; therefore, the numbers are growing more slowly than in the cities. The most remarkable change in age structure will occur within the next ten years, when the generation of baby-boomers—those born during the second half of the 1940s—retires (Sisäasiainministeriö 2005:8).

This chapter deals with Finland's, and in deeper analysis, Lapland's, unbalanced regional development and shows which regions are vulnerable in population processes. Population vulnerability is examined relative to such variables as natural population development, domestic migration and international migration patterns. We also examine whether immigration could be the solution to reverse the trend of an ageing population in Lapland. This study is a part of an anticipated project entitled *International*

---

[1] The basic study data were obtained from the official publications of Statistics Finland

Migration, Need of Labour and Effects of Immigration on Education Supply, funded by the European Social Fund (ESF), the Finnish Ministry of Education, and the Institute of Migration.

Concept of Vulnerability in Regional Development

Traditionally, a region's vulnerability can be assessed in terms of natural factors, namely birth and death rates. Their relationship is an indicator of vulnerability: in the worst case scenario, the death rate exceeds the birth rate. With a higher death rate, the region slowly withers away, losing growth potential. Elderly people are often observed to stay within their area of residence until nearly the end of their lives, in which case we can speak of ageing in place. In extreme situations, the permanent population of country villages are disappearing as the last of the local elderly die.

Internal migration is a dynamic variable affecting regional population structures in terms of fluctuations in number and composition (some regions lose part of their population, while others are winners in terms of the change in the number of residents). When migration occurs concurrently with natural changes in population, there is a multi-dimensional picture of the region's situation whether either process is negative or positive. Regional vulnerability may culminate in a situation that, in extreme cases, may be called regional death. This concept is consistent with Myrdal's (1957) theory of cumulative causation, in which regional growth patterns are assumed to be unbalanced. Myrdal pointed out vicious circles of cumulative interactions—for instance, negative development in migration balance creates negativity in other indicators. Cumulative causation in the nuclear area is driven by raw materials, population flows, and capital flows. Findlay (2005:431) reveals that populations are often exposed to multiple vulnerabilities: one dimension of vulnerability increases the likelihood of another. In other words, various indicators may culminate in a vulnerability.

One striking feature of modern societies is the geographic concentration of economic activity. The classic concept of agglomeration economies emphasizes the 'positive externalities,' or external economies of scale, scope and complexity, that result from the co-location of businesses. For example, firms enjoy access to a more extensive labour pool and find specialists with greater ease. Workers, in turn, benefit from a greater choice of potential employers and from better career prospects (Turok 2005:21).

The regions are part of a global world, and waves of migration may occur from across borders. Regions differ in their appeal, and in this respect, some are winners and others losers when it comes to receiving migrants. With respect to regional development, it is significant whether regions can attract and retain human capital. A region's local development potential consists of a variety of resources; the most important include human resources and their structure. A region needs people, both natives

Chapter 7: *Migration and Population Dynamics in the Regions of Finland—Special Analysis of Lapland*

and immigrants, of different educational backgrounds, who can serve in various economic sectors. The local potential of a region can be positive, or the region can be vulnerable, depending on the local resources and historical background. A region's vulnerability is not necessarily permanent; there can be a phase of positive development as a result, for instance, of strong economic input and investment, that create new conditions for the region.

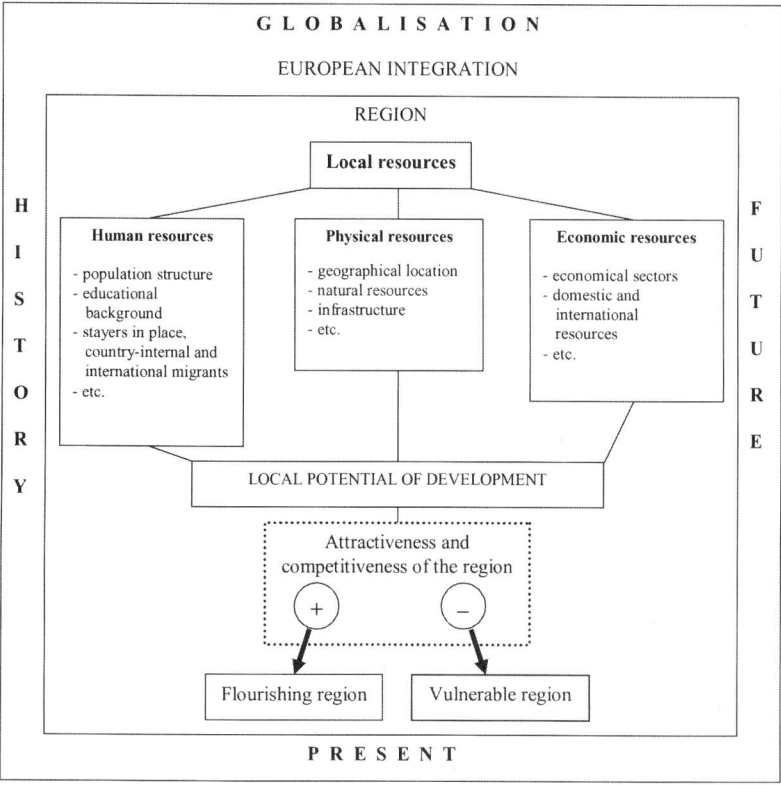

Figure 1. *Framework for local resources and potential of development.*

Smaller, more peripheral cities compete quite differently than large cities, since the former have a more restricted set of policies and lack the opportunity to match national capitals and world cities. The fact that places compete does not imply that they compete equally. As a result, negative attitudes often accompany competition, especially within the disadvantaged places (Malecki 2005:28).

As a whole, the dynamics of regional development—the positive side being regional appeal and competitive ability, and the negative side being vulnerability in these respects—consist of many elements, which Figure 1 illustrates. In this broader context, the degree of vulnerability varies over time and space: a region's present-day standing is linked to its past, which forms the basis for its present situation as well as for its future. A region consists of its own variety of resources. Some, such as natural resources and location are given, while others, such as human resources as a result of natural population growth and migration, always vary. Central to this chapter is the examination of various essential indicators of human resources, which are next discussed.

Lapland's Demographic Position in the National Context

First it is important to compare population development in Lapland to that in other counties of Finland. Changes in population development occur quite unevenly in the counties. Some receive new residents, while others are losing even their own. The county of Uusimaa, which hosts the capital of Helsinki, has been and will be the most appealing in Finland. It received 140,000 new residents during the last ten years and will likely welcome an additional 100,000 during the next decade. The percent changes from 1994 to 2004 and the projected change from 2004 to 2014 vary from -10 % to 12 % (Fig. 2). Counties showing negative future population development are primarily located in Northern and Eastern Finland, including Lapland. Residents are drawn especially to the large university cities of Tampere (in the Pirkanmaa county), Turku (in the county of Varsinais-Suomi) and Oulu (in the county of Northern Ostrobothnia), in addition to the previously mentioned Uusimaa county and its capital conurbation.

In 1995, although most of the counties in Finland were experiencing an excess of births, they also suffered country-internal migration loss at the same time (Figs. 3 and 4). In only four counties were there more people being born than dying, and more people migrating in than out. These counties are situated in South-West Finland and there are three big centres of growth and local labour market areas to which workers commute: the capital Helsinki in Uusimaa, Turku in Varsinais-Suomi and Tampere in Pirkanmaa. In terms of population development, the most serious situation was in South-Eastern Finland, because in those counties there was both a higher death rate and a deficit in country-internal migration.

Chapter 7: *Migration and Population Dynamics in the Regions of Finland—Special Analysis of Lapland*

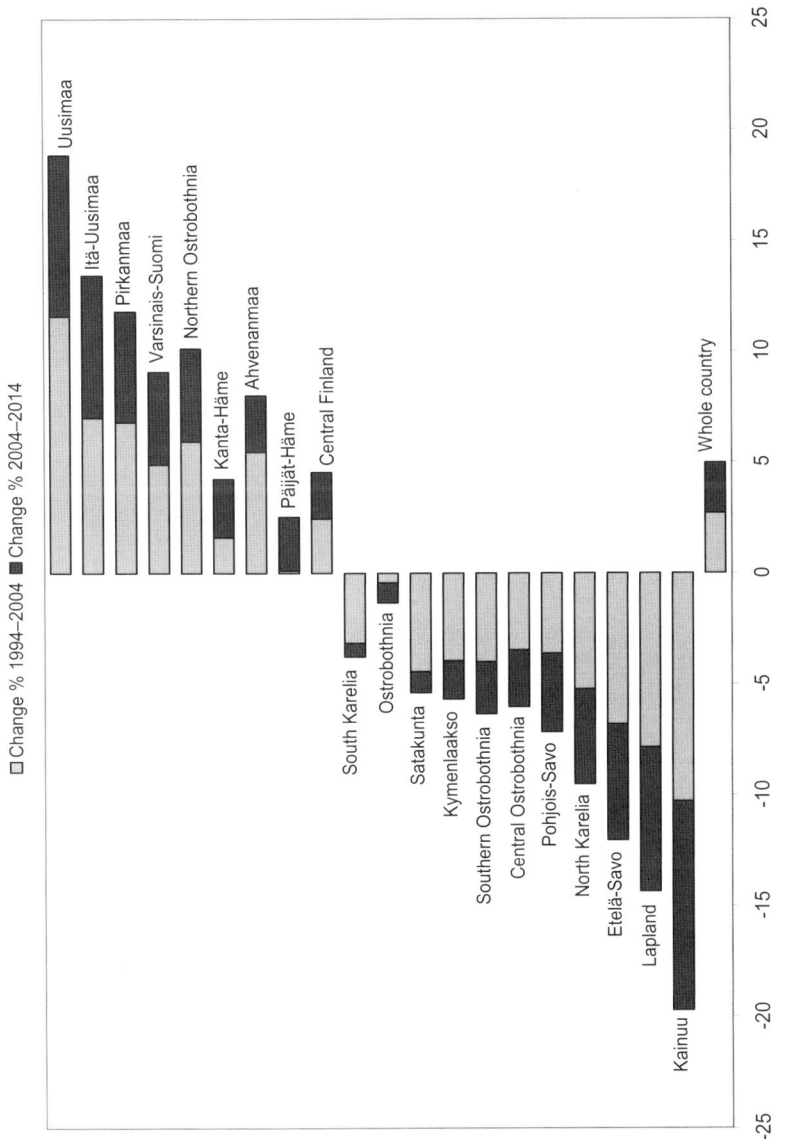

Figure 2. *Percent changes of the populations in the counties of Finland from 1994 to 2004 and projections from 2004 to 2014 (Data: Statistics Finland)*

An examination of population development in 2004 revealed that there are now more counties with excess of deaths and migration loss than in 1995. The area of negative population development has widened to all Eastern Finland as well as to Satakunta in South-Western Finland. As an equalizer, the number of counties with excess of births and migration gain has almost doubled. The situation in Lapland has been the same during the ten year period: natural population development is positive with an excess of births, but net country-internal migration remains negative. However, in any given area, such as a county, the centres of strong population growth may be sufficient to show the entire county as a positive growth area.

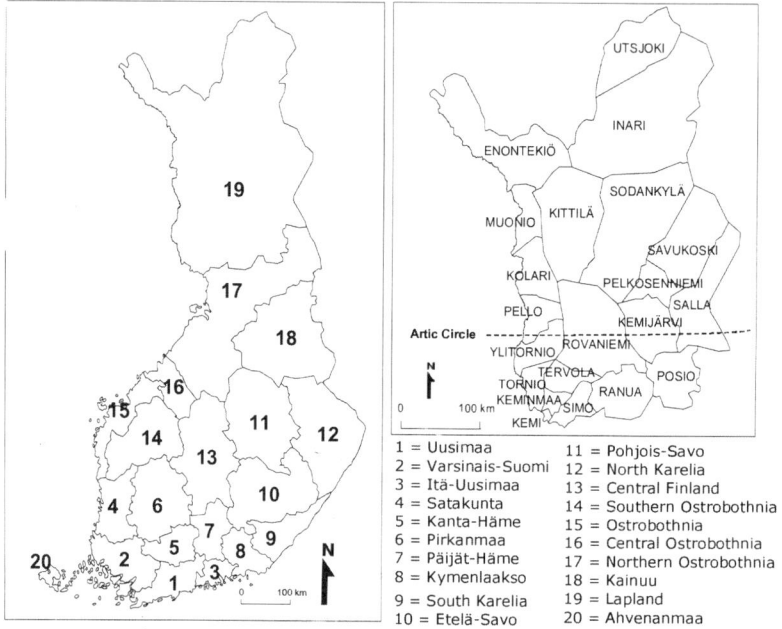

Figure 3. *Counties of Finland and municipalities of Lapland.*

Chapter 7: *Migration and Population Dynamics in the Regions of Finland—Special Analysis of Lapland*

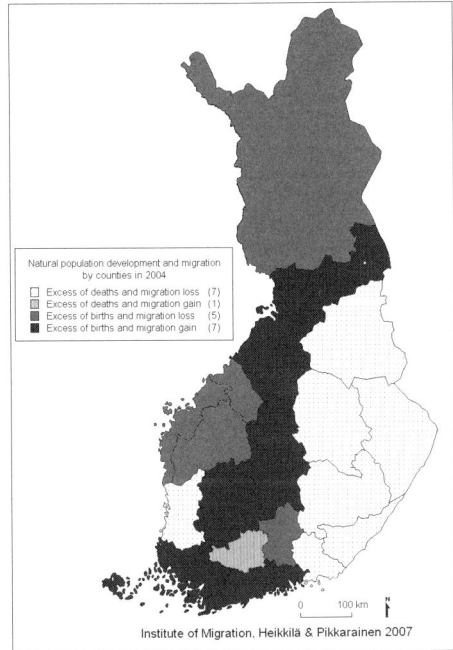

Figure 4. *Natural population development and country-internal migration in 1995 and 2004 by county (Data: Statistics Finland).*

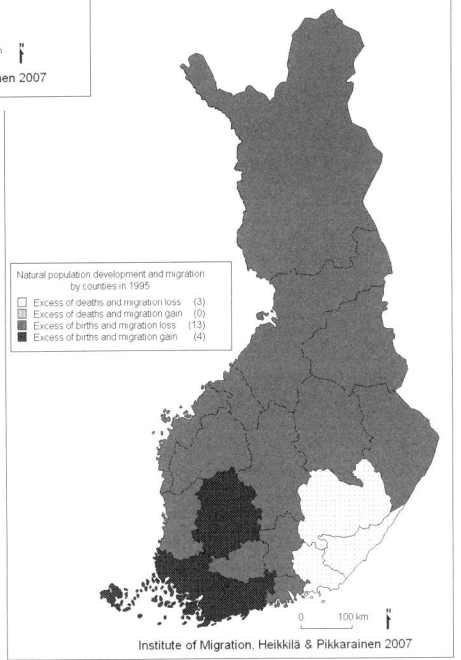

Finland is facing demographic regional development in different stages. There are areas in which natural population change, country-internal migration, as well as immigration, are all positive, such as in Pirkanmaa and Itä-Uusimaa (Fig. 5). Within Northern Finland, the county of Northern Ostrobothnia has the most positive balance of natural population change, due, among other factors, to the large Laestadian families who live there. At the other end of the scale are counties for which these indicators, excluding immigration, are negative. Most of these counties with negative population changes are located in Eastern Finland. By far the worst situation is in Kainuu where there is a high country-internal migration loss. Looking at the proportion of immigrants in each county, the highest rate is found in Ahvenanmaa, where there are a lot of Swedes, and in the capital area in Uusimaa, which attracts foreigners because is a place to meet their fellow countrymen. Relative to the county as a whole, in 2004 Lapland showed a slight positive natural population change, but net country-internal migration is the third worst of all the counties in Finland.

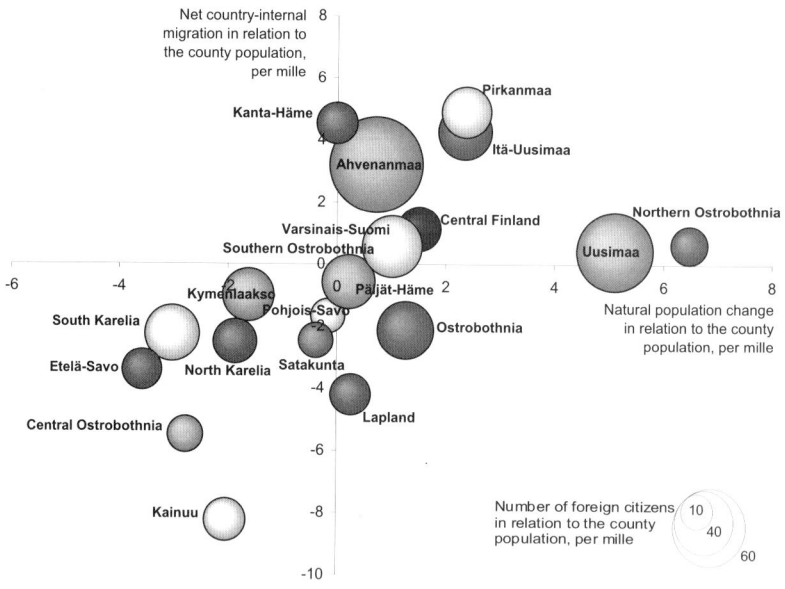

Figure 5. *Population changes in Finland's counties in 2004.(Data: Statistics Finland).*

Chapter 7: *Migration and Population Dynamics in the Regions of Finland—Special Analysis of Lapland*

Lapland's Migration and Population Processes

The population of Lapland decreased by almost 8 percent (15,739 persons) during the period 1990 to 2006 (Fig. 6), by which time the population was 184,935. Natural population growth shows births exceeding deaths but in 2002, 2003 and 2006 there were more deaths than births. This contrasts with earlier years when, for example in 1991, there was an excess of 1,000 births over deaths. Lapland's population can be said to be vulnerable with regard to natural growth since it is no longer showing a net gain; rather the human resource base is decreasing.

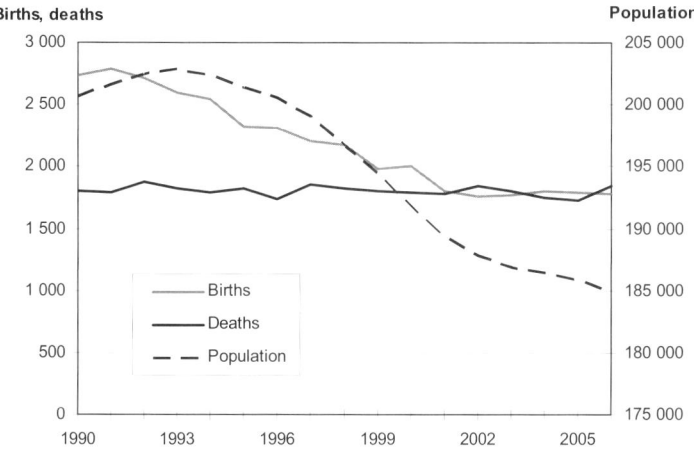

Figure 6. *Births, deaths and population development 1990–2006 in Lapland (Data: Statistics Finland).*

There are regional variations in domestic and international migration dynamics within the Lapland region. In 1990, Rovaniemi, the main centre of Lapland, gained in domestic migration but other cities and other municipalities faced net migration loss (Fig. 7). International net migration was positive for all three categories of regions.

In 2000, country-internal migration turned negative even for Rovaniemi when 606 more individuals moved out than in. In-migration increased by 34 % percent from 1990, but out-migration had been negative for Rovaniemi, because it increased by 92% in the same period. Other cities and municipalities also faced losses in country-internal migration. These losses, in absolute terms, have been highest for other municipalities, that is -1,460 individuals. International net migration however, was positive only for other municipalities with a gain of 21 persons.

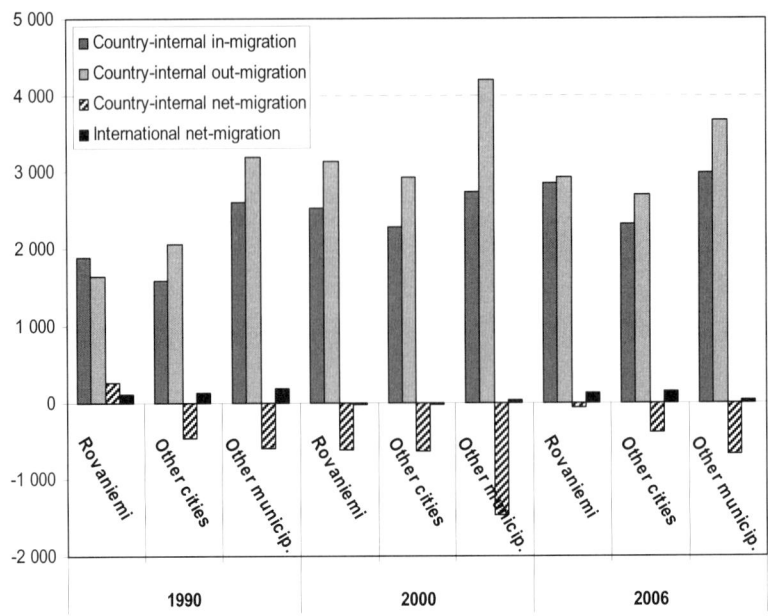

Figure 7. *Country-internal migration and international migration in Rovaniemi, other cities and other municipalities in Lapland 1990–2006. (Data: Statistics Finland).*

Country-internal migration numbers from 2006 are more balanced and net migration loss also fell in different types of regions in Lapland. Other municipalities, however, lost the largest number (-677 persons), from country-internal migration. For international migration, the balance has been positive for all types of regions, but the numbers are still too small to change total migration balance to a positive. Rovaniemi is attracting a younger population to the University of Lapland and other educational institutions.

Lapland's regional demographic development was heterogeneous in 2006 (Fig. 8). It is notable that there was a large group of municipalities in which both natural population change and country-internal migration were negative. The most negative development in relative terms was in Pelkosenniemi; the most positive in natural population change was in Utsjoki, Tornio and Rovaniemi. In country-internal migration, Kittilä was the only municipality in Lapland that experienced a gain. There is a large alpine skiing centre in Levi in Kittilä and there are a lot of attractive tourism jobs for new-comers. Each municipality has immigrants but the smallest relative proportion is in Savukoski (0.8 per thousand of population) and the highest in Muonio (16.2 per thousand). The areas, which are vulnerable according to many population indicators, can be said to have multiple and

Chapter 7: *Migration and Population Dynamics in the Regions of Finland—Special Analysis of Lapland*

thus multidimensional vulnerability. Many of these areas are in Lapland: Muonio, Pello, Sodankylä and Ylitornio are municipalities that experienced population loss in natural population development, country-internal migration and international migration in 2006.

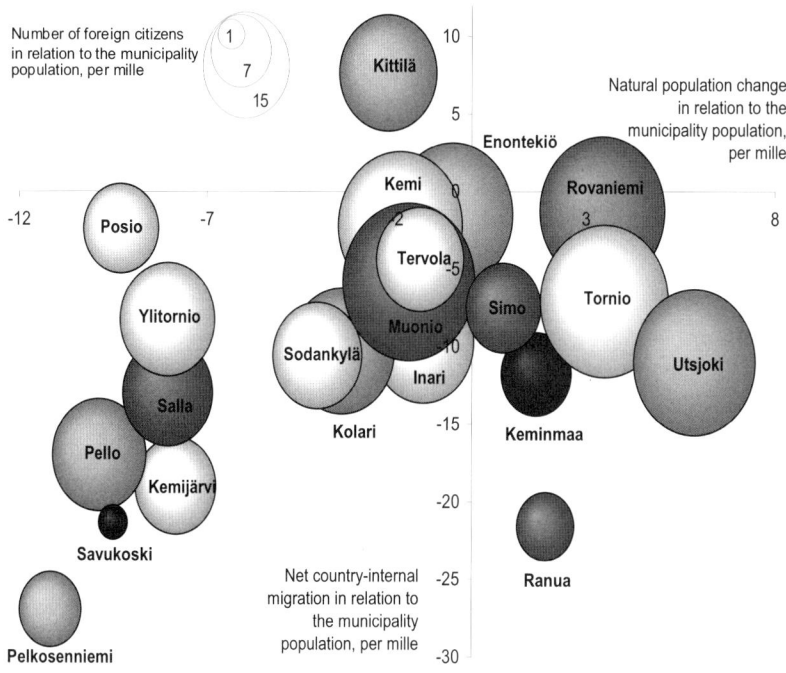

Figure 8. *Population changes in Lapland's municipalities in 2006. (Data: Statistics Finland).*

An examination of country-internal migration flows between municipalities in Lapland during the period 2000 to 2006 shows that the largest migration flow was from Keminmaa to Kemi city at 1,492 persons. The second largest was an opposite flow from Kemi to Keminmaa at 1,379 persons. Kemi thus experienced a small net gain in migration relative to Keminmaa. These flows may be explained by the fact that Kemi and Keminmaa are neighbour municipalities and migration within the same labour market area is usually high.

Migration between cities is also remarkable in Lapland, since the next largest flow has been from Tornio to Kemi (899 persons). These two cities are located close to each other in the South-Western part of Lapland. People from Sodankylä have been moving toward Rovaniemi (812 persons) and Rovaniemi also attracted migrants from Kemijärvi (770 persons). Lapland shows the same trends as the country as a whole: urban-to-urban migration is dominant in country-internal migration.

Conclusion

As regards renewing population through migration and economic development, the competitiveness of Finland's regions vary substantially. According to Kitson *et al.* (2005), competitive regions are able to: a) attract skilled, creative and innovative people; b) provide high-quality cultural facilities; and c) encourage the development of social networks and institutional arrangements that share a common commitment to regional prosperity. These factors are cumulative and, in regional development, show themselves to be positive impulses.

According to Kitson *et al.* (2005), Finland's most competitive areas are counties and centres of growth in Southern Finland, as well as Northern Ostrobothnia and its regional centre Oulu. These areas spread economic activity and positive impulses to extend local labour market areas where people go to work. The centres of growth attract original Finnish residents as well as immigrants. Municipalities that are vulnerable in terms of population growth and economic development are located in many parts of Finland (*see* Heikkilä and Pikkarainen 2008). These areas are not attractive to migrants and are unlikely to experience a positive balance of country-internal migration.

Population development varies more greatly in Lapland as a whole: there are winners and losers in natural population growth and country-internal migration. A positive sign is that all municipalities are attracting immigrants. Overall, population is concentrating in the cities; many people are moving between urban areas. Worth mentioning is the development of the Euroregion which consists of Tornio in Finland and Haparanda in Sweden. The close proximity and extensive collaboration between these two cities is something unique in all of Europe—concrete collaborations which began in the 1970s. Bilingualism is considered an asset in the region. These cities are two of a few where the population is growing and construction is brisk. IKEA's decision to build a location in Tornio–Haparanda has prompted great interest in the region; attracting 2 million shoppers each year. There are plans to enhance business activities in the region by 2010, creating an estimated 1,000 or more new jobs. The Tornio–Haparanda-region is the 'hot spot' of Northern Finland and Sweden at the moment (Rasku 2007:12–16).

Chapter 7: Migration and Population Dynamics in the Regions of Finland—Special Analysis of Lapland

Difficult as it might seem to turn cumulative negative, and thus vulnerable, development into opportunities for growth, the example of Tornio–Haparanda is offering new possibilities for Lapland. Tourism is also playing an important role, as evidenced in Kittilä and its positive country-internal migration balance. This economic area is providing seasonal work for local people and outsiders, even from Southern Finland. However, even a city can be vulnerable in its development, as has occurred in Kemijärvi. A few years ago, Kemijärvi was featured in news headlines because the Salcomp company moved its facilities to China. It was shocking that globalization had hit a specific region in Finland and that educated people had lost their jobs—sometimes two individuals from a single family.

Under these circumstances, the current situation testifies that international migration has not been a means of restoring positive population growth to vulnerable areas. It must also be stressed that finding a first job in Finland's labour market has been difficult for working-age immigrants, since many have been unemployed or outside the labour force (Heikkilä and Pikkarainen 2008). In the future, however, Finland will need to attract working-age migrants from all over the world and also use the existing labour pools in the country to fill the labour deficit caused by the loss of large cohorts. It will need immigrants for a variety of sectors, and compete for them with other ageing societies. Redistribution of immigrants to all regional levels—from global to local—will be critical to regional advancement.

References

Findlay, A.M. (2005). 'Editorial: Vulnerable Spatialities,' pp. 429-439 in *Population, Space and Place, Special Issue: Population and Vulnerability: Making Sense of Vulnerability* 11: 6. John Wiley & Sons, Ltd.

Heikkilä, E., and M. Pikkarainen (2008). Väestön ja työvoiman kansainvälistyminen nyt ja tulevaisuudessa. Siirtolaisuusinstituutti, Siirtolaisuustutkimuksia A 30. 219 s. http://www.migrationinstitute.fi/pdf/Siirtolaisuustutkimuksia_A30_ESR.pdf Summary: Internationalization of Population and Labour Force from the Present to the Future. http://www.migrationinstitute.fi/pdf/A30_summary.pdf

Karjalainen, E. (1989). Migration and regional development in the rural communes of Kainuu, Finland in 1980-85. *Societas Geographica Fenniae Nordicae, Nordia* 23(1): 1-89.

Kitson, M., R. Martin, and P. Tyler (2005). Regional Competitiveness: An Elusive yet Key Concept. *Association of Regional Observatories*, 3-9.

Malecki, E.J. (2005). Jockeying for Position: What It Means and Why It Matters to Regional Development Policy When Places Compete. *Association of Regional Observatories* 25-29.

Myrdal, G. (1957). *Economic Theory and Under-Developed Regions*. London.

Rasku, A. (2007). A developing twin city at the arch of the Gulf of Bothnia. Par Avion 2/2007: 12-16.

Sisäasianministeriö (2005). Väestön ikääntymiseen varautuminen sisäasianministeriön hallinnonalalla. Keskustelualoitteet, Sisäasianministeriön julkaisuja 36/2005. 60 p.

Turok, I. (2005). Cities, Regions and Competitiveness. *Association of Regional Observatories* 18-24.

8

Who Moves and Why: Stylized Facts about Iñupiat Migration in Alaska[1]

Stephanie Martin

Introduction

This research is part of a larger project on indigenous migration in the Arctic. The aim is to understand why people migrate, as well as the effects of migration on individuals, households, and communities. The larger project compares factors in migration in Canada with those in northern Alaska. This chapter summarizes what we can learn from existing survey data and presents general observations from northern Alaska. We extend migration research by looking at indigenous migration in the context of wage earnings, subsistence hunting and fishing, and family ties.

This research focuses on Iñupiat in northern Alaska, one of Alaska's three Eskimo groups. Figure 1 shows the study region—the North Slope, Northwest Arctic, and Bering Straits regions.

---

[1] **Acknowledgements** The National Science Foundation funded this project, Understanding Migration in the Circumpolar North (ARC-0639211), and earlier projects on which this is based: Migration in the Arctic (ARC-0457662), Survey of Living Conditions in the Arctic (OPP-120174), and Social Transitions in the North (DPP-9213137 and OPP-946351).

The United States Bureau of the Census provided access to data. The research that forms the basis of this paper was conducted while project researchers were given Special Sworn Status to use data the US Census Bureau at the Center for Economic Studies. Research results and conclusions expressed are those of the author and do not necessarily reflect the views of the Census Bureau. The data used in this paper have been carefully screened by the US Census to insure that no confidential data are revealed.

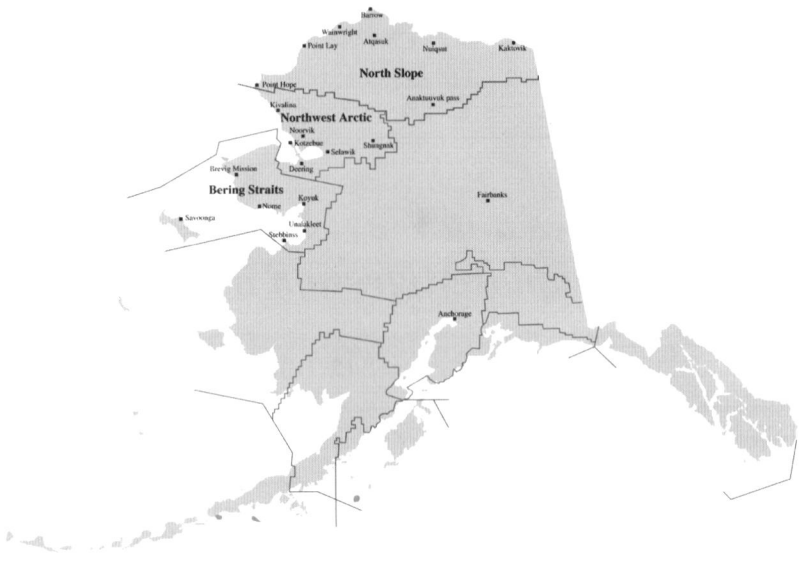

Figure 1. *Study region.*

In 2000, the population of the study region was about 24,000. Three towns (population 3,000 to 5,400) and 33 villages (population 130 to 700) are spread out over about 150,000 square miles (389,000 sq. Km.). Iñupiat make up about 80% of the population in towns and more than 90% of the population in most villages.[2] Local economies are 'mixed' in the sense that households rely on a combination of food from hunting and fishing, government income transfers, and wage earnings (Huskey 1992; Kruse 1991; Usher 1992; Wolfe and Walker 1987). Because of the Prudhoe Bay oil field, there are more jobs—with higher pay—in the North Slope borough. In other regions, most jobs are with state and federal governments and are concentrated in hub communities. Nearly all households engage in subsistence hunting and fishing. Subsistence involves place-specific knowledge and requires healthy local wildlife populations. Households hunt and fish together, share harvests, equipment for subsistence, cash, and market goods (Berman 1998; Huskey 1992; Magdanz and Utermohle 2002). One of the hypotheses is that even though jobs are scarce in villages, subsistence hunting and fishing and family ties make people less likely to leave. Our surveys asked about subsistence, family ties and sharing and give a more complete picture of migration than the US census does.

---

[2] Estimated from US Census 2000, race/ethnicity reported as Alaska Native/American Indian.

Survey data were also used to identify and describe return migrants. It is believed that return migration is essential for community viability. There are few opportunities for post-secondary education in remote communities. Only a small share of Iñupiat living in the region—3% according to US Census 2000—report having at least one year of post-secondary education. At some point, these people left and returned.

Because village populations are so small, migration can affect community survival. For some communities, out-migration is increasing at the same time births (and replacement population) are decreasing (Alaska Bureau of Vital Statistics 2005). Historically, in other regions of Alaska, many small communities of fewer than 100 have disappeared. Jones (1973) noted that in the 18th century there were several hundred small villages in the Aleutian Islands; by 1970, they numbered 24 (Alonso and Rust 1976).

Migration is a complicated process. It has economic, household, community, geographic, demographic, and time dimensions. Consistent with macro-economic literature, the term 'stylized facts' is used to describe general observations based on complicated facts (Kaldor 1961). Stylized facts are generally true, but there may be exceptions; stylized facts are drawn from census and survey data and used in the larger migration project to refine hypotheses and specify empirical models.

Data Sources

Data presented in this paper are taken from US Censuses 1990 and 2000 and several smaller surveys conducted in northern Alaska from 1978 to 2002. The US Census covers a larger geographic area than the surveys and contains migration information for Iñupiat regardless of where they moved. The surveys are limited to people whose migration destination is northern Alaska—people living in northern Alaska at the time of the survey. These smaller surveys provide a detailed picture of individual migrants. In particular, they tell us why people migrate and give information about their employment, family ties, social support, and traditional activities.

The earliest data about migrants are from a 1978 survey conducted by the North Slope Borough (NSB) and the Institute of Social and Economic Research (ISER). The sample includes 332 randomly selected respondents in six communities. In 1988 the borough expanded the survey to a census and implemented it at 5 year intervals. Not all years have migration questions.[3] Researchers from the University of Washington conducted the Social Transitions in the North (STN) surveys in 1993, 1994, and 1995. STN is a panel survey covering 171 randomly selected respondents in four communities in the Northwest Arctic Borough. The

---

[3] The 1998 and 2003 NSB surveys do not have specific questions about migration.

Survey of Living Conditions in the Arctic (SLiCA) conducted by ISER in 2003 includes 663 randomly selected respondents in 20 communities in the Nome census area, Northwest Arctic, and North Slope boroughs. The SLiCA survey also includes Siberian Yupiit and Central Yupiit people from communities in the Nome census area. Also in 2003, ISER, the Alaska Department of Fish and Game (ADFG), and the National Park Service (NPS) conducted a census of 74 households in the community of Buckland, located in the Northwest Arctic Borough. The Buckland census was designed as a wildlife harvest and social network survey but also contains migration information.

In this chapter, census data is used to provide a general overview of Iñupiat migration in Alaska, and survey data are used to examine migrants in more detail and generate stylized facts. The census classifies migrants differently than surveys. Census data cover the entire state and define migrants as people who have moved during the 5 years prior to the census. Census data were used to count people leaving northern Alaska (our study region), people moving to northern Alaska, and people moving within northern Alaska. The survey data are restricted to northern Alaska and cover a longer time period. We classified survey respondents as either stayers (people who have never left their community), return migrants (people who moved back to places where they were born and raised —DaVanzo and Morrison 1981), or in-migrants (people who moved into a northern Alaskan community for the first time). Missing from survey data are Iñupiat who have moved out of northern Alaska, including those living in Anchorage and Fairbanks (about 15% of the total Iñupiat population) (US Census 2000 Public Use Microsample).

Overview of Iñupiat Migration

People are more mobile. Figure 2 shows the increase in the total number of migrants—people moving out of northern Alaska and into northern Alaska—as reported in the US Census. The number of Iñupiat leaving northern Alaska from 1995 to 2000 (1,615) increased over that from 1985-1990 (1,140). The out-migration *rate* also rose slightly, increasing from 8.7% to 9.1%. Over this same time period, the number of people who moved to northern Alaska also increased. From 1995 to 2000, 1,010 people moved to northern Alaska compared to 780 from 1985 to 1990. Although the number is rising, the rate of in-migration dropped slightly from 5.9% to 5.7%. Migration is not new. Alaska Natives have been moving among communities for a long time (Lantis 1984; Alonso and Rust 1976; Kruse and Foster 1986).

Chapter 8: *Who Moves and Why: Stylized Facts About Iñupiat Migration in Alaska*

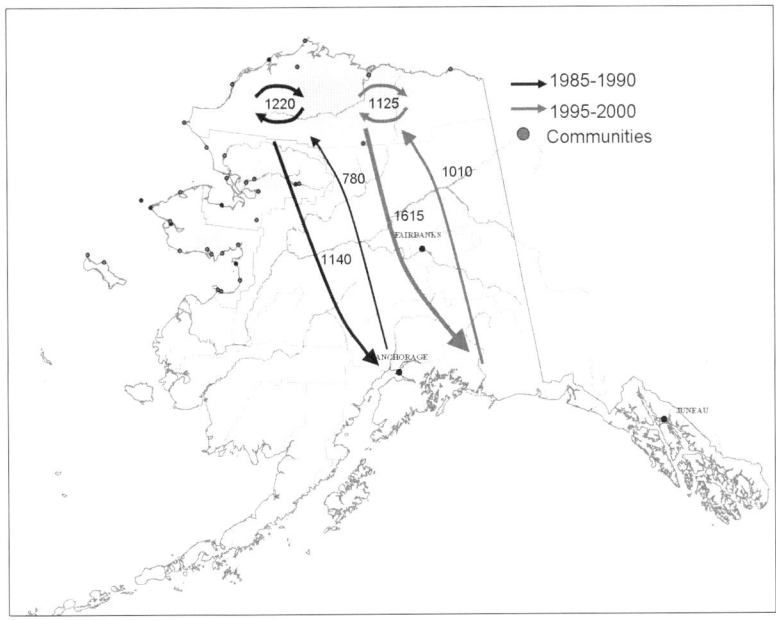

Figure 2. *Iñupiat migration to and from northern Alaska.* Source: US Census of Population and Housing (1990, 2000)

More females are leaving and more males are returning. Figure 3 shows that from 1985 to 1990, for every 10 people who moved from northern Alaska, about seven returned (US Census 1990, 2000). The pattern was the same for males and females. However, from 1995 to 2000, more females left and more men returned. Gender differences in migration are important for this study. Hamilton and Seyfrit (1994:192) coined the term, 'female flight' to describe the disproportionate out-migration of young Native women from remote rural villages. Reasons for gender differences in migration are described in the stylized fact section of this chapter.

Increasing numbers of Iñupiat are leaving northern Alaska for Anchorage or Fairbanks. Table 1 shows that most Iñupiat leave northern Alaska for Anchorage. Between 1995 and 2000, about half of all out-migrants moved to Anchorage—a slightly larger share than from 1985 to 1990 when 45% moved to Anchorage. The number of Iñupiat moving to Fairbanks also increased from 6.9% between 1985 and 1990 to 7.4% between 1995 and 2000. The number of Iñupiat moving outside Alaska declined from 15.7% to 12.7% during the same time period.

Migration in the Circumpolar North

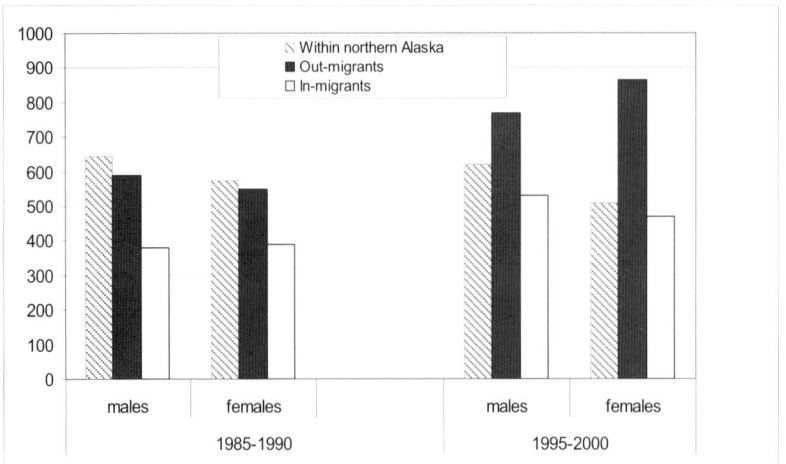

Figure 3. *Gender differences in Iñupiat migration 1985-1990 and 1995-2000.*
Source: US Census of Population and Housing (1990, 2000).

In summary, census data show increased migration over time. More females are migrating out of northern Alaska and fewer are migrating in. More males are migrating both out of northern Alaska and into northern Alaska. Increasing numbers of people are moving to Anchorage and Fairbanks. Census data do not answer questions about why people move, why they return, and the effects of migration on northern Alaskan communities. Stylized facts were developed using responses from the survey data.

Table 1. Out-migrant Destinations.

	1985-1990	**1995-2000**
Anchorage	44.8%	51.4%
Fairbanks	6.9%	7.4%
Other Alaska*	32.6%	28.5%
Outside Alaska	15.7%	12.7%
N=	**1,149**	**1,615**

Source: US Census of Population and Housing (1990, 2000)
*Other Alaska includes boroughs adjacent to Anchorage.

Stylized Facts About Iñupiat Migration

Stylized Fact Number 1:
Push and pull factors are different for males and females.
Push factors are features of origins. Pull factors are features of destinations. Lee (1960) identified push and pull factors in migration, and stated that they affect people differently. In the case of northern Alaska, pull factors draw people to Anchorage and Fairbanks. In many cases, push factors act as negative forces, keeping people in communities. In the 1980s, authors specifically linked gender differences and push–pull factors stating that the causes of female migration are different from those of male migration (Fawcett *et al.* 1984; Thadani and Todaro 1984). Understanding gender differences in Iñupiat migration is particularly important because villages have small populations (average 350). Differential out-migration changes the gender balance in communities which has important implications for community development.

Table 2. Top Reasons for Wanting to Leave Communities.

	Males	Females
Place too small, not enough to do	27%	18%
Get a better job	26%	16%
Own or children's education	12%	24%
To be near family	10%	18%
Sample size n=	108	179

Source: SLiCA (2003)

Out migration push-pull factors
Pull factors: Men leave for jobs, women leave for their education or their children's education. One survey (SLiCA) asked people if they had considered leaving their community and why. The survey data show that more women (46%) than men (38%) reported that they had considered leaving their community. This does not necessarily represent those who actually left, but it does help us understand reasons people leave. Table 2 shows the top reasons men and women give for wanting to leave their communities (push and pull factors). Men report that they want to leave for jobs and/or to live in a bigger community. Women report that they want to leave for their own or their children's education. Opportunities for a four-year degree in northern Alaska are limited to one small rural college in each of the three hub communities. State universities are outside northern Alaska altogether. Out-migration for education, however, may decrease over time. Prior to the 1980s, many rural communities did not even have high schools. Now, not only are there high schools in many communities, rural university campuses, and technical training schools in the towns, but on-line university

courses allow people to pursue post-secondary educational opportunities without leaving their community.

Push factors: Men stay in northern Alaska for hunting and fishing, while women stay for family reasons. These are push factors working in reverse, keeping people in northern communities. Table 3 shows the reasons people stay in northern Alaska. The responses are from both people who want to leave and people who don't want to leave. The table shows gender differences in push factors. A larger share of women than men report that they stay in northern Alaska for family reasons. More men than women report that hunting and fishing are primary reasons why they stay. Subsistence hunting and fishing require place-specific knowledge and property rights. Subsistence activities provide households with food and help maintain traditional culture. Men engage in subsistence activities more than women. This makes the cost of migration higher for men, who lose the opportunity to subsistence hunt and fish in their local communities. Although women don't include it in their reasons for wanting to leave, being a victim of violence may make women want to leave. Using SLiCA data, we found significant correlations (p=.204, sig. <.0001) between responses to questions about being a victim of sexual or other assault and wanting to leave the community.

Table 3. Top Reasons Why People Stay.

	Males	Females
Be near family	49%	59%
Hunting and fishing	23%	14%
Jobs	11%	10%
Like it here	12%	9%
Sample n=	279	371

Source: SLiCA (2003)

Return migration push–pull factors
Fewer women return because they marry and/or get jobs while away from northern Alaska. Although men and women both have educational and employment motives for leaving their communities, they often have different outcomes at their destinations. Women marry and/or get jobs which keep them from returning home. It is not possible to specifically track marital and job status of Iñupiat who have moved from northern Alaska to urban Alaska. Instead, we look at US Census and PUMA files for 'Eskimo'[4] men and women living in urban Alaska. About 71% of Eskimo women living in urban Alaska have been married—even though they may

---

[4] 'Eskimo' is broader than 'Iñupiat.' It also includes Yupiit and Siberian Yupiit people from western Alaska.

Chapter 8: *Who Moves and Why: Stylized Facts About Iñupiat Migration in Alaska*

be separated, divorced or widowed. This compares with 55% of men (US Census, Public Use Micro-sample PUMS, 2000). Eskimo women in urban areas are more likely to be employed—81% percent reported working, compared with 79% of males. Alaska Native men also have higher university drop-out rates than Alaska Native women, which might make them more likely to return home (Kleinfeld and Andrews 2006).

More men than women report that they return to be with family. Overwhelmingly, people return to be with their families. Table 4 shows that a larger share of men (68%) than women (58%) reported family as the main reason for returning.

Table 4. Top Reasons for Returning.

	Males	Females
To be with family	68%	58%
For job	10%	13%
Didn't like other place	8%	5%
Sample n=	114	138

Sources: SLiCA (2003), Buckland (2002).

Stylized Fact Number 2:
Many men who return do as well or better than people who never left.
Survey data in Table 5 show a transition taking place in northern Alaska that favors male return migrants over men who never left. In the past, most of the jobs in northern communities were held by people who had always lived there. Return migrants and immigrants didn't fare as well in the job market as stayers. The data for 2003 show this is changing. Male return migrants are now more likely than stayers to have jobs.

Table 5. Male Employment by Migration Status.

	Stayers		Return Migrants		In-Migrants	
	%	Sample n=	%	Sample n=	%	Sample n=
1978	74%	79	79%	38	70%	40
1993	92%	24	64%	11	64%	33
2003	73%	67	87%	117	65%	135

Sources: NSB (1978, 1993), SLiCA (2003)

The growing success rate of returning males is in contrast to high drop-out rates and low employment for Native men in urban areas. Survey data show that return migrants, men in particular, fare as well or better than people who never left. Of Iñupiat men in northern Alaskan communities with college-level educations, 86% are return migrants (SLiCA 2003,

Buckland 2003). This is a change from 1978 when most of those with college-level educations (67%) were in-migrants (NSB 1978). Male return migrants engage in fewer subsistence activities than men who never left, but the difference is narrowing. Figures 4 and 5 show men's subsistence participation[5] by migration status[6] in 1978 and 2003, respectively. Figure 4 shows a distinct difference between stayers and return migrants, with more stayers engaging in subsistence activities than return migrants.

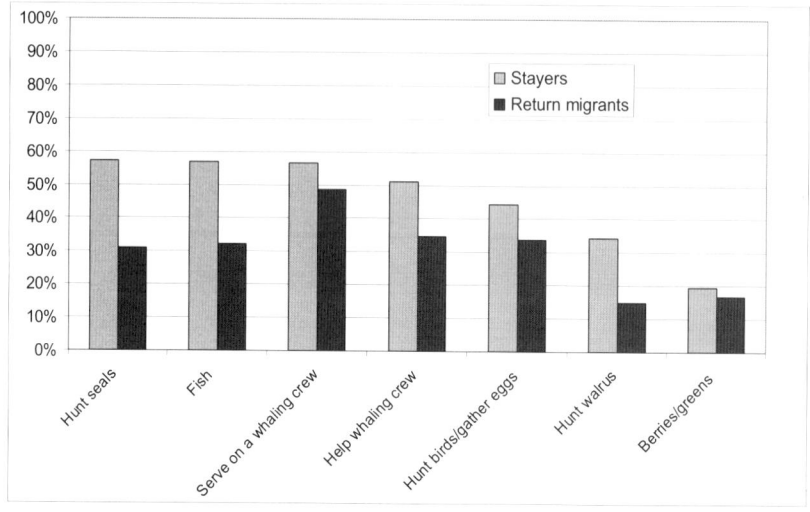

Figure 4. *Male subsistence participation by migration status, 1978.* Source: NSB 1978

By 2003, the gap between stayers and return migrants is nearly closed, with a few exceptions. Figure 5 shows that, compared to men who never left their community, as many return migrants reported fishing, hunting seals, land mammals and birds. However, fewer male return migrants reported being on a whaling or walrus crew or helping a whaling crew.

---

[5] The 1978 figure does not include land mammal hunting or preparing caribou meat. A ban on caribou hunting was in effect because of a sharp drop in the caribou population.

[6] In-migrants participate in fewer subsistence activities than either stayers or return migrants. Leaving them out makes the figures easier to understand.

Chapter 8: *Who Moves and Why: Stylized Facts About Iñupiat Migration in Alaska*

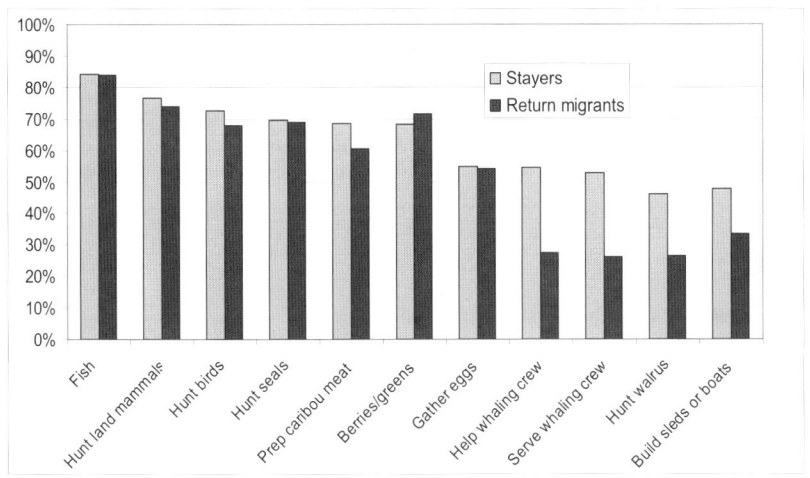

Figure 5. *Male subsistence participation by migrant status, 2003.* Source: SLiCA (2003)

Male return migrants report strong family ties and high social support comparable to or better than stayers and in-migrants. They also report high satisfaction with their lives. Table 6 shows that returning male migrants have comparable or higher social support and stronger family ties than stayers and in-migrants.

Table 6. Percentage of Adult Males Reporting Strong Family Ties and High Social Support.

	Strong Family Ties	High Social Support	Sample n=
Stayers	41.4%	51.1%	53
Return Migrants	38.9%	59.3%	112
In-Migrants	24.2%	53.3%	113

Source: SLiCA (2003)

Other research shows that family ties and social support are important factors contributing to life satisfaction (Martin 2004). This is evident in Table 7 which shows that 93% of male return migrants report being satisfied or very satisfied with their life as a whole. Male return migrants report higher satisfaction with their lives than stayers (86%) and in-migrants (81%).

Table 7. Percentage Reporting Being Satisfied or Very Satisfied with their Life as a Whole.

	Percent	Sample n=
Stayers	86%	53
Return migrants	93%	112
In-migrants	81%	113

Source: SLiCA (2003)

Stylized Fact Number 3:
Migration shapes sending communities.
It is important to look beyond the number of people leaving to understand the effects of migration on communities. Education is one way that return migrants benefit communities. Return migrants make up the largest share, about seven out of 10, of the college-educated Iñupiat people in northern Alaskan communities.

Table 8. Education Level in Northern Communities by Migration Status, 2003.

	Less Than High School	High School Diploma	Some Post-Secondary	Bachelor's Degree and Higher
Stayers	43.7%	18.8%	20.2%	1.8%
Return migrants	21.3%	42.2%	45.9%	68.7%
In-migrants	34.9%	39.0%	33.8%	29.5%
Sample size n=	207	311	163	38

Source: SLiCA (2003), Buckland (2003)

The increasing number of women leaving and not returning is creating a gender imbalance which, in turn, has implications for community-level well-being. According to the 2000 US Census, several communities in our study region have very few young adult women. Figure 6 shows age/sex composition of four communities in northern Alaska where women aged 20 to 24 make up less than 2% of the total population. In Alaska, there are more social problems in communities with fewer women (Hamilton and Seyfrit 1994; Hamilton et al. 1996). It is unclear whether women leave because there are social problems or there are social problem because women leave.

Chapter 8: *Who Moves and Why: Stylized Facts About Iñupiat Migration in Alaska*

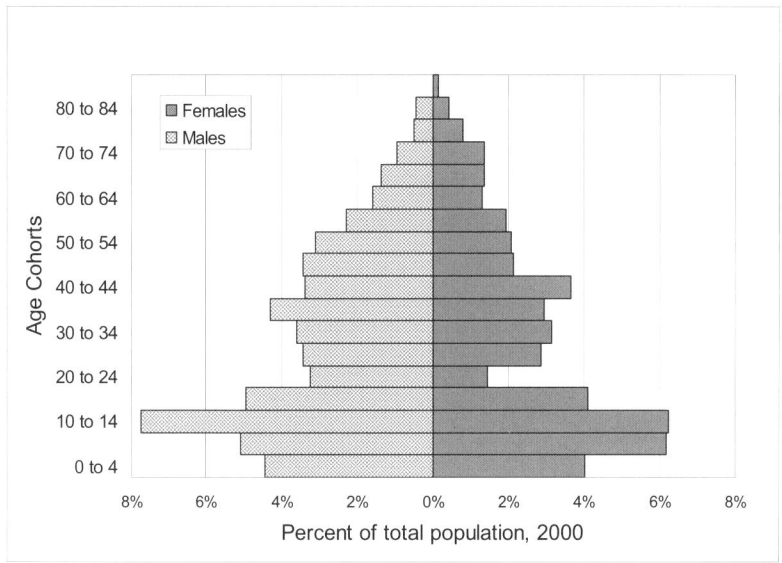

Source: US Census of Population and Housing (2000).

Figure 6: *Age/sex profile of 4 northern communities with few Iñupiat women aged 20 to 24.*

Stylized Fact Number 5:
A key influence on Iñupiat migration is the sending of subsistence food from rural to urban areas. Of households who send subsistence foods to people in other places, between 20% and 30% send food to Anchorage or Fairbanks (NSB 1998, SLiCA 2003; Buckland 2003). Sharing food with relatives and friends in urban areas helps Iñupiat maintain family ties and social support. This may be a key factor enabling return migration. It is also a factor that distinguishes northern Alaska from other migration flows, both international and rural–urban within the U.S. where migrants send remittances back to their original communities.

Summary

According to survey data, jobs and education are the main reason Iñupiat men and women leave northern Alaska communities. The pull of jobs and educational opportunities is stronger for women than men. Subsistence hunting and fishing and family ties make men less likely than women to migrate. More women than men leave, and once they are in urban areas, Iñupiat women are more likely than Iñupiat men to find jobs and marry. Fewer women return. However, men who return fare better than those who never left. They are better educated, more likely to be employed, are satisfied with their lives, and do as much subsistence hunting and fishing as those who never left. Gender differences in Iñupiat out- and return migration have long-term effects on communities. In some places, very few young adult women remain, possibly exacerbating social problems, and contributing to population decline.

References

Alaska Bureau of Vital Statistics (2005). *Annual report*. State of Alaska.
Alonso, W. and E. Rust (1976). The evolving pattern of village Alaska (Study No. 17). Prepared for the Federal-State Land Use Planning Commission for Alaska.
Berman, M.D. (1998). 'Sustainability and subsistence in arctic communities.' Paper prepared for presentation to the Western Regional Science Association, February.
Damas D., ed. (1984). *Handbook of North American Indians*. Washington, DC: Smithsonian Institution.
DaVanzo, J.S. and P.A. Morrison (1981). Return and other sequences of migration in the United States. *Demography* 18: 85-101.
Fawcett, J.T., S.-E. Khoo, and P.C. Smith (1984). 'Urbanization, migration and the status of women,' in Fawcett J.T., *Women in the cities of Asia: migration and urban adaptation*. Boulder: Westview Press.
Hamilton, L. and C.L. Seyfrit (1994). Female flight? Gender balance and outmigration by Native Alaskan villagers. *Arctic Medical Research* 53: 189-193.
Hamilton, L.C., R.O. Rasmussen, N.E. Flanders, and C.L. Seyfrit (1996). Outmigration and gender balance in Greenland. *Arctic Anthropology* 31: 89-97.
Huskey, L. (1992). *The Economy of Village Alaska*. Supported by the Henry M. Jackson Foundation. Anchorage, Alaska.
Jones, D.M. (1973). Patterns of village growth and decline in the Aleutians (ISER Occasional Papers No. 11). University of Alaska Fairbanks, Institute of Social, Economic and Government Research.
Kaldor, N. (1965). 'Capital accumulation and economic growth,' in F.A. Lutz and D.C. Hague (eds.), *The Theory of Capital*. New York: St Martin's Press.
Kleinfeld, J. and J.J. Andrews (2006). The gender gap in higher education in Alaska. *Arctic* 59(4): 428-434.
Kruse, J.A. (1991). Alaska Iñupiat subsistence and wage employment patterns: understanding individual choice. *Human Organization* 50: 317-326.
Kruse, J. And K. Foster (1986, March). Changes in rural Alaska settlement patterns. *Alaska Review of Social and Economic Conditions* 23(1). University of Alaska Anchorage, Institute of Social and Economic Research.
Lantis, M. (1984). 'Aleut,' in D. Damas (ed.), *Handbook of North American Indians*. Washington, DC: Smithsonian Institution.
Lee, E.S. (1966). A theory of migration. *Demography*. 3: 47-58.

Chapter 8: *Who Moves and Why: Stylized Facts About Iñupiat Migration in Alaska*

Magdanz, J. and C. Utermohle (2002). *The Production and Distribution of Wild Food in Wales and Deering, Alaska.* Technical Paper Number 259 Alaska Department of Fish and Game.

Martin, S. (2005). Determinants of well-being in Iñupiat and Yupiit Eskimos: do communities matter? Ph.D. diss. University of Texas at Dallas.

Thadani, V.N. and M.P. Todaro (1984). 'Female migration: a conceptual framework,' in Fawcett, J.T., *Women in the Cities of Asia: Migration and Urban Adaptation.* Boulder: Westview Press.

Usher, P. (1992). "Modeling subsistence systems for social impact assessment" Report prepared for the Grand Council of the Cree of Quebec. Ottawa.

Wolfe, R. and R. Walker (1987). Subsistence economies in Alaska: productivity, geography and development impacts. *Arctic Anthropology* 24: 56-81.

9

Migration and Socio-Economic Well-Being in the Russian North: Interrelations, Regional Differentiation, Recent Trends, and Emerging Issues[1]

Andrey N. Petrov and Tatiana Vlasova

Introduction

Migration is one of the basic demographic events (birth and death are the others) that directly influence the size of population in a given area. Migration both affects and is affected by economic, social, environmental, and political events. An increase in population mobility can be a symptom of economic crisis, social instability, and/or deteriorating quality of life.

Migration is a complex process that can be associated with multiple factors. Interregional migration is often seen as an economic phenomenon, particularly in discussions of labour migration. An act of migration, from an economic perspective, may result from dissatisfaction with current economic conditions at the origin or from a desire to take advantage of perceived benefits at the destination. Migration can be a reaction to a political phenomenon, as with refugees seeking a place of safety. Recently, linkages between migration and environmental factors are receiving increased attention, as in the cases of 'environmental refugees' and migration from ecologically fragile areas. Migration rates can also be

---

[1] This paper is partially based on themes, thoughts and figures produced in Tatiana Vlasova's presentation 'Interrelations of migration issues with demography and quality of life in the Russian North' at the Workshop *Migration in the Circumpolar North: Lessons Learned, Questions Remaining*, University of Roskilde, Denmark, June 10-12, 2007.

associated with natural resource depletion, climate change, desertification or floods, and land use changes.

The impacts of migration rest not only in the numbers, but in the composition of migration flows. Such characteristics as age, sex, fertility level, educational background, occupation, and skill levels of migrants have profound implications for development in both the sending and the receiving regions. Human capital drain or gain, abundance or shortage of labor, and depletion or growth of the local tax base, are among many economic impacts.

An analytical study of migration requires choosing a model that adequately represents migration processes in Russia's hinterland. Selecting one of the economic models would be a convenient option, whether based on wage gradients (e.g., the Harris-Todaro model, with wages and unemployment as key variables) or more elaborate utility-based approaches (Stillwell and Congdon 1991). However, such models have limited capacity to reflect such unique combinations of factors as seen in the post-socialist Russian North. Sutherland and Hanson (2000), who applied the Harris-Todaro model to migration in early post-soviet Russia, not surprisingly conceded that 'real wages' and unemployment rates were not particularly good predictors of migration flows in the mid-1990s. Petrov (2007) demonstrates that economic models are expected to have even weaker explanatory power for Arctic Indigenous populations. The limited ability of wage-based models to accurately portray migration patterns in the Russian North is likely to be associated with the importance of other factors, beyond wage and labour market situation. Available evidence suggests that costs of living, housing conditions, health issues, climatic severity, and poor public services may have profound influence on migration behaviour in the North (World Bank 2001; NEI 1998; Heleniak 1999). In sum, to understand migration processes in the Russian north a more comprehensive approach to identifying possible socio-economic factors is needed.

In this contribution, rather then singling out particular economic factors and events, migration processes are placed in the wider context of *socio-economic well-being* of northern populations, in an effort to unveil a more comprehensive and holistic picture of interrelationships between socio-economic conditions and migration patterns. Although there are a few studies that have examined geographies of migration in the Post-Soviet North (Heleniak 1999, this volume; NEI 1998; Semenov and Petrov 2001; World Bank 2001), there is only fragmentary evidence of exact mechanisms of migration, since most models restrict socio-economic factors to labour market and income variables, thereby omitting other important components of well-being. Even less is known about the long-term implications of mass out-migration to local socio-economic and demographic systems in the North.

This contribution focuses on interrelations between migration and the socio-economic well-being of northern populations. Our research polygon includes 14 northern regions of Russia (*see* Fig. 1). First, we develop typologies of migration trends and socio-economic conditions in northern regions of Russia. Then we analyze the impacts of socio-economic well-being on migration processes in the 1990s. Third, we examine the effects of mass out-migration on socio-economic well-being. Last, we discuss recent migration trends and their relationship with changing socio-economic conditions in the northern periphery, i.e., we consider whether a boom in the resource sector and increased in-migration result in improved socio-economic conditions. To illustrate past and present tendencies, examples from various regions are used, however most of them concern the Republic of Komi, the region with which the authors are most familiar.

Background: Migration Crisis in the Russian North

The Russian North is a remarkably populated part of the Circumpolar world. The 2002 census indicated that 10.8 million people lived in the northern regions,[2] which constituted approximately 7.5 % of Russia's total population (Fauzer 2005:96), compared to 1.9% in Canada and 0.3% in the USA, where approximately one million people live. The Russian North is home to the Arctic's largest cities and industrial complexes, which concentrate the largest labor force in the circumpolar north and provide the lion's share of industrial production (AHDR 2004).

It is well documented that after the collapse of the USSR the population of the Russian North has been declining (e.g., Heleniak 1999, 2003; Semenov and Petrov 2001; Heleniak, this volume). According to the 2002 Census, the population of the Russian North during the intercensal period (1989-2002) decreased by about 1.4 million or 16%, with all but two regions registering a net population loss (Rosstat 2002). These losses are 1.4 times higher than population gains during the preceding decade. Between 1989 and 2002, five northern territories lost more than a quarter of their population: Chukchi Autonomous Okrud (AO) (67.3%), Magadan oblast' (53.4%), Koryak AO (37.5%), Evenki AO (29.2%) and Taymyr AO (28.9%). Another three regions (Kamchatka oblast', Murmansk oblast' and Nenets AO) faced declines of 20% to 26%. Only Khanty-Mansi and Yamalo-Nenets AOs had population increases of 11.8% and 2.5%, respectively.

It is worth mentioning that even relatively prosperous regions of the North, such as the Khanty-Mansi and Yamalo-Nenets AOs had enormous

---

[2] This figure refers to the 'regions of the Far North and equated areas' The total population of the 14 regions included in the current study area is just over seven million.

migration losses. Because of considerable compensating in- and out-migration flows, these losses are masked by net migration figures. One, however, should not be misled on this: at least 65.0% of people residing in Yamalo-Nenets AO in 1989 left the region by 2002; for Khanty-Mansi AO the figure was 51.2% (Rosstat 2002). The instability of the population base severely undermines demographic potential and human capital assets in these regions.

Interestingly, the Census shows a more profound population loss in the North than do annual statistics. Heleniak (2003) estimated these discrepancies as -27.6% in Chukchi AO, -20.2% in Magadan oblast', and -10.7% in Koryak AO. Although these differences could be partially attributed to the difference in dates (01 January 2002 for the annual statistics and 09 October 2002 for the Census), the major issue related to non-registered out-migration, under-counted by annual Rosstat datasets.

From 1989 to 2002, most migrants from the northern regions moved to European Russia, specifically to the Central, North-West, Volga and Southern federal districts. Among the leading destinations were Krasnodar krai, the cities of Moscow and St. Petersburg, and the Moscow, Leningrad, Vologda and Rostov oblasts (Rosstat 2002). Migrants from the northern Far East often moved to the southern part of the region and south of Siberia. Migration from the North to European Russia joins a larger migration flow from Russia's east to the west. In the 1990s, a statistical propensity of migrants to move from Siberia-Far East to Central Russia was the highest in the nation. According to an available estimate, migration in the opposite direction was 172 times less likely (Andreev and Rakhmaninova 1999).

Mass out-migration in the North (*see* Fig. 1) started as early as 1990-1991, but was especially intensive during the *first period* of the migration crisis between 1992 and 1994 (Fig. 2). During *the population flight* of the early 1990s, the annual loss in some regions (the most devastated by the rapid economic collapse were Chukchi AO, Magadan, Kamchatka, Murmansk oblast', and Yakutiya) reached 10-15% of the population. In 1992, out-migration from Chukchi AO amounted to 165 persons per 1,000 residents. The total net migration loss in the northern regions from 1992 to 1994 was between 400,000 and 500,000 (Goskomstat 1997).

During the *second period (stabilization*: 1995-1998/99) the out-migration somewhat receded, although it continued to be high (Fig. 2). Most likely, this slowdown was the result of several factors, including a partial depletion of migrant stock (the most mobile of migrants moved within the first few years), relative economic stabilization, and (most notably) the unbearable moving costs vis-a-vis limited assets available to potential movers.

Chapter 9: *Migration and Socio-Economic Well-Being in the Russian North*

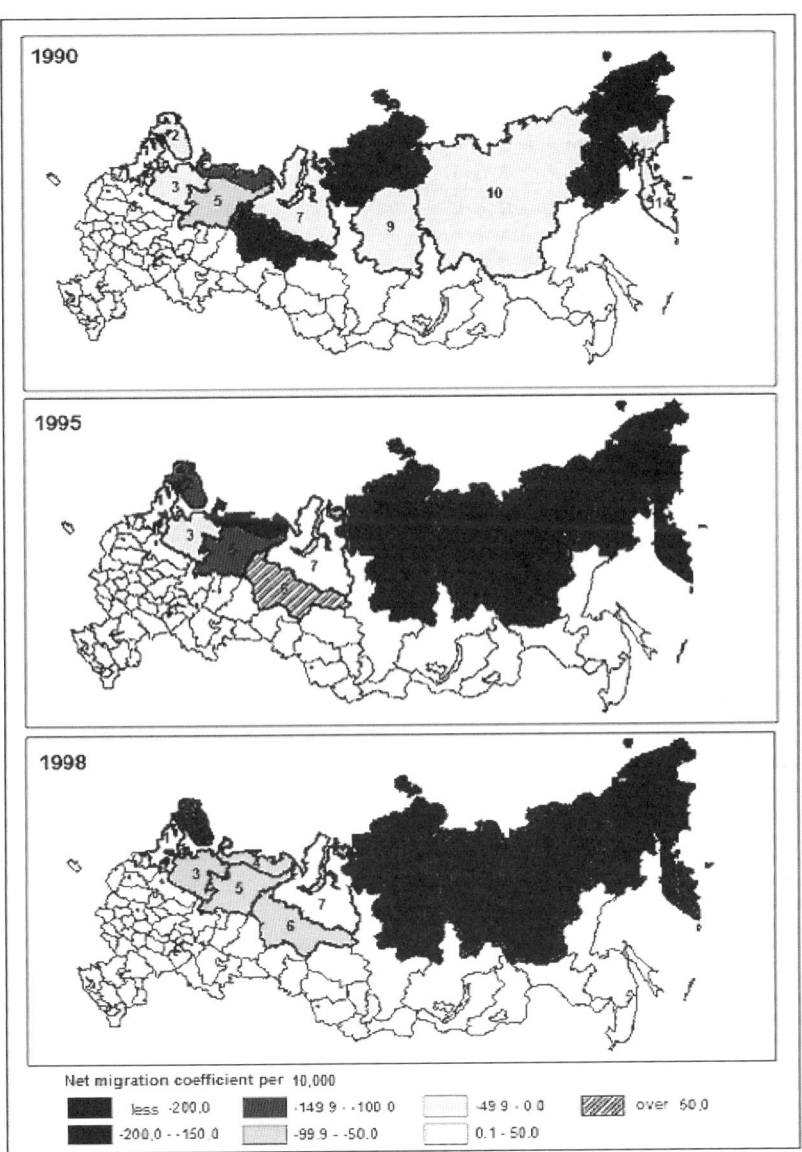

Figure 1. *Net migration coefficients in selected years* (Source: Goskomstat, various years). *Notations*: 1–Republic of Karelia, 2–Murmansk oblast', 3–Arkhangel'sk oblast', 4–Nenets AO, 5–Republic of Komi, 6–Khanty-Mansi AO, 7–Yamal-Nenets AO, 8–Taymyr (Dolgan-Nenets) AO, 9–Evenki AO, 10–Republic of Sakha (Yakutiya), 11–Magadan oblast', 12–Chukchi AO, 13–Koryak AO, 14–Kamchatka oblast'.

In 1997-1998, out-migration registered yet another increase (Fig. 2), which resulted in the second wave of out-migration from the North (although not all regions experienced this wave). If the first wave could be attributed to immediate consequences of the economic crisis when new labor in-migrants lost all incentive to remain in the North and quickly returned to the mainland, the second wave was associated with industrial restructuring, the non-payment crisis, and, most importantly, massive layoffs. The latter signified the final phase of over-employment that emerged as a result of the continuous loss in production volume and productivity in the early 1990s. Even if one considers the rather low output/labor and output/population ratios of the Soviet period as a 'norm,' by the mid-1990s the loss in production resulted in 4.5 million northerners (both workers and families) becoming an economically 'excessive' (surplus) population. However, many still held jobs (albeit they might not have been paid), driving the output/labor ratios down further.

The 'surplus workforce' phenomenon (that became an acute problem during the crisis, but is rooted back to the Soviet extensive industrialization, when a large workforce was attracted to the North to compensate for the lack of mechanization needed to fulfill production plans [Agranat 1992; Semenov and Petrov 2001]) was the major, but not the only driving force of intensive out-migration from the North. However, until about 1997, the actual loss of jobs was not as important a factor as one could expect, because of widespread hidden unemployment (up to 1.5 million in our estimate). In 1997-1998 the number of employed fell by 1.2 million and productivity started to rebound. Mass out-migration due to restructuring in the labor market was exacerbated in 1998-1999 by the August 1998 default crisis. This last wave of out-migration was generally over by 2000 (Fig. 2).

Lay-offs created an army of unemployed and an economically non-participating population. In fact, despite an overall population decline from 1991-1998 the non-participating population increased from 6.7 to 7.8 million, and the dependency ratio grew from 53% to 67%. Having lost their savings to price liberalization, left without primary incomes and frequently surviving on subsistence household production, many northerners lacked the financial means to out-migrate, i.e., they became 'hostages of the North' (Lynch 2003). This group (estimated in the millions) is a primary target of resettlement programs sponsored by federal and regional governments and international organizations (e.g., the World Bank). More importantly, the accumulation of the delayed demand for out-migration is a sign that the potential for out-migration and population loss in the North has not yet been exhausted (Kontorovich 2000). Growing mobility, spurred by economic satiation, may feed continuing out-migration.

Chapter 9: *Migration and Socio-Economic Well-Being in the Russian North*

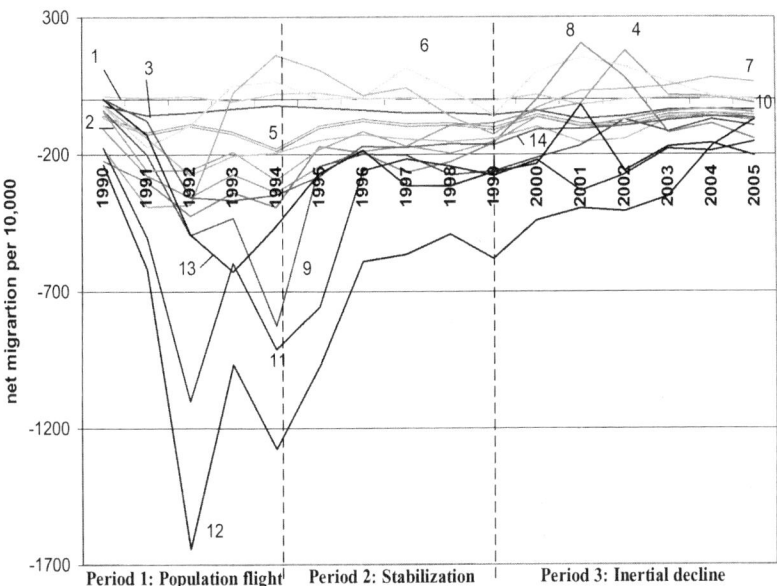

Figure 2. *Net migration coefficients in 1990-2005* (Source: Goskomstat, various years). Notations as in Figure 1.

Another change in migration flows from the North was caused by the longer-term implications of the default (1998). Due to the sharp drop in the ruble exchange rate, the financial possibilities of export sectors quickly rose, especially in the oil and gas industries. Moreover, shifts in the global market toward the growing value of raw materials and commodities favored resource economies (as much as the opposite trends devastated Russia's economy in the late 1980s and 1990s). As a result, in the early 2000s out-migration from the North decreased threefold (from 475,000 to 160,000), while in-migration increased as the labor market improved. The decline in out-migration was also related to the fact that many people who wanted and could out-migrate had already done so (Thompson 2004). In addition, a stabilization of migration processes (and relative improvement in underlying socio-economic push factors) was very uneven among and within regions (Fig. 2).

Despite recent positive tendencies, out-migration still dominates in the North, although the region now loses only 0.3-0.4% of the population annually, compared to over 2.0% in the 1990s. Most regions (which are neither oil nor gas powerhouses) continue to experience net population losses. In 2000, few oil and gas producing regions (Yamal-Nenets, Hanty-Mansi, Nenets) demonstrated positive net migration. By 2005 oil and gas districts either had very low net migration coefficients (Khanty-Mansi -3.0 per 10,000 and Nenets -14.0), or high in-migration (61.0 in Yamal-Nenets). In 1990 the net migration coefficient in Yamal-Nenets was -143.0, while in 2005 it was +61.0. Still, many depressed regions (Taymyr and Koryak AO, Magadan oblast') have negative net migration. In most territories, migration continues to be the main factor causing depopulation and a major contributor to the on-going demographic crisis (Semenov and Petrov 2001). For instance, in 2004 migration loss in the Komi Republic amounted to 5,900 people. This constituted 58% of the total population decline or about 0.6% of total population (FAGSKR 2004).

To summarize migration trends in the North during the years of the crisis, a typology of regions was developed using average net migration rates (ANMR) between 1990 and 1999. The results (Fig. 3) illustrate the degree of migration-driven deformation experienced by regional demographic systems, i.e., they show how strongly the regional demographic systems have been affected by out-migration.

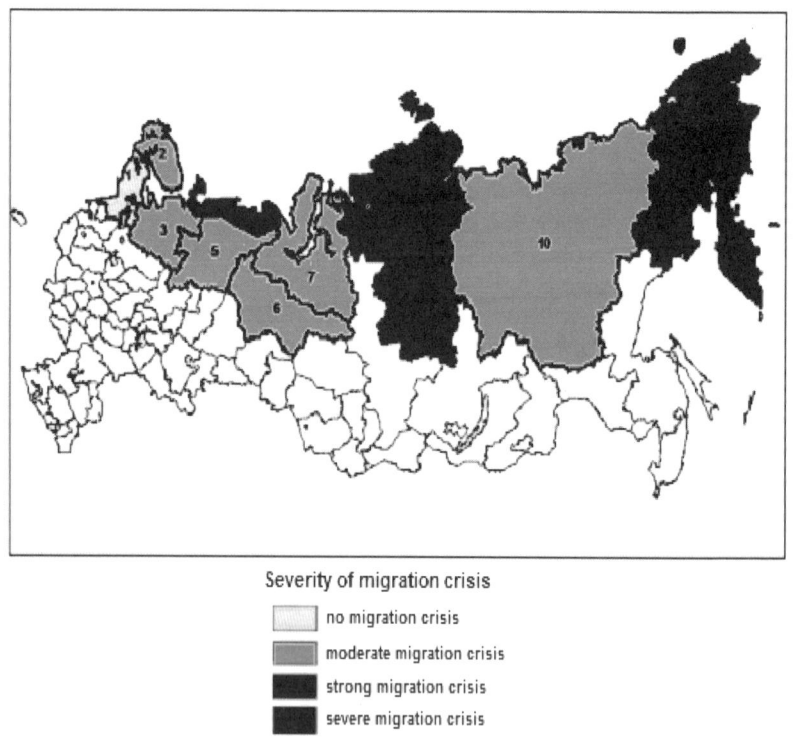

Figure 3. *Types of regions by severity of migration crisis in the 1990s*

We identified *four types* of regions: 1) Regions with little evidence of a migration crisis (ANMR above 0) include only the Republic of Karelia (which in terms of migration was more similar to Northwestern Russia than to other Northern regions); 2) Regions with moderate forms of a migration crisis (ANMR between 0 and -200) include the Republics of Komi and Sakha (Yakutiya), Magadan, Archangel'sk and Murmansk oblast's, Khanty-Mansi and Yamalo-Nenets AO; 3). Regions with a strong migration crisis (ANMR between –200 and –400) consisted of four economically marginal territories; and, 4) regions which experienced a devastating migration crisis (ANMR exceeding -400) included the Chukchi and Koryak AO and the Magadan oblast.

Socio-Economic Hardships and Well-Being in Northern Regions

Cost of Living

One of the most notorious economic problems that can be seen as a strong push factor of out-migration from the North is cost of living. Although the cost of living in the North is expected to be higher than in the mainland, differentials experienced in the 1990s reached unprecedented levels, and thus, despite possible high wages, real incomes plunged. (This exacerbated the real income gradient between the North and South, and, according to the economic models of migration, increased the propensity to out-migrate). If in the northern regions of Canada and in Alaska cost differentials are usually about 1.5, for the northern regions of Russia it is not uncommon to have three-fold cost differences (Fig. 4).

Cost hikes in the North, in addition to the usual reasons characteristic of all remote areas, were driven by systematic failures of the northern delivery system throughout the 1990s. An acute deficit of goods, fuel, and sometimes groceries was the major driver of ever-increasing prices. Of course, the liberalization of prices in the early 1990s itself reduced the cost subsidies created by the Soviet non-market pricing system. But it not only contributed to price hikes, it also made production of goods and food products at local Arctic enterprises (which earlier were directly or indirectly subsidized) increasingly costly (and sometimes impossible). As a result, the price of a standard food basket in the North (determined by Rosstat for every Russian region) in 1998-1999 was 1.1 to 3.1 times the Russian average. It was especially high in the most remote Chukchi, Evenki and Koryak AOs. Price increases during the 1990s (sometimes drastic due to periodical delivery failures) were most noticeable in peripheral Koryak AO, Taymyr AO, and Kamchatka oblast.' Only in the 2000s did northern regions see a slow, but gradual decrease in cost differentials.

Migration in the Circumpolar North

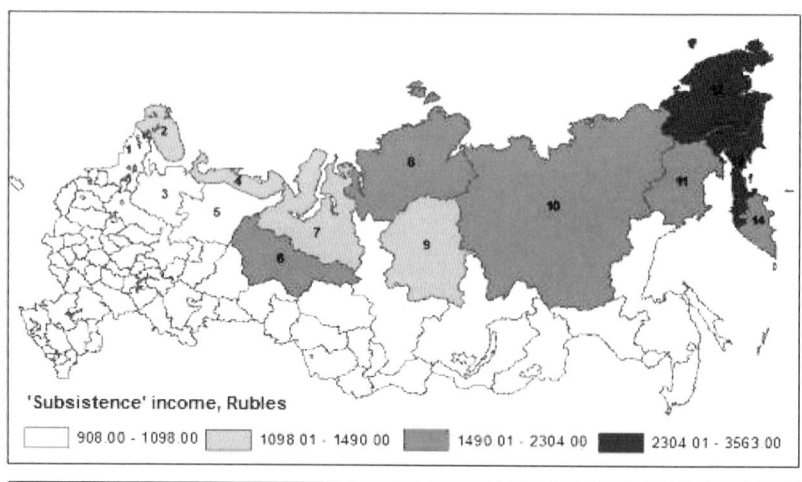

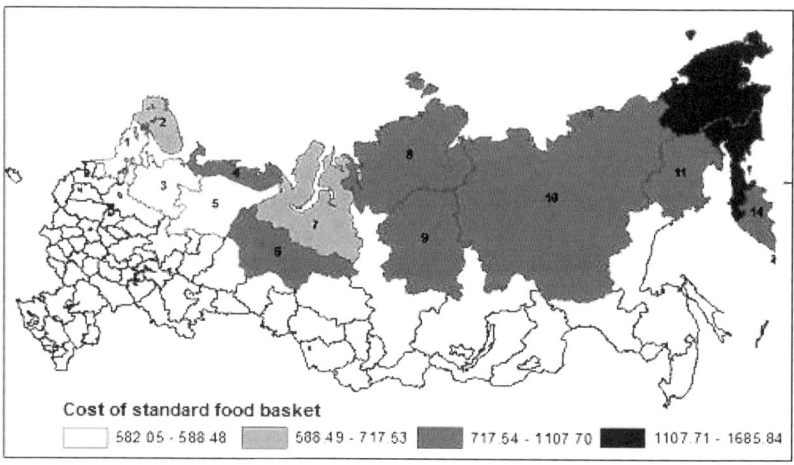

Figure 4. *'Subsistence' income and cost of standard food basket in the Russian North (1999)* (Source: Goskomstat 2000, all figures in Rubles)

Income Inequality and Poverty

Inequality in incomes is one of the most urgent problems in Russia (Hanson 2001; Fedorov 2002). Moreover, it is well documented that inequalities between and within regions have been increasing, and the gap between 'have' and 'have-not' regions and population groups has been widening (Bradshaw and Vartapetov 2003). Several northern regions, such as Khanty-Mansi and Yanal-Nenets AOs have high per capita GDP figures and average incomes, but also have skewed income distributions, when many or most people experience different levels of poverty. In fact, these okrugs and the Komi Republic have the highest Gini coefficients in Russia, after the city of Moscow and Samara oblast' (Rosstat 2006). In the Komi Republic, the income of the poorest 10% in 2004 was 1,600 rubles per month, compared to 27,800 for the richest 10%. The differential between the richest and the poorest was thus 1:17.1 (FAGSKR 2004). Moreover, incomes of the poorest group were growing slower than incomes of the richest group. This further exacerbated differentiation in material well-being: the richest group is sharing an ever larger percent of total income (in 2000 the 20% richest residents accounted for 45.3 % of total income while in 2005 their share increased to 48.2%).

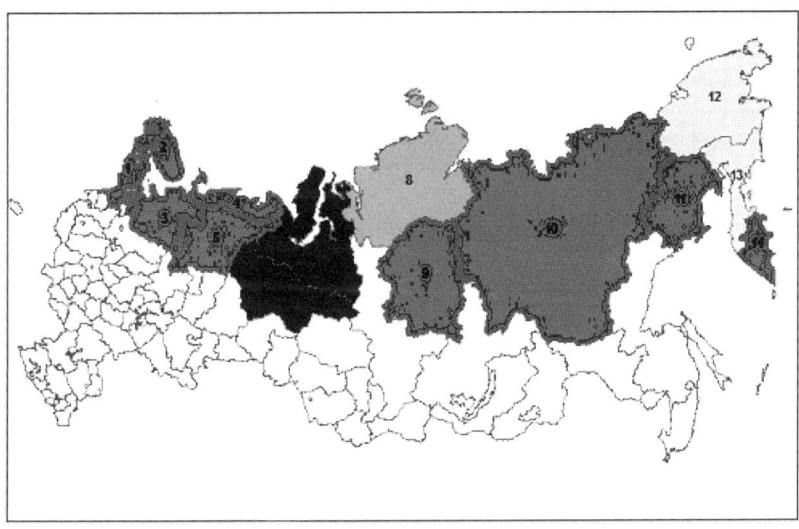

Ratio of average money income and 'subsistence' income

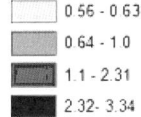
0.56 - 0.63
0.64 - 1.0
1.1 - 2.31
2.32 - 3.34

Figure 5. *Ratio of average monetary income and 'subsistence' income in 1999.* (Source: Goskomstat 2000)

During the decade of crisis, extreme poverty plagued most of the northern regions. The ratio of average income and 'subsistence' or 'minimum' income (definition in Appendix 1) is frequently used as a proxy for 'real wages' to illuminate the economic hardships of northerners. While few oil and gas regions demonstrated high ratios (although given income polarization, poverty in these regions was also substantial), there were a number of territories in which incomes were substantially below subsistence levels. In fact, by the late 1990s, only five regions had a higher ratio than the nation's average. More revealingly, in several regions the 'minimum' income ('required' for subsistence) was much greater than the average reported income (in fact, 2.0 times in Koryak and 1.3 times in Chukchi AO).[3] In another five regions, the average income barely covered the minimum (Fig. 5). As economic theories of migration would suggest, comparatively low real wages alone would generate a strong migration push.

In the 1990s, poverty in most northern regions exceeded the national level. As recently as 2000, 89% of the population in the Evenki AO and 50% in the Chukchi AO had incomes below a 'subsistence' income. Despite recent improvements in the economic situation (now these figures are 'only' 57.5 and 25%, respectively), the problem of mass poverty is still urgent across the North. In the Komi Republic, with one of the lowest levels of poverty in the North, the proportion of the population with incomes below the poverty line in 2003 was 19%, and the per capita income of those people constituted only 69% of the 'subsistence' income (FAGSKR 2004:13).

Unemployment and Non-Participation
High unemployment among non-Aboriginal populations is rarely observed in resource frontier regions. One obvious reason is that jobless people (excluding Aboriginal northerners) quickly leave remote areas to seek employment elsewhere. It is extremely difficult to address unemployment locally because the northern labor market is usually very truncated and inflexible. In Russia, mass lay-offs and limited mobility of financially squeezed populations created an army of unemployed northerners. In the mid-1990s, unemployment rates (calculated using International Labour Organizaton—ILO methodology)[4] in many northern regions quickly rose above Russia's rate (Fig. 6). Notwithstanding recent economic growth and a decline in unemployment, the unemployment rate in nine of 14 territories still remains above the country's average (Rosstat 2006). It is especially high in Taymyr AO (14.0%), Nenets AOs (11.4%), Kamchatka oblast' (9.5%), and the Republics of Komi (11.5%) and Sakha (8.9%). However, recent years have seen a substantial decrease in unemployment rates across the North. This decrease is related to intensive out-migration in preceding years, labor market restructuring, and a new resource boom.

---

[3] These figures, however, do not consider the traditional sector, barter, and unofficial incomes.
[4] The difference between International Labour Organization-based indicators of unemployment and registered unemployment is substantial. The unemployment level in northern regions by ILO standards is two to four times higher than registered unemployment [in Komi Republic in 2005 it was 11.5 % vs. 2.8% (Rosstat 2006)]. This may be explained by the fact that many people in remote areas are not registering as unemployed.

Chapter 9: *Migration and Socio-Economic Well-Being in the Russian North*

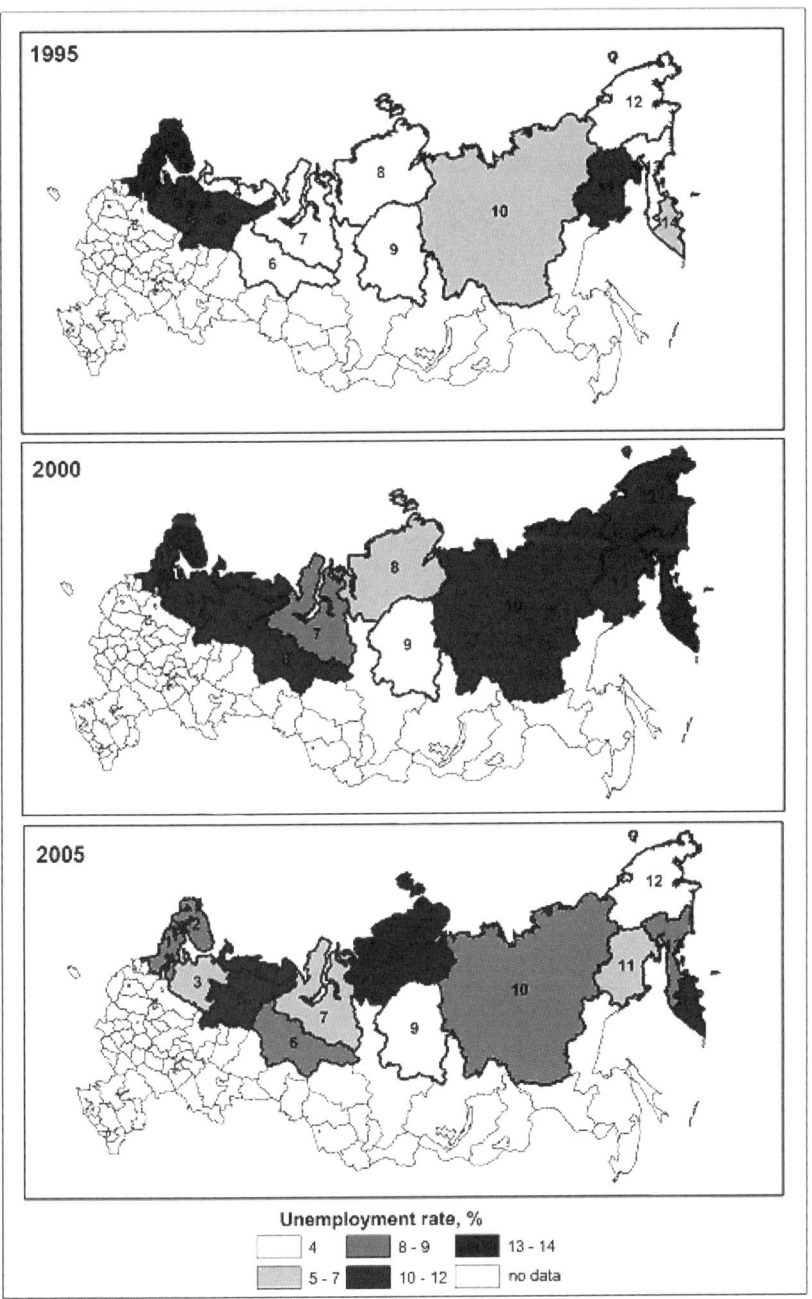

Figure 6. *Unemployment rate 1995-2005.* (Source: Rosstat 2006).

Interestingly, the booming oil and gas regions of West Siberia (Fig. 6) have rather high unemployment rates at just below the national average (7.6%). Despite an improving job market, the level of unemployment in these regions is slow to decline. It seems that positive net migration registered in these jurisdictions is not associated with progress in socio-economic well-being with respect to employment. This important observation may be an illustration of a decoupling effect, when a resource sector to a large degree uses in-migrant labor and simultaneously (due to small multiplier effects) creates a limited number of jobs in local non-primary sectors.

Even more severe than the problem of unemployment is the problem of non-participation. Employment rates have been falling throughout the 1990s—from 48.0% in 1991 to 33.0% in 1998 (data for regions of the Far North and equated areas)—leaving two-thirds of the total population to be unemployed or non-participating. In the Komi Republic, the percentage of the non-participating population rose sharply from 12% in 1992 to 22% in 2003 (FAGSKR 2004). Of course, there is a 'shadow' economy—household production, subsistence agriculture, hunting and other alternative (and informal) forms of employment—which are likely to affect this figure, but still employment levels are notably low. Before the crisis, rather small employment and high non-participation rates were attributable to the young age structure. In the 1990s, mass lay-offs, ageing and the 'hostages of the North' phenomenon discussed earlier, contributed to increasing non-participation and, thus, dependency ratios.

Summarizing *the geographies of economic hardship*, one can distinguish two polarizing groups of regions: 'haves' (Khanty-Mansi, and Yamal-Nenets AOs) and 'have-nots' (Magadan, Archangel'sk, Kamchatka obtast,' Chukchi, Koryak, Taymyr, Evenki AOs), with a third group at an intermediate position (Komi, Karelia, Sakha and Murmansk oblast). During the 1990s and 2000s the discrepancy between the two poles of economic prosperity (measured in income/living costs dynamic) increased, suggesting that the gap between haves and have-nots had widened (as in Russia itself [Bradshaw and Vartapetov 2003]).

Social Services and Infrastructure

The organization of social services (such as healthcare, public education, culture, social care, etc.) and the development of necessary infrastructure have always been problematic in the North (Wood 1987). A shortage of basic services and facilities was notorious throughout Soviet times, a problem that emerged as a result of rapid and poorly planned population growth and urbanization in northern regions. In the 1990s, even the scarce infrastructure experienced a fast degradation. The crisis most negatively affected cultural and health services. Between 1990 and 1997, the per capita number of hospital beds declined 10%, the number of doctors fell by 5%

and the number of nurses, in most regions, by 10-25%, whereas morbidity increased by 10% (Goskomstat 2000). Most drastically, the healthcare system 'shrunk' in the Evenki AO, Koryak AO, Kamchatka and Murmansk oblasts and the Republic of Sakha. In addition, the crisis eroded special medical services and childcare support systems. For example, at the peak of the crisis, the northern regions winessed closures of 139 obstetric care centers (1993-1996), 24 children policlinics (1994-1996) and a 20% decrease of available spaces in pregnancy care facilities (Goskomstat 2000).

The number of clubs and libraries also substantially declined. Theater and museum attendance fell between two and five times (depending on the region). Local publishing activity decreased dramatically, contributing to an increasing 'information hunger' in remote regions. These deteriorating conditions adversely affected social cohesion in the North by exacerbating social discomfort and the feeling of isolation and disconnectedness from the 'mainland.' They most likely amplified the "frustration of living in the North" cited by many migrants as a reason to out-migrate (NEI 1998).

Despite a shortage of or an inadequate quality of existing housing, new construction in the 1990s almost completely stopped, falling nearly five times. Although the housing problem was somewhat relieved by depopulation, many regions still had not reached the nationwide 'norms' on per capita footage. The lack of proper building maintenance in conditions of severe climate and permafrost quickly dilapidated housing stock. For example, in 2004 40% of Noril'sk's existing stock required repairs (Noril'sk 2005). In addition, northerners were subjected to systematic interruptions of municipal services, including wintertime heating shutdowns and electricity blackouts (Kontorovich 2000). Not surprisingly, 70% of respondents to the World Bank survey pointed to inadequate housing conditions as a possible reason to out-migrate (World Bank 2001).

Socio-Economic Well-Being
Instead of focussing exclusively on particular variables to evaluate economic well-being in the northern regions of Russia, we opted to develop an integrated socio-economic well-being index (SEWI). The SEWI is a sum of location quotients of several socio-economic variables (normalized by respective national means): percentage of residents with incomes below 'subsistence' income, ratio of average income and 'subsistence' income, unemployment rate, morbidity rate, and food consumption basket. We did not consider absolute values of income or prices as they are always higher in the North. Previous studies discussed some difficulties with using official Russian statistics for analyzing socio-economic conditions, in particular issues related to questionable methodologies of collecting and representing data (e.g., Bradshaw and Vartapetov 2003). For instance, official unemployment figures frequently underestimate real unemployment, and

'subsistence' income does not properly reflect the real cost of living. However, these data have to be used, as they are the only available source.

The geographic distribution of the SEWI in 1998 is presented in Figure 6. (We chose 1998 as a year of illustration, because, while post-socialist reforms had already fully unfolded, the post-default tendencies had not yet progressed.) A SEWI of 100 indicates that all socio-economic characteristics of a region are at or exceed the national average (benchmark). The Sakha Republic has a maximum SEWI of 50 (meaning that only 50% of the indicators make the national benchmark) and two more regions reached 40%. The remaining regions scored 30 and below, including six regions with an SEWI of 10. This typology clearly demonstrates the depth of the socio-economic crisis in the Russian North. The particular severity of economic hardships in northern territories is well documented in various case studies (Lynch 2003; Round 2006). Low composite levels of well-being most certainly will contribute as push factors of migration. In the following section, we turn to a preliminary analysis of the interrelationships between socio-economic wellness of population and migration from northern regions, using both composite (the SEWI) and several individual measures of well-being.

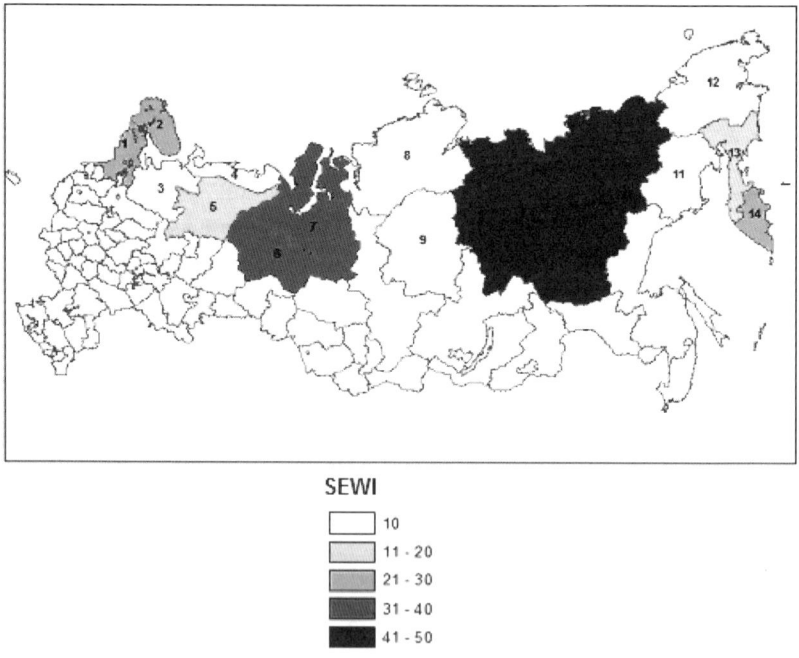

Figure 7. *Socio-economic well-being index in the Russian North*

Chapter 9: *Migration and Socio-Economic Well-Being in the Russian North*

Toward an Understanding of the Interrelationships Between Economic Well-Being and Migration: A Preliminary Empirical Analysis

Some evidence regarding socio-economic factors of migration from the North has already been collected and has pointed to a number of important observations. The World Bank survey of region–participants of the restructuring program (Magadan oblast', Noril'sk, Vorkuta) in 1999 provides important insight into people's motives and possible driving forces of migration. Most northerners (72% of whom considered out-migrating) referred to some aspects of socio-economic well-being as likely factors that would affect their decision to move: 45% cited the lack of income to buy food, and 39% the lack of money to purchase clothing. Three fourths of respondents spent 75% of their budget on food. Seventy percent reported unsatisfactory housing conditions (World Bank 2001). However, relatively few northerners gave a great deal of weight to employment, with only 6% of respondents mentioning a job opportunity elsewhere as the reason to migrate (Heleniak 1999).

Economic problems coincide with other push factors, such as the severity of the northern environment, isolation, and family ties. The survey of migrants (who moved from northern regions to Pskov, Rostov, Novosibirsk oblast's and Bashkortostan) conducted by the Netherlands Economic Institute showed that a "desire to return to the South" (52%) and climate severity and health issues (38%) were the leading causes of migration. Low income and unemployment were mentioned by 27% of the respondents (NEI 1998). The weight of economic factors was even lower for migrants born in the North (19%), who emphasized the frustration of living in the North, discomfort, and family circumstances.

The survey results suggest that migration from the Russian North is a very complex process affected my many factors. Most importantly, the evidence indicates that (in contrast to conventional economic models) social and economic hardships at the origin, not economic benefits at destination, are likely to be the primary drivers. Consequently, an analysis of migration factors should emphasize socio-economic conditions in northern regions. Our study focuses on regional-level socio-economic factors, and particularly on socio-economic well-being, which, as implied by surveys, have a profound influence on migration decisions in the North. Based on data for 14 northern regions (Rosstat, various years), this section presents an exploratory analysis of relationships between economic well-being and migration in the 1990s.

As mentioned earlier, at this stage we are not aiming to develop a comprehensive model of migration from fourteen regions of the North. Instead, we use a set of statistical techniques to collect more evidence about socio-economic well-being as a factor of migration. We adopt a structural push–pull factor model as a means to consider socio-economic factors as inducing or limiting the propensity of individuals to migrate, given that individuals' behaviour is governed by the rationale of maximizing quality of life (not just real income). Since motivation for migration from the North is highly complex (Heleniak 1999; NEI 1998), we do not expect socio-economic factors to be sufficient to fully explain migration flows. However, we do anticipate our analysis to be more exhaustive than traditional wage/income gradient models. Our modeling exercise focuses on migration processes in the 1990s, as it was the period of most intensive population loss.

The initial choice of variables was driven by the conventional logic of economic migration modeling (Stillwell and Congdon 1991). The net migration rate was taken as a dependent variable. Among individual socio-economic indicators, we selected several specific socio-economic variables: average earnings and income, 'subsistence' income, cost of a standard food basket, and unemployment rate (*see* definitions in Appendix 1). We used both income and earnings figures to illuminate the role of non-wage incomes (social subsidies, monetarized household and traditional economies, etc.) After analyzing traditional variables, we closely examined the relationships between migration and the SEWI, as it is a more comprehensive measure of socio-economic well-being.

Table 1. Correlation Between Net Migration and Selected Socio-Economic Indicators.

	NMR	MIN	FOODCOST	EARNINGS	INCOME	UNEMPL1	UNEMPL2
NMR	1.000	-.720**	-.808**	-.294	.111	.399	.555*
MIN		1.000	.924**	.523	-.036	-.291	-.503
FOODCOST			1.000	.505	-.093	-.501	-.667**
EARNINGS				1.000	.777**	-.456	-.334
INCOME					1.000	.182	.056
UNEMPL1						1.000	.677**
UNEMPL2							1.000

Notes: all data for 1999, UNEMPL2 for 1998 (Rosstat, 2004); UNEMPL1 is the unemployment rate in the year of migration, UNEMPL2 in the year preceding migration; ** significant at 0.01 level, * at 0.05 level (two-tailed).

The cross-correlation matrix (Table 1) suggests that the net migration coefficient is more strongly associated with two socio-economic variables: current cost of living and unemployment (in the previous year).

Interestingly enough, the correlation with income is not significant. Moreover, earnings (i.e., official salaries) is not only an insignificant variable, but has an unexpected effect (high earnings would be associated with out-migration), which is opposite to that expected for level of income. This again points to the fact that cost of living, not wages, drives migration in the North. It also drives home the point that the policy of high wage incentives, practiced in Soviet times to attract permanent migrants to the northern regions, was inevitably fruitless (Agranat 1992). The impacts and magnitudes of relationships suggest that both unemployment and high cost of living are likely to be strong push factors stimulating out-migration.

With respect to the SEWI, even a simple visual analysis of Figures 3 and 6 reveals a correspondence between this index and migration. If more formal measures of association are considered, the correlation between the SEWI and the average net migration coefficient for the 1990s is approximately 0.50, which, given the small sample, is a good result. Interestingly, the strength of correlation is noticeably higher in the Asiatic North (0.67) than in the European North, suggesting that the effect of socio-economic conditions on migration process in the Asiatic North may be higher. Theoretically, this is a plausible argument, because in regions of the Asiatic North, most residents are migrants with notoriously high mobility attracted by economic incentives introduced a relatively short time ago (largely since the 1960s) ; and, on the other hand, the severity of the economic crisis was outstanding. Thus, migration processes in these regions are extremely sensitive to changes in socio-economic well-being in general and the labor market dynamic in particular.

In order to navigate among possible socio-economic factors of migration, we performed the principle components analysis. The original variables list remained unchanged with only the addition of the SEWI. Admittedly, the initial set of variables was relatively short, so rather than shorten the variables list, factor analysis was used to group variables for their correct individual interpretation. Despite the fact that some of the individual variables were already used to calculate the SEWI, we were interested in whether the latter (which also considers more 'social' parameters such as morbidity) would exhibit equally strong covariance with all the main economic characteristics. The net migration coefficient was later also included as a variable to examine the covariance between net migration and socio-economic indicators.

The analysis (PCA with varimax rotation) identifies two principle components with eigenvalues higher than one and accounting for 83.8% of common variance (Table 2, test 1). The first component can be called the *economic stability–hardship factor,* because it includes both living cost indicators and unemployment rate. Our tests show that if the net migration coefficient is entered as one of the covariates (Table 2, test 2), it has the highest factor loading in this component, suggesting that the covariance of net migration with these variables is the strongest. These results corroborate the correlation analysis discussed above. The second component is the *socio-economic prosperity factor* with high loadings of income, wages and the SEWI. If the net migration coefficient is entered, its loading on component two is small (it is high for the natural growth coefficient, but this is beyond the scope of our analysis). The conclusion of the factor analysis is that while there are two major latent dimensions of socio-economic wellness, migration in the 1990s, as expected, was primarily related to the economic stability and hardship components of well-being.

Table 2. Groups of Socio-Economic Factors of Migration.

Indicators	Factor-groups			
	Test 1		Test 2 (with NMR as covariate)	
	Economic stability–hardship	Socio-economic prosperity	Economic stability–hardship	Socio-economic prosperity
FOODCOST	.973	-.05	.973	-.03
MIN	.915	.04	.907	.05
UNEMPL	-.773	.08	-.748	.06
INCOME	-.0.02	.958	-.0.02	.954
SEWI	-.297	.828	-.297	.823
EARNINGS	.565	.791	.565	.805
NMR	----	----	-.865	.154

Notes: Principal components with Varimax rotation and Kayser normalization; UNEMPL is the unemployment rate in the preceding year.

Keeping the identified factor groups in mind, we now turn to developing a regression model. An empirical regression model is a typical instrument used to operationalize theoretical models of migration—push–pull factor models in particular (Stillwell and Congdon 1991). We use a simple OLS linear regression model.[5] Although, initially, all the above variables were considered, the final regression equation excluded highly correlated and collinear variables (income and earnings, 'subsistence' minimum and food basket price). The purpose of fitting the linear regression model was to attempt to explain net migration using indicators of socio-economic well-being. Observations in previous sections provide important evidence that such dependency between migration and well-being is likely to exist. Our expectation is that the model will have a relatively good explanatory power, although it will be limited by the socio-economic nature of included variables, thus omitting other causes of migration.

---

[5] We did not run a more typical log-transformed version of a regression model since our dependent variable (net migration) has negative values.

The net migration coefficient is chosen as a dependent variable, and six socio-economic indicators as regressors (all for 1999). Given that MIN and FOODCOST and INCOME and EARNINGS form the same latent factors (Table 2), they introduce multicollinearity. To ensure the model's quality, one variable from each pair has to be excluded. Since FOODPRICE and INCOME had higher factor loading in the PCA, we opted to retain them and delete the other two. Regression analysis uses a backward stepwise procedure that iteratively eliminates statistically insignificant regressors, thus improving the model's quality. After these adjustments were made, the backward stepwise linear regression procedure was run. The resulting equation is:

$$NMR = 69.6 - 0.26*FOODCOST + \varepsilon \quad (1)$$

The model retained only one variable, namely, the standard food basket cost; all other variables were filtered out as statistically insignificant. Although the explanatory power of this model is moderate ($r2=0.65$), it is highly statistically significant with no multicollinearity effect. The result is very interesting, because it suggests that the price of food (a proxy of living costs and accessibility of main necessities), not unemployment or wage levels, was the most important factor in migration. This reiterates an earlier observation that living costs, especially food prices, were the main push factor of migration from the Russian North. This migration was, in fact, sometimes 'forced' by circumstances, that is, when people became 'economic refugees' as they out-migrate, having no opportunity to provide for themselves at the origin. Conversely, as demonstrated by Canadian and US experiences, only a gradual decline in living costs can stabilize northern populations and ensure that human capital is adequately reproduced (Agranat 1992; Petrov 2006).

The regression model demonstrates that during the crisis, migration processes in the North were more tightly associated with short-term socio-economic conditions, such as price fluctuations. High prices may have worked as triggers of migration (which induced other economic and non-economic incentives), while other factors provided an additional push for out-migration to occur. Because our model is not devoid of shortcomings (most obvious are the small sample size and the limited number of variables), findings presented in this section should be treated as preliminary and carefully studied further and confirmed with more elaborate analyses.

Contemplating Consequences of Out-Migration: Ageing and Loss of Human Capital

Whereas economic factors of mass out-migration from the North have received some attention, much less is known about the economic consequences of this trend. A most evident result of out-migration is the loss of labor force, and, more importantly, human capital (including the 'brain drain'). Given that mobility is always age- and gender-specific, migration-driven deformation may cause significant changes in the age–sex structure of a population and labor force, which could significantly jeopardize future economic development. There are some theoretical and empirical indications that depopulation in the frontier also leads to considerable long-term economic losses associated with decreased consumption (Petrov 2007).

Age characteristics of migration from the Russian North are quite typical for frontier regions in crisis, but they sometimes contradict Ravenstein-style 'laws.'[6] According to existing surveys, the majority of out-migrants are of working age. Lusin and Korchak (1999) estimated the share of working-age migrants as 70% of total flow, of which 60% belong to the 16 to 25 age cohort. Similarly, Komi data (FAGSKR 2004) demonstrates that the working-age population constitutes 60-70% of total migration losses (63.5% in 2003). Heleniak (1999) presented data on out-migration from selected northern regions indicating five main out-migrating groups: 30-45 years of age (labor migrants and spouses), 55-58 years of age for men and 51-57 years of age for women (retirees), 20-23 years of age (young specialists), 17-18 years of age (students) and 6-8 years of age (children of the first group).

It is also interesting to note who does not migrate. The late 40s to early 50s age group was least likely to migrate. One of the interpretations of this fact refers to the 'sitting-in' syndrome, when people do not move until they receive (or become eligible for) 'northern' retirement packages. Overall, the outflow of the younger economically active cohort, and often stable pre-retirement and retired population resulted in a rapid ageing of the population and depletion of demographic and labor force potential.

Although most northern regions were still demographically much younger than the rest of Russia (the percentage of people over 60 years of age in all regions combined was 10.7% compared to 21.0% in all of Russia), ageing in the Russian North was extremely rapid. In some regions, the share of persons in older age groups increased several fold: for example, in Chukchi AO it was threefold. If, in the late 1980s, 11 regions were considered demographically 'young,' by 1996 only four territories would be described in that way. The dependency ratio rose concurrently, and brought

---

[6] *See* Ravenstein (1885); Tobler (1995).

additional economic burdens such as pensions and social services for one million retirees.

The intensive out-migration of young people and the limited mobility of older persons (due to high costs of moving, attachment to localities and social networks, or the 'sitting-in' syndrome[7]) was the major factor that induced rapid ageing of the population as a whole. The Northern labor force also matured, partially because younger workers migrated to the mainland. This is especially worrisome given the upcoming baby-boom retirement wave. In sum, the North lost its demographic 'capital.'

Mass labor migration from the North has also undermined the quality of human capital. Not only has the labor force aged significantly, but it has tended to be less skilled and less educated. In contrast to many other peripheries, formal levels of education in the Russian North historically have been higher than Russia's average, albeit still far below the country's urban core. However, among the educated labor force, the structure of educational attainment has shifted toward lesser levels of training, particularly to professional post-secondary non-university degrees. All northern regions show below average proportions of university-educated personnel (Rosstat 2006). Whereas Russia's labor force during the 1990s and 2000s has been becoming more educated, the educational assets of many northern regions have been depleting.

The 'brain drain' was especially noticeable in territories with the strongest out-migration: Koryak, Evenki, Taymyr, Chukchi AOs, and the Republic of Sakha lost the bulk of their human capital. Only a handful of regions experienced the growth of 'talent' (e.g., Karelia, the only northern region with positive migration trends through the 1990s). On the other hand, the process of regaining 'talent' is very problematic even in booming resource regions: the 'brain gain' registered in West Siberia appears to be quite limited (levels of personnel education between 1998 and 2005 show only marginal growth [Goskomstat 1999; Rosstat 2005; 2006]). In addition, northern regions lack in their capacity to advance education and training locally, making the local labor supply ill-equipped to respond to a possible growth in employment demand if the resource boom continues, or to a further industrial restructuring, if the boom turns bust.

Recent Trends and Policy Questions

Despite recent improvements in macroeconomic conditions in most of Russia's regions (including the North), many socio-economic problems persist. As we alluded to earlier, new economic opportunities have not alleviated these problems, in fact, they have sometimes exacerbated them.

---

[7] See more on this matter in Thompson (2004), and Round (2006), this volume.

For example, the gap between the richest and poorest populations in northern regions continues to increase, and unemployment and non-participation remain extremely high, while income to cost of living ratios outside the oil and gas island of Western Siberia are at or below average. It may be argued that this situation is a reflection of the 'resource curse' or 'Dutch disease' that increasingly infects Russia's resource-dependent economy (Ahrend 2005). The concentration of resource royalties in the hands of the Federal Government, after regions lost their rights to retain the bulk of their 'resourse windfall' in 2004 (Kriukov *et al.* 2004), deprives even oil and gas rich territories of the ability to use their advantage to address local needs.

Although out-migration has been generally declining and in-migration increasing since 2000, most regions continue to register a net population loss (Fig. 2). This is partially attributable to continuing difficult socio-economic conditions in the North and low levels of well-being compared to the 'mainland.' Another source of loss are government resettlement programs designed to move 'excessive' populations from the North (Thompson 2002; World Bank 2001; *see also* Heleniak this volume). If, in the 1990s, these programs were merely declarative schemes, they recently became more tangible (although most remain ineffective). However, Russia still lacks a comprehensive approach to dealing with demo-economic issues in the North. The regulations adopted by the Russian Government and, in particular, the *Concept of the state support of economic and social development of the regions of the North* (2000), emphasize the need to regulate northern migration by improving labor market conditions and economic well-being. They advocate such measures as prioritizing local employment, implementing contracting and other forms of labor market regulation, changing the wage indexation system, supporting out-migration of retirees, enhancing fly-in fly-out methods of resource exploitation, etc. (Pravitel'stvo 2000). In other words, there is a growing understanding that both market and non-market mechanisms are needed to overcome the socio-economic crisis (Kotlyakov and Agranat 1994)—a winning combination illustrated by the Canadian and U.S. experiences (Agranat 1992; Petrov 2006). However, a comprehensive *regional* demo-economic policy targeting the Russian North is yet to be developed.

On another point, the resource boom of 2000 that helped northern regions begin recuperating from the devastation of the 1990s, will inevitably end. If the stability of oil and gas prices is an uncertainty, resource depletion is an unavoidable problem. Production of Soviet-era oil and gas fields is poised to decrease in the near future, and the availability and profitability of new reserves is uncertain (Dienes 2004). Therefore, adopting northern economic systems to meet the challenges of an eventual slowdown in the resource sector and depopulation is, arguably, the most important long-term issue of northern development. This makes studying mechanisms and implications of the migration crisis of the 1990s even more valuable. Many, including the authors, have argued that population is an important asset that may allow some northern economies to undergo a transformation to post-industrial, non-staple, more diversified forms (Agranat 1992; Petrov 2006, 2008). Others have pointed out that population also has a geopolitical role in guaranteeing Russia's sovereignty over remote areas (e.g., Kontorovich 2000). Thus, 'population development/planning' especially human capital development in geographic research, socially-oriented observations and policy-making in the Russian North should become as central issues as 'resource development' (Vlasova, 2009).

Concluding Remarks

Our preliminary analysis points to some important conclusions. First, socio-economic well-being is an important factor of migration in the Russian North: socio-economic variables considered in this survey explained at least 65% of net migration from northern regions. Among these variables, two latent factors were identified that contributed to population change in the 1990s: stability–hardship and economic prosperity. Although de-industrialization and deteriorating labor market conditions have served as crucial factors of out-migration, our model demonstrates that critical changes in socio-economic wellness associated with the crisis, particularly with increased living costs and fallen real wages, had more significance as 'triggers' of migration in the 1990s. These patterns, to a degree, deviate from the conventional 'logics' of migration processes. As noted earlier, the north-to-south migration in the Russian North violates some of the 'Ravenstein laws' and fundamental assumptions of the gravity model (Petrov 2005, 2006). Such systematic differences need to be further explored.

Secondly, we argued that to better understand migration mechanisms in the North it is necessary not to cherry-pick particular economic parameters (wage, unemployment, etc.), but to consider socio-economic well-being as a complex phenomenon, which includes an array of social and economic attributes. In this paper, we merely started implementing this approach by developing the Socio-Economic Well-being Index (SEWI) and using it as a variable in our models. Not surprisingly, we found that the level of well-being in the 1990s in most northern regions (even oil and gas rich regions) was exceptionally low. Future work should focus on designing an even more comprehensive parameter that would measure the quality of life in all its material and non-material complexity. The quality of modeling results will greatly improve if this measure includes indicators directly representing household and individual behaviors.

Among other points, this contribution offered an historical model of the migration crisis in the North covering three periods (1992-1994, 1995-1998/99 and post-2000). In each of the periods, migration processes differed in intensity, pattern, or mechanism. We also developed a cumulative typology of northern regions by measuring the degree of migration crisis throughout the 1990s.

A study of past and present migration trends in the North has an important audience among policy-makers and political elites. After a decade of financial disarray, federal and regional governments in Russia have entered a period of relative fiscal stability in which regional development projects (given the political will) can receive necessary funding and support. However, a comprehensive approach to dealing with the immense problems of the northern regions is yet to emerge. From what has been discussed in this paper, it is clear that it is no longer appropriate (nor strategically viable) to continue with either Soviet-style or neo-liberal policies of prioritizing short-lived economic interests for the socio-economic well-being of northern populations. The federal and regional states have to exercise both direct and indirect (market-based) regulation of migration with a strong emphasis on improving the quality of life of all northerners. Optimizing shares of local and 'imported' workforce, permanent and short-term, full-time and part-time forms of employment, is a necessary first step forward.

On-Going and Future Research
Issues of migration, socio-economic well-being, and quality of life in the Russian Federation have to be more deeply and widely studied within a multidisciplinary scientific framework. Such research also needs to consider the perceptions of local and indigenous people carried out within socially-oriented observations (ASI, 2009; Vlasova 2010). These types of research and observations, are serving to increase knowledge of trends in migration, living conditions of northern residents under the impacts of climate change, biodiversity, globalization, socio-economic changes, and political responses are now being carried out within several multidisciplinary International Polar Year (IPY) projects. The IPY Arctic Social Indicators (ASI) Project and IPY PPS Arctic—N 151 are the examples of these. They are devoted to the investigation of complex human–nature interactions occurring in the forest–tundra marginal zone of the Russian Federation, the United States, Canada, and Scandinavia. Some of these interactions will be directly observed in processes of population migration.

Acknowledgements

The authors are indebted to Lee Huskey and Chris Southcott, the organizers of the *Migration in the Circumpolar North: Lessons Learned, Questions Remaining* workshop at Roskilde University, Denmark, June 10-12,

2007.This research has been supported by the Russian Academy of Sciences Presidium Programme 16.2 (coordinator V.M.Kotlyakov), by the Research Council of Norway within IPY PPS Arctic project (coordinator Annika Hofgaard) and by the College of Social and Behavioral Sciences Summer Research Grant at the University of Northern Iowa.

References

Agranat, G.A. (1992). *Vozmozhnosti i real'nosti osvoeniya Severa: Global'nye urok.* (Possibilities and realities in developing the North: Global lessons). Moscow: VNIITI.
AHDR (2004). *Arctic Human Development Report.* Steffansson Arctic Institute, Akureyri
ASI (2009). *Arctic Social Indicators Report.* Steffansson Arctic Institute, Akureyri
Ahrend, R. (2005). Can Russia Break the 'Resource Curse'? *Eurasian Geography and Economics* 46(8): 584-609
Andreev, E.M. and M.V. Rakhmaninova (1999). Vnutrennyaya migratsiya v Rossii v proshlom i nastoyaschem (Internal migration in Russia in the past and present). *Voprosy Statistiki* 5: 53-63.
Bradshaw, M. and K. Vartapetov (2003). A new perspective on regional inequalities in Russia. *Eurasian Geography and Economics* 44(6): 403-429.
Dienes, L. (2004). Observations on the problematic potential of Russian oil and the complexities of Siberia. *Eurasian Geography and Economics* 45(5): 319-345.
FAGSKR (2004). *Uroven' zhizni naseleniya Komi. Analiticheskaya zapiska.* (Standards of living of Komi population. An analytical report). Federal Agency of Government Statistics of Komi Republic, 42 p.
Fauser, V.V. (2005). Naselavie i demografichskoe razvitie Severa Rossii (Population and demographic development of the Russian North), pp. 96-106 in V.N. Lazhnzev (Ed.), *Sever kak ob'ekt kompleksnykh regional'nykh issledovanii.* Syktyvkar: KSCUBRAS
Fedorov, L. (2002). Regional inequality and regional polarization in Russia, 1990–99. *World Development* 30(3): 443-456.
Goskomstat Rossii (1997). *Rossiiskii Statisticheskii Ezhegodnik 1997 g. (Russian Statistical Yearbook 1997).* Moscow: Goskomstat.
Goskomstat Rossii (1999). *Trud i zanyatost'.* (Labor and employment). Moscow: Goskomstat.
Goskomstat Rossii (2000). *Rossiiskii Statisticheskii Ezhegodnik 2000 g.* (Russian Statistical Yearbook 2000). Moscow: Goskomstat.
Hanson, P. (2001). 'Regional Income Differences,' pp. 419-444 in B. Granville and P. Oppenheimer (eds.), *Russia's Post-Communist Economy.* Oxford, UK: Oxford University Press.
Heleniak, T. (1999). Out-migration and depopulation of the Russian North during the 1990s. *Post-Soviet Geography and Economics* 40(3): 155-205.
Heleniak, T. (2003). The 2002 Census in Russia: Preliminary Results. *Eurasian Geography and Economics* 44(6): 430-442.
Kontorovich, V. (2000). Can Russia resettle the Far East? *Post-Communist Economies* 12(3): 365-384.

Kotlyakov, V.M. and G.A. Agranat (1994). The Russian North: problems and prospects. *Polar Geography* 18(4): 285-295

Kriukov, V., V. Seliverstov, and A. Tokarev (2004). 'Federalism and regional policy in Russia: problems of socio-Economic development of resource territories and subsoil use,' pp. 96-127 in P.H. Solomon, Jr. (ed.), *The Dynamics of 'Real Federalism'. Law, Economic Development, Indigenous Communities in Russia and Canada.* Toronto, Canada: University of Toronto, Centre for Russian and East European Studies.

Lusin, G. and A. Korchak (1999). 'O regulirovanii migratsionnykh prozessov na Severe Rossii (On the regulation of migration processes in the Russian North),' pp. 56-61 in *Sever i rynok: formirovanie ekonomicheskogo poryadka.* Apatity: KSCRAS

Lynch, D.F. (2003). 'Hostages of the North: marginality with vengeance,' pp. 305-318 in W. Leimgruber, R. Majoral and C-W. Lee (eds.), *Policies and Strategies in Marginal Regions.* Burlington, VT: Ashgate.

NEI (1998). *Migration from the Russian North: Profile. Mechanisms of Migration and Adjustment in Recipient Regions.* Rotterdam: Netherlands Economic Institute.

Noril'sk (2005). Informatsionno-analiticheskie materialy o deyatelnosti munitsipalitetov v 2004 gody i planakh na 2005 god. Associatsiya Sibirskikh i Dal'nevostochnykh gorodov. http://www.asdg.ru/asdghtml/iam/2005/02/

Petrov, A.N. (2005). 'Modelirovanie vliyaniya udalennosti i transportnoi dostupnosti na migratsinnye protsessy na Rossiiskom i Kanadskom Severe (Modeling the effect of remoteness and transportation accessibility on migration processes in the Russian and Canadian North),' pp. 138-143 in Yu. N. Gladky (ed.), *Gumanitarnaya geografiya v 21 veke.* St. Petersburg: Epigraph.

Petrov, A.N. (2006). *Geopopulyatsionnye prozessy na Rossiiskon i Kanadskon Severe v 90e gody 20 veka.* Avtorefeat. (Geo-population processes in the Russian and Canadian North in the 1990s. A Synopsis.) St. Petersburg. 22 p.

Petrov, A.N. (2007). When people matter more than gold: Modeling economic effects of rapid depopulation and aging in the shrinking frontier economy (Yukon). A paper presented at the Canadian Population Society Annual Meeting, May 31-June 2 2007, Saskatoon, SK.

Petrov, A.N. (2007). Revising the Harris-Todaro framework to model labour migration from the Canadian northern frontier. *Journal of Population Research* 24(2): 185-206

Petrov, A. (2008). A talent in the cold? Creative class and the future of the Canadian North. *ARCTIC – Journal of the Arctic Institute of North America* 61(2): 162-176

Pravitel'stvo RF (2000). O kontseptsii gosudarstvennoi podderzhki ekonomicheskogo i sotsial'nogo razvitiya rayonov Severa. (On the concept of the state support of economic and social development of the regions of the North). Postanovleniye #197 ot 07.03.2000.

Ravenstein, E. (1885) The Laws of Migration. *Journal of the Statistical Society of London* 48(2): 167–235.

Rosstat (2002). *Vserossiiskaya Perepis Naseleniya. TT. 1-14* (All-Russia Census of Population. Vol. 1-14). Moscow: Rosstat.

Rosstat (2005). *Trud i zanyatost'.* (Labor and employment). Moscow: Rosstat.

Rosstat (2004). *Regiony Rossii 2004.* (Regions of Russia 2004). Moscow: Rosstat.

Chapter 9: *Migration and Socio-Economic Well-Being in the Russian North*

Rosstat (2006). *Regiony Rossii 2006*. (Regions of Russia 2006). Moscow: Rosstat.
Round, J. (2006). Marginalized for a lifetime: the everyday experiences of gulag survivors in post-Soviet Magadan. *Geografiska Annaler* 88B(1): 15-34.
Semenov S.P. and A.N. Petrov (2001). Demograficheskii krizis na Severe Rossii: istoki i geografiya. (Demographic crisis in the Russian North: roots and geography). *Izvestiya Russkogo Geograficheskogo Obshchestva* 133(3): 86-91
Stillwell, J., and P. Congdon, eds. (1991). *Migration Models: Macro and Micro Approaches*. London–New York: Belhaven Press.
Sutherland, D. and P. Hanson (2000). 'Demographic responses to regional economic change: inter-regional migration,' in P. Hanson & M. Bradshaw (eds.), *Regional Economic Change in Russia*. Northhampton, MA: Edward Elgar.
Thompson N. (2002). Administrative resettlement and the pursuit of economy: The case of Chukotka. *Polar Geography* 26(4): 270-288
Thompson N. (2004). Migration and Resettlement in Chukotka: A Research Note. *Eurasian Geography and Economics* 45(1): 73-81
Tobler, W. (1995) Migration: Ravenstein, Thorntwaite, and Beyond. *Urban Geography* 16(4): 327–343.
Wood, A., ed. (1987). *Siberia: Problems and Prospects for Regional Development*. New York: Croom Helm.
World Bank (2001). Project appraisal document on a proposed loan in the amount of US$80 million equivalent to the Russian Federation for a Northern Restructuring Project. Human Development Sector Unit, Russia Country Department. Washington, DC: World Bank.Vlasova T.K. (2009) Experience in developing approaches and methods for socially-oriented observations of the North: the integration of interdisciplinary science and public opinion. In V.A. Chereshnev (ed.). *Russian Northern Innovation Strategy. Social development of northern regions*. Materials of the 5th Northern Social and Environmental Congress, Moscow, April, 21-22, 2009. Moscow, p.67-79. (in Russian).
Vlasova,T.K. (2010). Integrated Arctic Socially-oriented Observation System (IASOS) Network. In *Sustaining Arctic Observing Networks (SAON). Inventory of Arctic Observing Networks. Russia. Russia country Report.* March 2010. Chapter 14: 53-55.

Appendix 1. Variables and definitions

Variable	Description	Definition
MIN	'subsistence' or 'minimum' income	Cost of consumption basket, including food, durable goods and services necessary for sustaining health and livelihood of a person, plus mandatory charges and fees. The value is determined by the law passed by federal or local legislature.
FOODCOST	cost of a standard food basket	Cost of standard food basket comprising 25 different items of groceries.
EARNINGS	employment earnings	Total annual amount of received salaries divided by the number of employees and by 12 (does not include social assistance payments).
INCOME	monetary income from all sources	Monthly incomes from entrepreneurial activity, salaries of hired workers, social assistance (pensions, compensations, stipends, etc.), dividends, and other sources of income (total annual income divided by 12).
UNEMPL	unemployment rate (ILO)	Ratio of unemployed (in a given age-group) and economically active (participating) population in that age group, %.
NMR	net migration rate	In-migration minus out-migration divided by the mid-year population (per 10,000).

Source: Rosstat (2006)

10

How the North Became Home: Attachment to Place among Industrial Migrants in the Murmansk Region of Russia

Alla Bolotova and Florian Stammler

Introduction

Inhabitants of industrial cities in the Russian North often say: *Sever tyanet* (the North 'lures' us in). You can hear this phrase among those who live in the North, as well as those who moved to more southern regions, but return from time to time to visit relatives and friends. Most people in the Russian North are first- or second-generation migrants, so they do not have deep family roots there. Current inhabitants either moved to the North themselves or their parents (grand-parents in the oldest towns) moved there. Most did not plan to stay, but expected to earn money for several years, with the idea of returning to their place of origin. However, as the years passed, many changed their plans and settled in the North. We find such patterns in many environments of labour migration world-wide, be it the 19th century Polish migration to industrial cities in West Germany (Rhoades 1978; Klessmann 1978; Eder 2003), the millions of 'Gastarbeiter' who migrated from Turkey to Germany after WWII (Horrocks and Kolinski 1996), immigrants to England's steel and mining cities, or France's North African population. What is different in the Russian North—among other things—was that the first generation of labour migrants arrived to uninhabited or sparsely settled places and had to adapt to harsh climatic conditions.

Despite these difficulties, the majority of these former migrants are still living in the North, even though some regions have experienced massive out-migration (Heleniak 1999, 2003, 2008, this volume). This article provides an ethnographic description of how these migrants and their descendants develop an attachment to their northern places, and describes what attracts migrants to the North, and what inhibits their leaving as pensioners. Economic analysts focus on the material benefits that explain migration patterns in the North and elsewhere. The simplest model is that people move to improve income and cost of living (Huskey 2005). In Russia, state incentives for living and working in the North formed the main material regulatory instrument for migration (Stammler-Gossmann 2007). However, recent studies have emphasized non-material dimensions that have influenced decisions to move or to stay in the North (Thompson 2008; Round 2005).

Ethnographic evidence from the Murmansk region contributes to a deeper understanding of the social, cultural, and other non-material variables that may overrule even material incentives for relocation facilitated by the state. In fact, initial temporary state-induced relocation of large numbers of people to the North developed into a permanent settlement pattern. The relocation and settlement histories of Northerners tell us how this transforms identities of individuals, as well as communities in the Russian North as a whole. It is a process whereby an environment that is seen as 'harsh,' or 'hostile' by outsiders, and cities that are often considered neither beautiful nor worth living in, have become home for some people. By focusing on attachment to place among migrants who moved to work in the north, we omit those who want to leave the North.[1] This approach is driven by our theoretical interest in the principles of how people develop roots to places, spaces or communities—a matter of intensive sociological debate within and outside the North (Acebo-Ibanez 2007). We argue that rootedness and attachment to place are underestimated when analysing the efficiency of relocation programmes by state authorities, especially for non-working pensioners. Our research shows that often the original targeted relocation candidates choose to stay in the North, while transferring flats and other benefits of relocation programmes to their children in the hope for better chances in education or employment elsewhere.

Methods
Fieldwork for this article was conducted from 2006 to 2008 in the Murmansk region in the industrial towns of Kirovsk, Apatity, and Kovdor. These cities were chosen because they represent different types of industrial settlements characteristic of the region: Kirovsk and Kovdor are both single-industry towns, but established in different periods (Kirovsk in 1929, and Kovdor in 1953), which influenced the structure of the city population. Apatity developed as a town in the same period as Kovdor near a small railway settlement. It differs significantly from the other two settlements because, from the very beginning, it was founded as a kind of 'think tank,'

---

[1] The presence of a still significant potential for migration out of northern industrial cities that is 'stored' in the North for various reasons has been the subject of other research (Thompson 2004; Heleniak 1999) and will not be covered in this context.

Chapter 10: *How the North Became Home: Attachment to Place Among Industrial Migrants in the Murmansk Region*

that would provide scientific support for industries in Kirovsk and in the whole Murmansk region.

Seventy unstructured in-depth interviews were conducted focusing on relocation and life histories, complemented by the lead author's participant observation in the cities, six months in duration. This fieldwork focused primarily on the first and second generation of incomers, representing various social groups, such as mining specialists, scientists, administrative staff, blue-collar workers, and pensioners. The biographical method with very loosely structured interviews and careful participation by a researcher in reconstructing an informant's biography is well-suited to evaluate and compare different periods of life and their importance in forming human personalities. Secondary sources such as publications on local history and memoirs of first-comers to the region complement the data for this article.

We describe the principles that the Soviet state applied for inducing migration into the area. Stretching over several decades, empirical materials available for analysing the migration process vary significantly: for the first wave of newcomers who arrived in the 1930s we have only a few published memoirs and reminiscences of children (secondary sources). For this period, we therefore restrict ourselves to a general overview of how and why people arrived to new industrial towns in the Murmansk region. To analyse the second wave of migration (after 1950), it was possible to interview migrants themselves, which is why we focused on collecting first-hand narratives for that generation. Open life-history interviews reflect informants' relocation and settlement experiences—physical and mental. The main questions triggering their narratives were the following: What kind of people arrived? How did they arrive? How did they experience their first years in the North? and, What were the characteristics of the communities that developed?

While this methodological approach is generally suitable for providing qualitative insights into relocation and settlement histories, we have to consider some limitations and problems in our data. For example, most informants who came to the North in 1950s and 1960s are now about 70 years of age and have a rather positive image of the past, while perceiving the present more negatively. In Russia, this tendency is increased by low pensions that often hardly suffice for subsistence. Another problem encountered by others (Kaznelson 2007) is that some informants who experienced forced resettlement as children are still afraid to relate traumatic events dealing with their or their parents' relocation in Soviet times. Despite political changes in the country, some people are so accustomed to keeping the dark side of their family stories secret that they still avoid talking about these issues.

The Industrial Peopling of the Kola Peninsula

Murmansk was the first Russian northern region to be industrialised. Before the revolution of 1917, the region was very sparsely populated. Soviet authorities paid special attention to the region soon after, mostly because of the proximity of the Finnish and Norwegian borders and the strategically important ice-free port of Murmansk. The first Soviet geological expeditions to the area organized in the early 1920s by Alexandr Fersman uncovered rich mineral resources. A large-scale influx of people as a result of state-induced labour migration began with intensive industrialisation in the late 1920s. Currently the majority of the population in the region lives in industrial cities founded between 1930 and 1970.

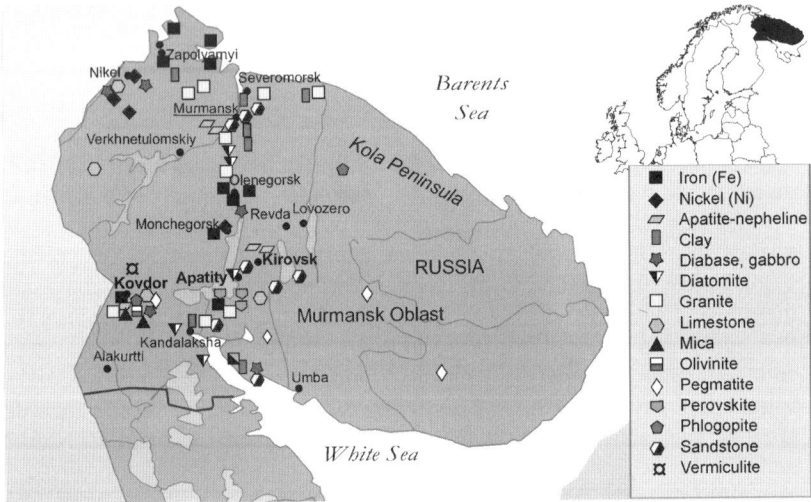

Figure 1. *Murmansk Oblast, main cities and mineral deposits. Map: Arto Vitikka, Florian Stammler.*

The exploitation of the first deposits in the 1930s caused the first wave of in-migration. Two new industrial towns were established: Khibinogorsk was set up on the foothills of the Khibiny mountains to develop a giant Apatite deposit—a mineral used as fertilizer in agriculture. The settlement was raised to the status of a city in 1931 and was renamed Kirovsk in 1934. Monchegorsk was founded in 1937 as the base for Nickel mining. This first wave of migration increased the population of the Murmansk region 16.7 times, from 19,100 people in 1920 to 318,400 in 1940 (Bojkov 1983:30). As a result, the share of the rural population—often local Sami, Komi and Nenets reindeer herders and fishermen—decreased from 64.9% of the overall population in 1920 to 15.7% in 1939, whereas the

Chapter 10: *How the North Became Home: Attachment to Place Among Industrial Migrants in the Murmansk Region*

urban population in the same period increased from 35.1% to 84.3%. (Murmanskaya 2000:59). The second wave of in-migration was in the 1950s and 1960s, when cities such as Kovdor, Olenegorsk, Apatity and others were founded. The inflow of people continued during the 1970s and until 1981, by which time the population of the Murmansk region had skyrocketed to 1.006 million people (90.8% urban population; 9.2% rural), a 3.2 times increase since 1940 (Bojkov 1981:10). The periods these migration waves occurred significantly influenced the type of communities that formed in the new cities. Kirovsk is classified as a first wave city in our research, while Kovdor and Apatity were chosen as cities of the second wave.

First Wave of Newcomers—1930s: 'Komsomol Constructions'
The city of Khibinogorsk became the first large-scale construction site in the region. In the 1930s, the construction of industrial plants and towns in the proximity of mineral deposits proceeded rapidly, as the Soviet programme for forced industrialisation required the supply of additional mineral resources.

The peopling of industrial towns founded in the 1930s occurred in a uniform way: these cities were built by three main groups: the largest group was formed of *spetspereselentsy*, former peasants (*kulaki*) forcibly deported from central and southern regions of the USSR, under the framework of communist programmes of 'dekulakisation,' or 'liquidation of the kulaks as a class' (Kaznelson 2007). In 1931-1932 about 45 thousands *spetspereselentsy* arrived in the Murmansk region (Shashkov 2004:11). Gulag prisoners formed the second group, and specialists and contract workers the third. Officially, both Khibinogorsk and Monchegorsk were announced as Komsomol (Kommunist Union of Youth) constructions, assuming that they would be constructed by young enthusiastic people, coming voluntarily to settle in the North. In reality, the voluntary flow of people was smaller than the forced one. According to evaluations of Shashkov, 21,325 *spetspereselentsy* arrived in Khibinogorsk between 1930 and 1935, out of 44,292 inhabitants in the town. Spetspereselentsy comprised the main work force at the enterprises in Khibinogorsk—more than 60% of all workers (Shashkov 2004:12).

Many of those who came voluntarily (Komsomol members, specialists in mining, construction, NKVD–secret police staff) did not have much choice where to go either. They were sent by the authorities to a place where a labour force was needed at a particular time. Non-fulfilment of this kind of order was severely punished during Stalin's rule. Even though physical force was not applied for getting these labourers to the North, it was a completely state-induced relocation. A significant number of specialists were from Leningrad because at that time, administratively, the Kola Peninsula was part of the Leningrad region. Architects from Leningrad were particularly active in designing northern mono-industrial towns within the Russian Northwest (Kirovsk, Monchegorsk), and outside (Novyi Urengoi, Nadym). In Kirvosk and Monchegorsk, the legacy of Leningrad is still very strong, and inhabitants call their cities 'Mini-Leningrad' with pride.

The living conditions in the new industrial towns were extremely difficult for first settlers. Peasants deported from their villages in temperate regions arrived at a place with a very different, very harsh climate. Most of them were not able to bring anything with them, because all their belongings were confiscated in the process of 'de-kulakisation.' During the first few years, *spetspereselentsy* lived in tents. Later they moved into barracks, which they built themselves after work. Memoirs of spetspereselentsy give a strong impression of the living conditions for the first years in the North:

> In Khibinogorsk we had to live in tents. There were 60 people in one tent, without basic facilities, on common plank beds where people were sleeping, sitting, eating. In winter while sleeping, the hair got frozen to the plank beds, and it was not possible to sleep when it was raining, because the tent was leaking. So we spent the winter 1931-1932. After work settlers were building wooden shed barracks. Before the winter of 1933 we got a 12 m^2 room for two families in a barrack. (Kovaleva 1997:122)

Khibinogorsk was growing extraordinarily fast: a railroad connecting the future town with the main St. Petersburg–Murmansk line was built very quickly in 1929 by prisoners. In 1930 construction of an Apatite-enriching processing plant (*obogatitelnaya fabrika*) began, and it was completed very quickly in 13 months. *Spetspereselentsy* made up the main work force on all construction sites. Mechanisation was minimal; it was mostly manual labour that was used. The population of Khibinogorsk was very diverse, comprising 32 different nationalities (Shashkov 2004:27), the largest percentage Russians and Ukrainians.

Settlers from various places in the country were already living on the 25th kilometre: Russians, Tatars, Ukranians, Germans, and others. One person was given a place 70-80 cm width, each family was separated with a board 20-30 cm wide; there were two stoves in the tent, which were heated day and night. There were about 50-60 people living in one tent. That winter it was very cold and windy (Khyanninen 1997:137-138).

This extreme density of people, conditions of poor hygiene and cold climate led to a high mortality rate among the inhabitants of these tents in the early years:

Chapter 10: *How the North Became Home: Attachment to Place Among Industrial Migrants in the Murmansk Region*

On September 7th, 1930, we were brought to the mountains. They dropped us off near the road. We took a look around—everywhere mountains. There were two long one-story barracks in the place where Khibinogorskaya street is now. It is difficult to say how many people were living in this barrack. There was no way to think about hygiene there. Diseases started, every morning the dead were taken out. Everyday clothes were brought by carts to a kiln room in order to kill off the lice (Lebedik 1997:24).

In the very beginning, the living conditions of the voluntary contract workers and specialists were not radically different from the forced relocates, but the former were given the privilege to be the first to get a separate room or flat. Only the most important specialists would be given separate apartments.

Officially, the *spetspereselentsy* were not prisoners and they were not guarded, but their rights were significantly limited. For example, they had to register every month with the administration, and they were not allowed to leave town. Moreover, a certain percentage of their salary was deducted for services, and there were restrictions related to work and education in some institutions.

Here in the Khibiny mountains, we—deportees—moved without guards, we were only obliged to check in with the registry lists every month. We, *spetspereselentsy*, did not have passports, instead we got an identification certificate which did not give us the right to move beyond the city borders. Our material situation was incomparable with the material situation of free contract workers, who got all benefits statutory for the Far North. There was also a fee deducted from our salaries for maintenance of the NKVD (secret police) administration, which was guarding us. First they took 25%, then 15% and later 5% (Gudovskaya 1997:37).

It was difficult to talk about attachment to the North for those who were forcebly moved there and barely survived under inhumane conditions. However, in the few available memoirs of *spetspereselentsy*, we witness, in addition to grim feelings and sorrow, an awareness and pride of belonging and contributing to the process of creating a new town in harsh northern conditions.

We, 'kulaks,' were morally broken, dejected people. Thousands of people were starving and grieving in tents and barracks under the howling of the crazy northern wind, under

> wailing of the snowstorm and crying of our own little children shivering of cold in canvas tents, in simple timber barracks that were difficult to heat. We were working in daytimes ... away on the job (*на совесть*): we constructed roads, built the city, mined apatite, processed it on the enrichment plant which we built, we were struggling with snowdrifts, and all this was made by hands of kulaks. That's how it was, thousands of innocent people got convicted without court and examination, they were brought somewhere in freight-cars, as cattle (Gudovskaya 1997:37)

The city of Khibinogorsk in the vicinity of the Apatite mining enterprise developed very intensively during the 1930s. In 1930 the Kola Science Centre was established to support the mining and chemical industry with scientific research. The Centre also became an important base for further geological explorations on the Kola Peninsula. The mandate of the Centre, however, was broader than geology, and in 1931, a botanical garden was added. The town was growing step by step; first stone buildings were erected, used mostly for public social needs such as schools, clubs, laundry, sauna, hospital, fire-department, cafeteria, kindergarten, etc.

Most of the inhabitants, however, had to live without basic comfort in everyday life in the wooden shed-houses. Toilets were outside, the houses did not have running water or sewer systems, the kitchen was usually shared by several families, and inhabitants had to take turns keeping the fire burning on cold winter nights. Many people remember these times with nostalgia, emphasizing that under these harsh conditions people were very friendly and supportive of each other. They did not have any problems with stealing, nobody even locked doors when they went to work.

> Our life was hard, but we lived in friendship, just as normal people. I remember when we moved into a wooden house, there were three families keeping cows. It happened that hay for cows was drying in the backyard, it started raining and the whole house would go out and take away the hay. And there were no stealing at all—different from now, where even rugs are stolen (Melnikova 1997:86).

Thus, there are a lot of good and nostalgic memories, but this was not an ideal world. Many shared very limited and poorly equipped living spaces, which at times led to conflict.Suffering and hardships both brought settlers together and dissociated them.

Chapter 10: *How the North Became Home: Attachment to Place Among Industrial Migrants in the Murmansk Region*

> My parents and Grechkin's family were sharing one room, and they quarrelled and fought very often. There wasn't complete harmony in other families either (Zajtsev 1997:70).

Skills acquired from their places of origin at times proved instrumental for the survival of those who were forcibly separated from their homelands, and brought from villages to construct a home in what, for many, was a completely alien empty environment. Many settlers themselves believe that their work ethic and peasant's skills of working the land were of great importance in the new place as well. In order to survive hungry times, many settlers began to plant vegetables, though at the beginning this was seen as a crazy idea in the conditions of the Far North. After the first harvests, however, many 'new northerners' followed suit. Many people also kept cattle, goats, and pigs. Mushrooms and berries were collected and preserved in large amounts, which formed an important subsistence support.

> Just as we were used to work hard, we were also working a lot here. In order to subsist somehow we worked the land for garden plots, planted potatoes, cabbage, carrots, and turnips. We kept goats, later pigs. We went to the forest for mushrooms and berries and took a lot of them (Zubkova 1997:20).

Spetspereselentsy remember that the situation in the North in the late 1930s was even better than in villages in other regions, because people received their salaries regularly and it was possible to survive, while in rural areas people were starving. As a result, in many cases free relatives of *spetspereselentsy* moved to the North voluntarily, after they received news about better living conditions there.

Intensification of Industrialization in the 1950s–1960s
During WWII, most of Kirovsk's population was evacuated, but when the war ended, many of those who survived returned voluntarily. In the first years after the war, industrial cities of the region were not only reconstructed, but development increased considerably and became a mass phenomenon. Several new towns were founded; most of them grew around rich mineral deposits opened up by geological expeditions in the 1930s. Mono-industrial towns were prevailing, since this was the general orientation in the country at that time. In the early 1960s the city of Apatity was founded near Kirovsk. The goal was to move the Kola branch of the Academy of Sciences—the largest centre for basic and applied sciences in the Murmansk region—to the city and develop it further. The second reason for the establishment of Apatity was to place a second city near Kirovsk to further develop the mining complex and build more housing for workers:

Kirovsk is situated in the mountains, and space for construction in the valleys is limited.

The death of Stalin in 1953 led to a considerable decline of the GULAG system, which generated important changes in the working force of the North. Although the region needed an increasingly larger number of people to develop the mining industry and populate new cities, the forced re-settlement of people became politically inappropriate. Instead of forcibly relocating people, the Soviet Union developed a system of material stimulation, which induced people to leave their southern places of origin and relocate to the north. Those who came were mostly young people once they had completed their education, and contract workers: young people were 'allocated' to the north after their studies. This state-organised distribution of people across the country was a common practice throughout the Soviet Union and an important instrument used to manage the labour force. People were also stimulated by higher salaries and good career prospects, contract workers arrived mainly from villages, where life was still very harsh after the war, and therefore securing a work contract was a way to escape from the village. In addition to inter-regional state-induced population movement, the labour force within the region was also actively re-distributed. This was particularly true for construction workers, who could arrive first to one settlement, and then be relocated to the next construction site upon completion of the first. The city of Kovdor in the Far West of the Murmansk region is one example. Workers who built Kovdor arrived from sites in Kirovsk, Afrikanda,[2] or Revda.

Migration after WWII differed considerably from pre-war relocation not only because of the different role of the state, but also in terms of the social structure. In the 1930s, people had come mainly as whole families from their home regions, so several generations were represented: children, parents, and often grandparents. As a result, the early industrial towns became populated by groups of relatives cutting across different age groups. In contrast, migrants in the 1950s and 1960s were mostly young and single, starting a new life in a new place. Many newcomers decided to marry in the north and start their families there. We hypothesize that this different social texture of communities has influenced the collective sense of belonging for members of such places as Kirovsk and Kovdor.[3]

---

[2] There are two main versions of the strange naming of the settlement, and there is no agreement in the field regarding which one is true. One is that it was very hot there when the first geologists came and someone said—'it is like in Afrika, so hot!' As a consequence, people started to call the place Afrikanda. The second version is that there were some African or Cuban people working there and the name Afrikanda relates to their influence.

[3] Fieldwork and the in-depth analysis of the data are ongoing (as of March 2008).

Chapter 10: *How the North Became Home: Attachment to Place Among Industrial Migrants in the Murmansk Region*

Motives to Move to the North

In the 1950s and 1960s, workers for the industrial development of the Murmansk region were hired from all parts of the huge territory of the Soviet Union. Recruiting was undertaken primarily in rural areas, but also in towns in older industrial regions, like the Ural area. Most newcomers were initially attracted by various material benefits they could get in the North. First of all, earnings in regions officially considered as the Far North (Moiseev 2006) were higher than in other regions: special northern benefits were added to the basic salary for every year of work (*polyarki* or *severnye nadbavki* system). The idea of state-stimulated material benefits used to attract people to relocate to the North was applied in the same way for the whole country, but the names, percentages and coefficients changed over time and region (Stammler-Gossmann 2007; Epshtein 1963)

> The purpose of our move was clear ... of course... the initial incentives were of a quite mercantile character. I thought: well, I go to the North—there I earn within five years enough for the rest of my life (male, age 68, Kirovsk).

> I arrived with my friend also like this. She says: "let's go to the North, people say you can earn good money there". ... And we had a large family at home. Well, that's how we left (female, age 71, Apatity)

Another important reason for moving was the prospect of getting a separate flat, which was much easier in the North than in other areas. In mono-industrial towns, enterprises were closely connected to city administration and construction companies. Very often, flats in a building were distributed among people working for the same enterprise, so they became not only colleagues but neighbours. First evidence suggests that a feeling of community evolves among randomly assembled people from diverse origins from being connected both at work and at home..

> Most people came here because of housing. Not so much because of money as of housing (female, age 42, Apatity).

Many young people moved to the new cities in the Murmansk region immediately after finishing secondary or higher education. A system of state-organised distribution was implemented in most educational institutions at that time that would send people to places where a workforce of a particular profile was needed. Alumni with the best marks had the right to choose where to go; others were obliged to go where they were sent.

Employment contracts in this system usually lasted three years, after which people were free to leave for other places. However, many stayed and formed the backbone of Soviet industry.

One of the largest groups of newcomers to the North was villagers. Former peasants moved to work by contract because they wanted to escape from villages, where life still was very hard in the 1950s and 1960s. Therefore many interviews include strong narratives about the very poor life in the villages, where people were struggling with the consequences of Stalinist collectivisation of agriculture. People were starving, did not have enough clothes, or were working extremely hard just for a piece of bread. These hardships in the rural areas of the Soviet Union have been throughly studied from archival and statistical sources and more recently also through memories of survivors (Davies and Wheatcroft 2004; Kaznelson 2007). Peasants tried desperately to escape the villages to the cities by any and all means.

There are examples of people not even knowing that they were going to the North—they thought they were moving to Leningrad and ended up in the Murmansk region instead:

> Life was very hard after the war [...]. My neighbour says "they recruit people for construction there" [...]. Well, we went to the raion (local administrative centre) and signed up for construction work in Leningrad. My aunt, the sister of my mother and I. There was another acquaintance too. Then it turned out they didn't actually bring us to Leningrad ... How should we know? Lenspetsstroi was the name of our high-voltage electric lines. The headquarters were in Leningrad, but they brought us to Pinozero, to this place here. And what did we know? I tell you: four classes [of school education]. We didn't even watch any cinema before we were 15 years old. Well, what's up there in the village? We all worked like horses (female, age 73, Kovdor).

Aside from the material incentives for moving to the North, there were also some non-material reasons that influenced initial relocation decisions. The atmosphere in the entire country at that time was full of romanticism about the North and travelling in general (Vail and Genis 1996; McCannon 1998). People, especially the younger generation, were dreaming of going to far-away places—the further the better, as one informant said. For some, moving North was also a way to gain independence from parents and relatives. The most remote regions in the Far East, such as Kamchatka or Sakhalin were very attractive for young romantics. The Murmansk region was slightly inferior to these, but still very interesting.

Chapter 10: *How the North Became Home: Attachment to Place Among Industrial Migrants in the Murmansk Region*

First Impressions

While material incentives often established the initial attractiveness of the North, a whole range of other reasons from social to emotional contributed to movement and settlement decisions, once forced relocation was replaced by state-induced relocation in the Soviet Union. First impressions and the narratives provided by relocatees show this. Many young people moved to the North with romantic enthusiasm. The curiosity for the new and remote was paired with romanticism—perhaps dreams of meeting the love of one's life. Some young women moved to follow their boyfriends or married in the immediate advent of the move. The specificity and beauty of the natural northern environment was an additional attraction for those newcomers with an enthusiasm and interest in nature and various forest activities. Natural phenomena such as polar days, midnight sun, polar nights and northern lights made strong first impressions.

> I wake up at 2am, and it's daylight [...], and these clear names 'Arktika,' 'Severianka' [northerner...]. Somehow these were associated with romanticism. Because I am romantic to some extent [...] I also called and say: the forest is lighter, good visibility, a lot of mushrooms, lots of berries. An enchanting region somehow, very interesting (male, age 56, Apatity[4])

This informant first came to the Murmansk region to visit a friend. However, the interesting nature and the atmosphere of a young, intensively developing city of Apatity were so attractive that later he decided to move there.

Many of the newcomers did not know anything about the North before they moved. In the minds of many, the North was an endless hostile white desert, populated by polar bears. Narratives describing first impressions include reports on physiological adaptation to the specificity of northern nature and the harsh climate, which is something that everyone encounters in the very beginning and has to get accustomed to after arriving. There are many stories of people arriving without proper shelter from the cold in winter or from the mosquitoes in summer, which are remembered as as a shocking experience.

Former peasants who did not have professional training could only get work requiring few or lower qualifications, so their memories of the first years in the north are about very hard labour in the cold climate. Mechanisation of labour was minimal, and many operations requiring manual work outdoors were filled by women accustomed to outdoor work in their villages, and attracted to the North in large numbers. Men were more

---

[4] Interview taken by Olga Gerasimenko.

often trained to operate the first industrial equipment. Many of those who stayed for a long time say that the North itself selects people: those who were not tough enough to stand the hard work, or who did not adapt to the dynamic communal life of young incomers, returned to the South. The others stayed, and today are proud that they became, through 'the work of their own hands,' the backbone of the new Soviet northern population.

One of the most common remembrances of firstcomers to new towns is the feeling of living amid nature, where there are only few houses in the midst of the forest, and mushrooms as well as berries waiting to be picked right next to the houses, even during lunch breaks. While this is still the case in northern towns in Fennoscandia or Alaska, life in Russia's North today resembles urban life in any other corner of the country. Creating similar living standards for everyone all across the vast country was among the important development goals of the Soviet Union.

First impressions are important because they contrast what incomers encounter when they arrive in a new place. Mostly recollections are about climatic conditions for which new-comers were not ready. During the first few years, people tried to adapt to the new conditions: they got used to the weather, to different northern specificities such as polar days/nights, and they learned how to dress for the harsh climate. The earliest newcomers would have had special first impressions because they arrived at a time when the city did not yet exist. They contributed to its growth from a few houses in the forest to a modern town.

Temporality Becomes Permanent
Initially most people did not plan to stay in the North for long: many expected to stay one to five years, earn some money, and then return to their home regions. However, with this temporality in mind they kept extending their stay, as their conditions of life and plans changed. For the early newcomers from villages, the north first provided a stable food supply, and they knew they would not starve to death. Later, salaries increased and they were able to afford non-food items, while the situation in many of their home regions was still mainly about a struggle for survival. Knowing this, they extended their work contracts and stayed longer. The relative improvement of living conditions was particularly important for those who came from villages. Being young and full of energy, many met their partners in the North and started their families there. That is how the first generation of northern industrial city-inhabitants was born. While many had a hard time adapting to the new conditions, they gradually began to like it:

> I came in January, and cried, and cried. I said [to my husband] 'Let me go home, I go home now'. 'Ok, wait, I get an advance [salary], and send you home.' I say 'just for a day.' 'I get my salary—I send you home.' That's how we have been living—

Chapter 10: *How the North Became Home: Attachment to Place Among Industrial Migrants in the Murmansk Region*

for how long? From 1975 on. Now I don't want to go home any more. I started to like it here and don't want to go anywhere else. I wait for the winter to pass and for summer to come, in August, for mushrooms and berries...That's how it is. I quite like it (female, age 62, Kovdor).

For inhabitants of northern industrial cities, attachment to place is often related to their contribution to the very creation of the place. In their minds, the place was hostile, harsh and wild when they arrived, and as a result of their efforts, these places have become comfortable, modern and nice places to live. For example, incomers actively participated in establishing the infrastructure, and helped administration and other responsible organisations construct green zones. The latter are particularly indicative, as incomers become attached to the 'natural' environment that is actually constructed by them, while the natural environment outside the city was more often perceived as wild.

When we settled down here, the trees that grow around the house now were not there. All this we planted with our own hands. It happened that my husband goes to the forest, digs out birches and bird cherry trees and mountain ash, and brings back these seedlings. Now we get the neighbours and all went together... digging holes ourselves, and planting trees and bushes. And all, really everything ourselves [...]. We were young, and we wanted everything. And on other occasions, we would go out together and tidy up the leaves, sweep the yards, help the janitors (female, age 71, Apatity).

Activities such as planting trees in the city were often organised formally through industrial enterprises (or by housing committees). People would gather, typically on a Saturday, to jointly work outdoors in the city. All over the Soviet Union, these communal work unpaid sessions were called *subbotniki* (Saturday 'volunteer' work day). As they were organised by companies or authorities, these sessions were virtually obligatory, even though not necessarily negatively punished in case of disobedience. Many informants remember *subbotniki* with enthusiasm. Even though the rhetoric might have been inspired by Soviet propaganda, it was not only ideology that stimulated people to participate, but their wish and an obvious need to improve common conditions of living in the new town. Much work was done fully voluntarily. The new northerners planted trees, painted their houses, built places for common use, such as stadiums or places for skating, benches for pensioners at backyards, etc.

In the early days we had *subbotniki*. We tidied up the entire territory around us. Everything was clean and tidy. [...] Anyway, the whole house [community] was friends, everybody came to help always, nobody refused, nobody skived (female, age 83, Apatity).

In those cities that were created in the 1960s, such as Kovdor and Apatity, most in-comers were of similar age when they arrived—between 20 and 30 years old. Their memories of these times are full of nostalgia about their young years. They remember having great fun together. People were very friendly, hierarchies were not so much felt in everyday life, everybody was equal, most people worked for the same goals, and crime was minimal. Practically all incomers shared the experience of being far away from relatives, and many just started their own families either with fellow northerners or came as young couples. This joint hands-on experience at work and the strong feeling of a community of equals formed much of these people's biographies in their best years, and it is this time and this environment created by their own hands to which they developed an attachment.

We note that many of our interviewees have the brightest memories about their early adult period, when they started their work biography and a personal life independent from parental control.

A number of factors contributed to the influence of this period in the lives of those we interviewed and their choices.

- First, the experience of collectively overcoming hardships created solidarity.
- Second, this suffering took place at a time in an individual's biography when they were full of energy, enthusiasm and agency, geared toward finding the right direction to go in their lives.
- Third, they came to these places at a time when there was a cult of young energetic activists, whose achievements for common goals were highly honoured and celebrated.

The poor housing conditions also contributed to the social cohesion within communities of incomers. Many started their live collectively in tents, barracks, or communal housing, before they had children and their own flats. This is why members of that generation know each other very well. Even when they had separate flats, many were still socially very active. One of the arenas of this social activism was the neighbourhood or the community in the apartment-houses where people lived. They participated in various common activities organised to improve common and public places. These common events and shared activities were open to all, and everyone was welcome, regardless of nationality or social background.

> We were all like this: everything was done immediately: 'come on, come on let's do it, tidy up, clean up [...] ironing, painting.' All our neighbours were like that.
> Q: And did you know each other?
> No, we didn't. We just came here, met here, and started to do everything together. Everybody somehow became part of the group immediately (female, age 88, Apatity).

This community feeling was further facilitated by local settlement patterns in the neighbourhoods, where colleagues working for one company became neighbours in their apartment buildings. Spending the time at work and at home together contributed to feelings of community. Sometimes this caused a relative closeness of a micro community. One interview partner called this system 'clanness' (*klanovost*). The use of the word 'clan' hints at a type of bonding that resembles in its closeness the intimate ties and solidarity among relatives. This system was particularly strong in corporate housing, i.e., multi-story company apartment blocks or institutions, sometimes much like dormatories, managed by them, and inhabited by their staff.

Newcomers who arrived later did not see the cities in their very early developmental stages. One of our informants moved to Apatity in the early 1970s when it was still a young and developing city, but it already had all the necessary infrastructure. Since the city was planned according to standards of a socialist city, it included all communal services in each small district—something that made everyday life very convenient and also attached people to it:

> We [wife and husband] ended up in the North. Time and again, we thought about leaving, leaving again. But where would we head to? ...We got this housing here. And when a person gets housing, he starts getting attached to that place. And that's why I say: the north sucked us up. How did the North do that? Firstly, the city of Apatity in 1972 was a developing city, new construction, enlarged city-landscapes. ...How was it all arranged: There was a 'mikroraion' (neighbourhood), consisting of several houses, a kindergarten, a school. All this infrastructure was so convenient for the inhabitant that it really facilitated people to realise themselves. It is close to work, the kindergarten is close by, the school is *vis-à-vis*, the policlinic close by, the hospital not far away, the children's school of fine arts in the centre, and so is the

children's music school. It was everything. Look, all the shops are in easy reach. This infrastructure attaches people very much, very much (female, age 63, Apatity).

Indeed, in the construction of socialist cities the principle of *mikroraion* was specifically planned for conveniently organizing the inhabitants. In some cases, general plans were even specifically adapted to northern conditions. On the other hand, the generation that came when the cities were already built does not have the feeling of collective hardships, of hands-on experience in building a city out of the pristine forest. This shows that different generations develop attachments to place differently. We could even say they use diametrically opposite arguments. The earlier generation became attached because the North was so uncomfortable, they had to collectively overcome the hardships, whereas later generations, like those in the quote above, became attached because it was so convenient and comfortable to live in the North, in a readily constructed environment that enabled the realization of one's personhood.

Mikroraions and joint *subbotniki* of neighbourhoods might strengthen attachments. The big corporations in the industrial cities were often pivotal in establishing these units. On the other hand, the strong role of corporations in the cities also segregated neighbourhoods from one another. In Apatity, for example, staff of the Academy of Sciences had their corporate housing, as did staff of the hydro powerplant, and construction workers. Correspondingly, they had their own corporate events, their own *subbotniki*, shops, dining halls, kindergardens, telephone networks, transportation; in short, their own microcosm. Unlike western companies, Soviet corporations were what was called 'total social institutions' (Humphrey 1998:452, paraphrasing Clarke 1992), with an all-caring infrastructure for their employees. Therefore, in a way the strong corporate structure of the cities formed the identity of the inhabitants, who maybe felt they belonged as much to their companies as to their city. However, with post-soviet restructuring, the corporations outsourced almost all social activities, much to the favour of municipalities, which took over most of these responsibilities.

By inheriting these structures, the city could potentially inherit people's sense of belonging. The future viability of northern communities will depend partially on the cities' success in fulfilling this community fostering role. The two case study sites in this article do not allow for generally relevant conclusions, but we might hypothesize along the following lines:

a) mono-industrial cities with a declining industry or a bankrupt main enterprise have a 'community identification vacuum,' and if this is not filled by an alternative institution—be it a city authority or civil society—social cohesion will decrease, outmigration will become the preferred option, and smaller communities could be facing closure.

b) more prosperous cities with main enterprises in restructuring and outsourcing benefit from an organisation that is able to stimulate collective agency among inhabitants with now diverse employment and sources of income. Their main challenge is to be successful in economic diversification and still maintain a common sense of belonging among city inhabitants.

We carefully hypothesize that in cases where a city-wide organisation successfully maintaining the sense of community through a soviet-style 'total institution' enterprise (Clarke 1992), social cohesion can be stronger among residents, the idea of temporality can be overcome, and long-term viability of the city population as a whole might be achieved.

Feeling Home in the North?
We have shown how our interviewees experienced their relocation to the North as a process of becoming attached, in one way or the other. While one result of this temporality changing into permanence is the growing importance of these northern places for the incomers' biographies, another question is whether this has led to the North becoming their homeland.[5] For both the interviewees and the authors, this question turned out to be complicated, because the definition of 'homeland' is very diverse, and further hampered by language barriers. In fact, talking about 'homeland' in different languages significantly alters the dialogue, since the etymology of the very term is different. The most commonly used equivalent for 'homeland' in Russian is *rodina*. However, the terms differ insofar as the etymologic source of *rodina* is *rod*, which means clan, blood-related kingroup, but also *rodit,' rozhat,'* to be born, to give birth. Linguistically, none of these terms is linked to place, home, or house. As a result, talking about this in Russian, results in people reflecting more about where their kinship roots are, where they were born, or where their ancestors are buried, rather than where their houses are, where they built homes.

We therefore argue that many of our interview partners feel 'at home' in the North, even though they do not say that their *rodina* has moved with them to the North. More of our respondents might have answered that their homeland is in the North, if we had been able to convey the idea of homeland in Russian that is independent of blood and kinship ties. The Russian word for home is *dom*, which also means house. The term is equally symbolically charged, and feeling at home (*chustvo byt' doma*) is a

---

[5] For a discussion on what *rodina means* for young generation of inhabitants of northern industrial cities—*see* Rasumova (2006).

fundamental state of mind for all our respondents. However, linguistically the feeling at home (*byt doma*) and the homeland (*rodina*) are totally separate, which makes us wonder how much they are connected in the understanding of our respondents:

> There, in the Novgorod region is my rodina (homeland)[...] but this place has become my dom (home) (male, age 48, Apatity).

> All this Tyumen', Tverskaia ... I couldn't care less about it. We go there, it is our rodina, the graves are there, so what. It's nothing more than some obligations. There is no desire, no longing to go there whatsoever. What should we do there? (female, age 42, Apatity).

This suggests that the understanding of homeland and feeling at home are different qualities indeed, captured by the unrelated Russian terms. Caring for the graves of relatives in the South becomes an obligation on the *rodina*, which for the last quoted informant has become completely detached from the place where she feels she belongs. On the other hand, for many people the graves are a symbol of the place where they feel they most belong. Even though not intended in the first place, northern industrial cities such as Apatity, Kovdor, or Kirovsk have acquired this meaning, as now the second generation is getting older and already cares for the graves of their parents of the first generation. This contributes as a factor for resisting relocation efforts of today's pensioners to more temperate regions.

> My daughter is calling me to come, of course [to join her in another city]. Come on, mum, sell everything here. We buy you a one room flat.' But how can I leave now? My husband is now buried here, my son is buried here, my sister is buried here, my daughter in law is buried here. I cannot do that, I can't. I don't have the guts to leave all this behind and go away (female, age 80, Kovdor).

In this case, the *dom* and the *rodina* seem to have merged into one, which is probably the most complete criteria for attachment to place. With an increasing number of people feeling this way, the transient status of whole cities such as Apatity, Kovdor, or Kirovsk changes to permanent. Processes of out-migration, therefore, are not seen as an abandoning of the North anymore, but more like normal migration within families, which we find everywhere on the planet. It is worth noting that place of birth is not crucial in many of these. Many people who were born elsewhere, came to the North and spent their lives there, do not want to move back to their birth places. Along similar lines, many members of the first generation born in northern industrial cities do not necessarily develop a strong attachment to the North and decide to move elsewhere. In both cases we can say that mobility is greatest in young adult life. That mobility has made large-scale state-induced movement to the North possible; it also facilitates young northerners' out-migration.

Therefore, we suggest that both the inclination to stay in the North among first generation incomers, and the potential for out-migration among those who were born in the North underlines the importance of a person's physical engagement with their environment. The older generation feels attached to young northern cities that grew from the work of their own hands, whereas the younger generation grew up in the existing environment, and their contribution to their environment is still ahead—so they might well search out this self-realisation elsewhere.

That said, another at least equally important factor is the solidarity among northerners that started with the collective experience. As argued above, we suggest that jointly overcoming hardships, joint hard physical work, and collective joy in one's young adult years 'glues' people together and turns them from a number of randomly composed former inmates or deported labour migrants into a community with a sense of social cohesion. This creates extensive social networks that last well beyond the immediate collective habition of the North.

Among the older generation, knowing so many people in town, having shared a collective path with many of those who are decision-makers in companies and city administration today is a strong factor contributing to make them feel at home. In many interviews, people emphasize how especially friendly, open and hospitable Northerners are, and indeed the authors noticed that with their own entry to the field. We can therefore synthesize these two strains by arguing that an intimate knowledge of people with collectively shared experiences and of the places where these experiences happened creates strong social ties among northern residents and between people and places.

Response to Relocation Programmes

We argue that the sense of place among different generations of Northerners described above deserves to be considered in broader demographic planning, especially in relocation programmes that have been in place in the Russian North since the fall of the Soviet Union. Relocation programmes are one of several ways for the state to induce relocation without forcing it. These programmes were initiated by the World Bank, the Russian Government, and others in the face of mass out-migration, particularly from the Russian Far East (Heleniak 1999; Thompson 2004). In particular, the programmes target the 'surplus' population of the North and aim to encourage, mainly on economic considerations, pensioners and other non-working population to leave (Hill and Gaddy 2003). At the base lies the idea of the North as a resource colony, as a work place rather than a homeland. Our research has shown, however, that as a result of Soviet northern policy, the North has become a homeland not only for the indigenous people (Vitebsky n.d; Stammler 2005), but also for the majority population of industrial incomer-workers and their support (Thompson 2008, Round 2005).

We have shown above how it is particularly the generation who built industrial cities in the Murmansk region who are deeply socially embedded in the communities and most attached to these northern places. Most are now retired and eligible for participation in state or privately sponsored relocation programmes. However, as a result of their temporary status having turned permanent, many retired people now participate in the relocation programmes rather for their children than for themselves. Housing is, for most people in Russia, among the most important symbols of a successful life, and from Soviet times people were accustomed to acquiring housing for free. Now that they have to buy it in many cases, programmes providing substantial assistance to acquire housing are welcome in any region. Therefore, in some cases parents participate in relocation programmes, get housing in the South in their names, give this housing to their children, while they themselves prefer to stay in the North.

Over the last 10 years, the relocation programmes have changed; they vary considerably according to the source of funding (Thompson 2004). Under the early federal programmes, people could get a flat elsewhere and keep their flats in the North. Later it became obligatory to give up the flat in the North, in order to permanently remove 'surplus' people from these areas. However, as often in Russia (and probably elsewhere too), the inventiveness of people on the ground is rich and hard to overestimate. In order to avoid completely losing housing in the North, they might give up their old flat but buy a new one in the North, while at the same time use relocation assistance through one of the programmes.

Another change in the programme structure proves more difficult to deal with: while before people could get a ready-made flat somewhere in exchange for their housing in the North, now they get certificates for a certain amount of money, which is calculated based on the size of the family. These certificates can be cashed in with a bank when the contract for purchasing a flat is made. The procedure is more complicated, relocation candidates have to search for their flat themselves and do all the purchase paperwork, and often the sum on the certificate is not enough to cover the full cost of a flat, as market prices for housing are higher than what is calculated in certificates.

Chapter 10: *How the North Became Home: Attachment to Place Among Industrial Migrants in the Murmansk Region*

This shows that for several different reasons, participation in so-called relocation programmes does not reveal the potential of out-migration from the North in a straightforward way. Participation might be active because any support for housing is welcome, no matter where it is. Our research suggests that participation in programmes reveals a real need to improve housing conditions within families in general. Participation would be lower if relocation assistance would only be available when pensioners would physically move South through the programmes. On the other hand, the popularity of programmes would increase among relocation candidates if they operated more effeciently along two lines: if people could move to areas they really want, and if certificates would be enough to buy a flat in that desired region.

The discourse shows how difficult it is for people when they do participate and relocate back to the South. We will not analyse all the points in detail here, as it extends beyond the framework of this chapter. Nonetheless, the main reasons our research partners mentioned are the following:

- problems with health: some mention allergic reactions to southern climates, and problems of backward adaptation when they relocate from the North to the South. One widespread saying, confirmed by evidence among several of our respondents is that people die shortly after relocating to the South.
- several mention that it is particularly difficult to find something meaningful to do in the South, especially employment. Many Kirovsk, Kovdor and Apatity inhabitants are highly specialised in the mining sector, and would not find work in other places.
- we were told that it is not worth moving to the South for financial reasons, since the cost of food and other needs in some central and southern regions are not much lower than in the North. This might be particular to cities in Murmansk oblast, since they are comparably close to St. Petersburg and have the best-developed infrastructure in the Russian north, with railways and an extensive road network.
- In those cases where people relocate from the northern cities to small villages in the South, difficulties of re-adapting to the lack of comfort there is mentioned. The living situation in these villages is still very basic, for example concerning the quality of housing, sanitary hygiene, running water, heating and sewer systems.
- Many people have a hard time establishing or re-establishing their social networks in the South. Solidarity is mentioned as one of the most important advantages in northern city-communities, as the following example shows:

Where is the difference between Voronezh, where my mother and father are, and this city [Apatity]? A very big favourable difference is that the Voronezh people are very rude. They are not cooperative, rather troublesome (*sklochnye*). (female, age 42, Apatity).

We feel homesick to the North, of course [when we are not there...], because we have everything there: friends, colleagues, acquaintances, everybody. And there I am still a new person. They [children] have their life [...] Yes, the North pulls me, to the native place (*penaty*). (female, age 65, Apatity).

All these reasons confirm Round's (2005) and other arguments that planning demographic change in the North only along economic lines of efficiency does not necessarily bring the desired results. Our research shows that this tendency prevails even under-cover, in cases where participation in relocation programmes on paper is active, but in practice the benefits do not go to the target population, because many of them do not want to leave. Among the most important contributions of anthropology to our general advancement of knowledge has been that humans are not only economic beings. Social and cultural factors have to be considered on equal terms if we want to understand the patterns under which humans make decisions to move and settle.

Conclusion

The ways in which people link themselves as persons to other persons (the evolution of community) as well as to particular locations (attachment to place) is a matter of broad relevance to social science research in general. We have shown in this article several factors by which humans link themselves to these places.

This article presents the first and still preliminary results of a multi-year research project. We therefore restricted ourselves to presenting some evidence from fieldwork that has been undertaken in Murmansk Oblast, and dared a first attempt at analysing them for their relevance to our understanding of human movement and settlement. At later stages of the research, this material will be amended, enriched by comparisons with other regions, and more thoroughly analysed for theoretical debates about sense of place and urban anthropology. We explicitly acknowledge that there are many more factors to consider which go beyond the framework of this article. For example, we attempt to show why people do NOT leave, consciously leaving out the reverse, i.e., the reasons why people DO leave and what generates the migration potential from the North to more

Chapter 10: *How the North Became Home: Attachment to Place Among Industrial Migrants in the Murmansk Region*

temperate regions. More research will also reveal the multiple place-based elements of human identity, in this case multiple homes, between which people commute, or dual attachments of people to several places, which we find among fly-in fly-out shift workers in northern industry.

Two different arguments for attachment to northern cities— collective overcoming of hardships and discomfort *versus* collective enjoyment of the comfort of a modern city—can be seen as two sides of the same coin. On the one hand, it is the heroic survival that 'glues' people together; on the other hand it is the attachment to a microcosm that successfully protects from these hardships and creates a framework for finding oneself and one's place in a community. By looking at people's experiences, we have shown that the initially temporary (state-induced) relocation of large numbers of people became a permanent settlement pattern. While people in the 1930s arrived as whole communities and families to the North, migrants in the 1950s–1960s were mostly young and single, starting a new life in a new place. Many newcomers married in the North and started their families there. We hypothesize that the different social texture of communities has influenced the collective sense of belonging in places such as Kirovsk and Kovdor. These processes transform identities of migrants and their descendants, as well as communities in the Russian North as a whole. Intimate links to the North develop to the extent that people become reluctant to leave, even though they might not consider the North entirely as their *rodina* (homeland).

Interviews with former labour migrants as well as with some of their children born in the North indicate being born in a place alone is not the strongest prerequisite for feeling attached to that place. Rather, we have described how other determinants of belonging play an important role, for example the experience of having built the place with one's own hands, the experience of solidarity among incomers that developed into a dynamic community, exemplified by participation in voluntary work, *subbotniki*, and other collective events.

Places such as Kirovsk, Kovdor and Apatity even today can be seem 'harsh,' 'hostile,' grey, and boring to outsiders. Particularly, westerners arriving in such Soviet cities do not find many attractive features that could make life worth living there for them. However, as a result of the processes described above, these places that were so hostile for the incomers 50 years ago have become home for many. In fact, it is better to say people have made these places their homes, and this process created social cohesion among inhabitants. We have argued for particular linguistic sensitivity when doing research on 'homeland ' and 'feeling at home' in Russia, as the etymology of the very term carries such different symbolic meanings. The process of developing attachment has to be understood in the framework of state-induced relocation, which is how Kirovsk, Kovdor and Apatity were established. We suggest the process of becoming attached to place is a creation of physical and social space, which requires mental movement at least as much as physical movement from the South to the North. Responses of northern residents to recent programmes of state-induced relocation become better understood if we consider the complex processes described above.

References

Acebo-Ibanez, E.D. (2007). Metropolis, the Southern Cone of Latin America and the Antarctica. Representations of the environmental problems among young inhabitants of Buenos Aires. *Arctic & Antarctic International Journal of Circumpolar Sociocultural Issues* 1(1): 99-147.
Bojkov, V.YE. (1981). *Grani nashej zhizni. Murmanskaya oblast': tsyfry i fakty.* Murmansk: Murmanskoe knizhnoe izdatel'stvo.
Bojkov, V.YE. (1983). *Kolskij kraj: tsyfry i fakty.* Murmansk: Murmanskoe knizhnoe izdatel'stvo.
Clarke, S. (1992). Privatisation and the development of capitalism in Russia. *New Left Review* 196.
Davies, R.W. and S.G. Wheatcroft (2004). *The Years of Hunger. Soviet Agriculture 1913-1945.* Cambridge: CUP.
Eder, A. (2003). Polish Life in West Germany After 1945: A Case Study on Hamburg. *The Sarmatian Review* 23(online): http://www.ruf.rice.edu/%7Esarmatia/403/232eder.html
Epshtein, A.L. (1963). *L'goty dlya rabotauschikh v rajonakh Krajnego Severa I mestnostyakh, priravnennykh k rajonam Krajnego Severa.* Moskva: Izd-vo uridicheskoj literatury.
Gudovskaya (Zinchenko), L.E. (1997). 'Chto sokhranila pamyat,' pp. 34-41 in *Spetspereselentsy v Khibinakh: Spetspereselentsy i zakliuchennye v istorii osvoenia Khibin (kniga vospominanii).* Apatity: Khibinskoe obshestvo 'Memorial.'
Heleniak, T. (1999). *Migration from the Russian north during the transition period.* World Bank report no 20818. Accessed 23/06/2006 at http://www-wds.worldbank.org/external/default/WDSContentServer/WDSP/IB/2000/09/08/000094946_00082605593363/Rendered/PDF/multi_page.pdf
Heleniak, T. (2003). Geographic aspects of population aging in the Russian Federation. *Eurasian Geography & Economics* 44: 325-347.
Heleniak, T. (this volume). Migration and Population Change in the Russian Far North during the 1990s, chapter 4, in Huskey, L. & C. Southcott. *Migration in the Circumpolar North. Issues and Contexts.* Edmonton: CCI Press.
Heleniak, T. (2008) 'Changing Settlement Patterns across the Russian North at the Turn of the Millennium,' Chapter 2, pp. 25-52 in Rautio, V. and M. Tykkyläinen, (eds.). *Russia's Northern Regions on the Edge: Communities, Industries and Populations from Murmansk to Magadan.* Helsinki: Kikimora publications.
Hill, F., and C. Gaddy (2003). *The Siberian Curse: How communist planners left Russia out in the cold.* Washington D C: Brookings Institution Press.
Horrocks, D., and E. Kolinsky (1996). 'Migrants or Citizens? Turks in Germany between exclusion and Acceptance,' pp. i-xxv in D. Horrocks and E.

Chapter 10: *How the North Became Home: Attachment to Place Among Industrial Migrants in the Murmansk Region*

Kolinsky (eds.), *Turkish Culture in German Society Today, Culture & Society in Germany*. Oxford: Berghahn Books.
Humphrey, C. (1998). *Marx Went Away but Karl Stayed Behind (updated edition of 1983 Karl Mark Collective: Economy, Society and Religion in a Siberian Collective Farm)*. Ann Arbor: The University of Michigan Press.
Huskey, L. (2005). Challenges to Economic Development: Dimensions of 'Remoteness in the North.' *Polar Geography* 29(2): 119-125.
Kaznelson, M. (2007). Remembering the Soviet State: Kulak Children and Dekulakisation. *Europa-Asia Studies* 59(7) November: 1163-1177.
Khyanninen, T.I. (1997). 'Pust' ne dovedetsya vnukam,' pp. 136-140 in *Spetspereselentsy v Khibinakh: Spetspereselentsy i zakliuchennye v istorii osvoenia Khibin (kniga vospominanii)*. Apatity: Khibinskoe obshestvo 'Memorial.'
Klessmann, C. *(1978)*. Polnische Bergarbeiter im Ruhrgebiet 1870-1945: Soziale Integration und nationale Subkultur einer Minderheit in der deutschen Industriegesellschaft. Vol. 30. *Kritische Studien zur Geschichtswissenschaft*. Goettingen: Vandenhoek & Ruprecht.
Kovaleva, T.V. (1997). 'Agitatsiej nikto ne zanimalsya,' pp. 121-122 in *Spetspereselentsy v Khibinakh: Spetspereselentsy i zakliuchennye v istorii osvoenia Khibin (kniga vospominanii)*. Apatity: Khibinskoe obshestvo 'Memorial.'
Lebedik (Chuvashova), V.M. (1997). 'Stranitsy detstva,' pp. 23-25 in *Spetspereselentsy v Khibinakh: Spetspereselentsy i zakliuchennye v istorii osvoenia Khibin (kniga vospominanii)*. Apatity: Khibinskoe obshestvo 'Memorial.'
Moiseev, R.S. (2006). Nekotorye metodologicheskie i metodicheskie voprosy raionirovania Severa Rossii. *'Trudy' Kamchatskogo Filiala Tikhookeanskogo Instituta Geografii Dal'nevostochnogo Otdelenia Rossiiskoi Akademii Nauk ("Труды" КФ ТИГ ДВО РАН)* 6: 36-54.
McCannon, J. (1998). *Red Arctic: Polar Exploration and the Myth of the North in the Soviet Union 1932-1939*. New York and Oxford: Oxford University Press.
Melnikova, U.S. (1997). 'Togda my mogli postroit,' pp. 85-86 in *Spetspereselentsy v Khibinakh: Spetspereselentsy i zakliuchennye v istorii osvoenia Khibin (kniga vospominanii)*. Apatity: Khibinskoe obshestvo 'Memorial.'
Murmansk (2000). *Murmanskaya oblast na poroge 21 veka*. Murmansk: murmanskij oblkomstat.
Rasumova, I.A. (2006). '"Rodin—eto minimum kraj...": k probleme lokalnoj samoidentifikatsii zhitelej Severa,' pp. 39-45 in *Evropejskij sever v sud'be Rossii. XX vek*. Sborn. nauchnykh statej. Murmansk: Murmanskij gosudarstvennyj pedagogicheskij universitet.
Rhoades, R.E. (1978). Foreign Labor and German Industrial Capitalism 1871-1978: The Evolution of a Migratory System. *American Ethnologist* 5: 553-573.
Round, J. (2005). Rescaling Russia's Geography: The Challenges of Depopulating the Northern Periphery. *Europe-Asia Studies* 57: 705-727.
Shashkov, V.Ya. (2004). *Spetspereselentsy v istorii Murmanskoj oblasti*. Murmansk: izdatel'stvo Maksimim.

Stammler, F. (2005). *Reindeer Nomads Meet the Market: Culture, Property and Globalisation at the End of the Land*. Vol. 6. *Halle Studies in the Anthropology of Eurasia*. Münster: Lit publishers.

Stammler-Gossmann, A. (2007). Reshaping the North of Russia: towards a conception of space. *Arctic and Antarctic Journal of Circumpolar Sociocultural Issues* 1(1): 53-97.

Thompson, N. (2004). Migration and Resettlement in Chukotka: A Research Note. *Eurasian Geography and Economics* 45: 73-81(9).

Thompson N. (2008). *Settlers on the Edge: Identity and Modernization on Russia's Arctic Frontier*. Vancouver: UBC Press.

Vail, P. and A. Genis (1996). *1960ye: Mir sovetskogo cheloveka*. Moskva: Novoe literaturnoe obozrenie.

Vitebsky, P. (n.d.). The Arctic Is ... A homeland. Internet publication, accessed at http://www/thearctic.is/documents/homeland.pdf (22/05/2005).

Zajtsev, K.D. (1997). 'Izgoi,' pp. 69-73 *Spetspereselentsy v Khibinakh: Spetspereselentsy i zakliuchennye v istorii osvoenia Khibin (kniga vospominanii)*. Apatity: Khibinskoe obshestvo 'Memorial.'

Zubkova, F.V. (1997). 'Opyat' nas ushemlyaut.,' pp. 19-21 in *Spetspereselentsy v Khibinakh: Spetspereselentsy i zakliuchennye v istorii osvoenia Khibin (kniga vospominanii)*. Apatity: Khibinskoe obshestvo 'Memorial.'